PARLIAMENTARY
REFORM IN SWEDEN
1866–1921

Oxford University Press, Amen House, London E.C.4

GLASGOW NEW YORK TORONTO MELBOURNE WELLINGTON
BOMBAY CALCUTTA MADRAS KARACHI
CAPE TOWN IBADAN NAIROBI ACCRA SINGAPORE

PARLIAMENTARY REFORM IN SWEDEN

1866–1921

BY

DOUGLAS V. VERNEY

OXFORD

AT THE CLARENDON PRESS

1957

PRINTED IN GREAT BRITAIN

*'There are really only two countries which have
Constitutions of ancient origin,
England and Sweden'*

PONTUS FAHLBECK in 1904

Preface

SWEDEN is well known to foreigners as a social democracy. The Social Democratic party was the largest parliamentary group as long ago as 1914; the first Socialist Government took office in 1920; and, since 1932, the party has dominated both Government and Parliament. Shortly before the outbreak of war in 1939 considerable interest was being shown abroad in Swedish social and political life, and among the books published at this time were the Fabians' *Democratic Sweden* edited by Margaret Cole and *Sweden, The Middle Way* written by Marquis Childs. There is still, however, no detailed survey in English of the operation of Swedish political institutions.[1] The present account deals with the historical development of the machinery of government in modern Sweden, with particular reference to the reform of Parliament.

The period chosen for study is chiefly that from 1866 to 1921, the fifty-five years which form the great period of Swedish parliamentary reform. The Parliament Act of 1866, introduced by Louis De Geer, abolished the four Estates of Nobles, Clergy, Burghers, and Farmers and established in their place a bicameral legislature. It is from this time that the Swedish Parliament begins to develop as a modern legislative body. A second reform bill in 1907, coming into force in 1909, introduced general manhood suffrage in Second Chamber elections and modified some of the qualifications for election and membership of the senatorial First Chamber. (It may be noted that in Sweden the more popular chamber is the second.) In 1918 a third reform, coming into force by 1921, extended the franchise for both chambers to women and abolished plural voting for the First Chamber.

The three reform bills are important not only in themselves but in the wider context of the country's social, political, and constitutional development. For this reason, the book begins with an account of the Swedish Constitution, coming into force

---

[1] Until the publication of Dankwart A. Rustow's excellent *The Politics of Compromise: A Study of Parties and Cabinet Government in Sweden.* (Princeton University Press, 1955.)

in 1809 and establishing the separation of powers between the King and Parliament. It was hoped by some liberals at the time that Parliament would be reformed, but this did not happen for another two generations. In order to account for this delay and the significance of Swedish history upon the Parliament Act of 1866, the first two chapters are concerned with the operation of the Constitution before 1866 and the state of the unreformed Parliament of Estates.

Perhaps the most significant of the political and constitutional developments in the period from 1866 to 1921 was the change in the interpretation of the Constitution. Though the Parliament Act of 1866 retained the principle of the separation of powers, this was gradually broken down and executive power transferred from the King to his Ministers. They in turn came to depend increasingly on parliamentary support. Finally, in 1917, the year before the third and last reform bill, a Liberal–Social Democratic coalition government took office, relying for support on a majority in the legislature. It is this year which is considered by Swedish writers to be the watershed between the old separation of powers and the new doctrine of *parlamentarism*, or, as it might loosely and perhaps inaccurately be termed in England, 'parliamentary government'.

Much of the fascination of modern Swedish history lies in the great constitutional change which took place in this short span of time following 1866. Several chapters are therefore devoted to an analysis of the changing relationship between King, Ministry, and Parliament.

If any explanation is needed for the attention so markedly paid to the subject of parliamentary reform, which in itself is of considerable interest in comparison with British reform bills, it is that the passage of the three Reform Acts illustrates the changing political system and provides an insight into the actual operation of Sweden's political institutions.

I am indebted to Professor Lolo Krusius-Ahrenburg, my former colleague at Helsingfors, Finland, for first suggesting the subject of the Swedish Parliament, and to Professor Elis Håstad of the University of Stockholm for giving me initial encouragement and advice. Thanks are also due to the officials of the National Archives (*Riksarkivet*), and the Library of Parliament (*Riksdagsbiblioteket*) for their assistance. His late Majesty,

King Gustav V, graciously permitted me to examine the royal archives. In England, Professors K. C. Wheare and T. S. Simey have kindly read the typescript, as has Professor Merle Curti of the University of Wisconsin. I should like to thank my colleagues Dr. W. J. Rowe, Dr. Dennis Chapman, and Mr. John Pinsent for their criticism, and above all my friend Professor Edvard Thermaenius of Stockholm for his constant guidance and kindness throughout the preparation of the book. My wife, Diana, has contributed so much that my final word of appreciation is reserved for her.

D. V. V.

Department of Social Science
University of Liverpool

Contents

CHAPTER I

The 1809 Constitution

THERE are in Sweden four fundamental laws (*grundlagar*) upon which all other laws are based. The two most important are the Constitution or Instrument of Government (*Regeringsform*) which regulates the various branches of government, and the Parliament Act (*Riksdagsordning*) which outlines the composition and powers of Parliament. The other two fundamental laws deal with the freedom of the press and the succession to the throne.

The present Constitution was adopted in 1809, at the time of the loss of Finland to the Tsar and the invitation to Marshal Bernadotte to become king. There have been amendments to this document, but many of its provisions, which established a division of powers, remain much the same. When the Constitution was passed, the liberals hoped to supplement it by a radical reform of Parliament which would supersede the system of the four Estates of Nobles, Clergy, Burghers, and Farmers. A new Parliament Act was needed, but by the time it was framed, in 1810, enthusiasm for a thoroughgoing reform had waned, and the Parliament Act of that year retained the Estate system. The reform of Parliament affected both the privileges of the Estates and the fundamental laws: it therefore required the concurrence of the King and all four Estates. This was one reason for the delay and difficulty in accomplishing the reform.

It was not until 1866 that the Estates were abolished by the passing of a completely new Parliament Act, a measure which was as much a landmark in Swedish parliamentary history as the 1832 reform act in England. In a sense it was as though the work begun in 1809 was now completed. Many of the questions discussed in the 1860's were of a constitutional nature, and it is necessary, for a proper understanding of the Parliament Act of 1866, to know what were the provisions of the 1809 Constitution and to examine its operation in the period 1809 to 1866.

1. *Its form*

A draft Constitution was presented to Parliament within two weeks of the deposition of the deranged Gustav IV Adolf. In his report, Hans Järta, the secretary of the Constitution Committee of fifteen members, stated:

> The Committee has tried to construct an Executive Power which, within definite limits, will operate with singleness of purpose and full strength to carry out what it purposes; a Legislative Power wise and faithful in action but firm 'and strong in opposition; a Judicial Power independent of all except the Law and not autocratic in its interpretation of the Law. It has also tried to make these powers a safeguard and restraint upon one another: it has not let their authority overlap but has let each retain residual powers. The Constitution as suggested by the Committee shall rest on these grounds, the organs of State having their own sphere and counterbalancing one another.[1]

In accordance with this decision to establish a strong executive power, an Article was inserted in the Constitution to the effect that 'The King alone shall govern the realm' (A. 4). The word 'alone' signified that neither Parliament nor the Council of Ministers shared in the executive power. The King was responsible for foreign affairs and was empowered not only to carry on his own foreign policy and make alliances but to declare war if he found this to be necessary, provided that in each instance he consulted his Ministers (A. 11–13). (In constitutional documents before 1789 the declaration of war had also required the assent of the Estates.) In military matters, too, the King was supreme and was Commander-in-Chief of the armed forces (A. 14). On questions affecting them, he need consult only the appropriate Minister (A. 15). The King alone was responsible for the administration of the country, and appointments to the naval, military, and civil services were in his hands, including the final choice, from a list of three, of bishops and burgomasters (A. 29, 31). He could dismiss certain leading servants of the Crown such as Ministers and provincial governors (A. 35), but judges and civil servants retained their traditional independence and security of tenure (A. 36). The award of two votes to the King in the Supreme Court was a relic from an earlier period: he never in fact used them.[2] 'Laws and decrees

[1] *Constitutions-Utskottets Memorialer 1809–10*, Mem. No. 1, pp. 6–7.
[2] This provision (A. 21) has been repealed.

relating to the general economy of the realm', including commercial treaties, were within the competence of the Crown, which could act upon a recommendation from Parliament or, if it desired, submit such 'economic legislation' to joint decisions by Crown and Parliament (A. 89). (In the 1860's the fixing of railway rates and charges and the reform of local government were considered to be part of the King's power over economic legislation.) The King was forbidden to establish any monopoly (A. 60) or alienate Crown lands (A. 77).

Not only did the King wield executive power, but he possessed equal rights with Parliament in legislation (A. 87) except in those matters which were exclusively his, for instance the general economy (A. 89), and those which were exclusively within parliamentary jurisdiction, for example taxation (A. 57). This did not imply that the King actively took part in the legislative process. Indeed, the Estates and their committees were forbidden to deliberate in the presence of the King (A. 55). For the most part, his contact with Parliament was formal and confined to an Address at the beginning of each session. He could, however, summon a deputation of Parliament to hear its opinion concerning developments in foreign policy, and could inform it of matters which were important but confidential (A. 54). (This deputation was called the 'Secret Committee' though it was not part of the ordinary committee system.) He had power both to dismiss Parliament after it had been sitting for three or at most four months (A. 109) and to call it for extraordinary sessions (A. 49). There was no prorogation because each Parliament consisted of one session only. Three of the four Speakers were appointed by the King, the exception being in the Clergy Estate, where the Archbishop, a royal appointment, was ex-officio Speaker (A. 52).[1] The King also nominated the Secretary appointed to the Farmer Estate.[2]

Parliament could not call the King to account for his conduct (A. 3). The main check upon the King was his Council. Although Ministers were responsible only for advice, all executive acts were to be countersigned by a Minister. It was stated in Article 9:

Should at any time the unexpected event occur that the King's

[1] During the Era of Liberty, the Estates had elected their own Speakers.
[2] Riksdags Ordning A. 24.

decision would be plainly contrary to the fundamental or general laws of the realm, it shall be the duty of the members of the Council of State to make a vigorous protest against such decision. Any member who does not separately enter his opinion in the minutes shall be held responsible for the decision as if he had advised the King to make it.

This obligation, as well as a safeguard, of the Minister, was reaffirmed in Article 38:

Should a Minister presenting a matter think that any order of the King is in conflict with the Constitution, he shall remonstrate against it in the Council of State: if the King should still insist upon issuing the order it shall be the Minister's right and duty to refuse his countersignature thereto and, as a consequence, to resign from his office which he shall not resume until Parliament has examined and approved his conduct. In the meantime his salary and other emoluments shall continue.

Parliament controlled the Council of Ministers through its Constitution Committee, which examined the minutes of the Council of State (or King-in-Council), excepting certain matters affecting the security of the realm and foreign affairs, in which, as has already been noted, the King had special powers (A. 105). If the committee discovered that there had been a manifest violation of the fundamental laws or failure to refuse countersignature as indicated in Article 38, it was to instruct Parliament's Officer of Justice (*Justitieombudsman*) to impeach the Minister before the Court of Impeachment (A. 106). Where there was a less serious misdemeanour, such as failure by a Minister or even the whole Council of State to pay due regard to the welfare of the State, or failure to perform their duties with impartiality, zeal, ability, and energy, the Constitution Committee was to bring the matter before Parliament, which could request the King in writing to remove from the Council of State and from office the person or persons criticized (A. 107). The latter was known as the 'political responsibility' of Ministers in contrast to the 'juridical responsibility' of Article 106. It depended, however, on the concurrence of a majority of the Estates (i.e. three out of four), whereas the juridical responsibility lay within the competence of the Constitution Committee itself.

By these checks, Parliament was expected to be able to prevent unconstitutional action by the King. Just as the King was
given a share in the legislative function, so Parliament was
allotted some control over the executive. A further check
was provided by the regularization of such meetings as the
1809 Parliament; if necessary, Parliament could assemble without being summoned by the King (A. 49).

In many financial matters, Parliament had sole and absolute
jurisdiction. The most important of its privileges was emphasized
in Article 57: 'The ancient right of the Swedish people to tax
themselves shall be exercised by Parliament alone.' Parliament delegated some of its work to a Committee of Supply
(*statsutskott*), which discussed finance bills before they were
debated and voted separately upon in the four Estates.

Appropriations were granted for five years, the maximum
interval allowed by the Constitution between meetings of Parliament, but if the new Parliament failed to agree within four
months to a new Budget the King could dismiss the Estates.
Meanwhile the old scale of appropriations was to continue in
operation (A. 109). Under the 1809 Constitution the interval
was never exceeded, and the Budget was always passed. The
Crown continued to have its own sources of 'ordinary income'
(*ordinarie inkomster*) but customs duties were henceforth classified
as taxes (*bevillningar*) or 'extraordinary income' dependent on
parliamentary sanction (A. 60). The system of land taxes (*grundskatter*) remained one of the Crown's sources of 'ordinary'
income.

Control over expenditure was also defined. Supplies were
granted for each Estimate (*huvudtitel*) (A. 62) and neither ordinary nor extraordinary income could be transferred by the King
from one estimate to another (A. 64, 65). This seemed to indicate that the King's freedom to use even income from his own
sources was to be restricted.[1] In 1810 the new Parliament Act
established a body called the Parliamentary Auditors, consisting of members of the Estates.

Parliament continued to control the Bank of Sweden, the
oldest national bank in Europe, founded in 1688, and the sole
note-issuing authority in Sweden (A. 72). It also continued to
supervise the National Debt Office (A. 66). This had been set

---

[1] Herlitz, N., *Grunddragen av det svenska statsskickets historia*, p. 195.

up in 1789 to manage the National Debt and, incidentally, to prevent any repetition of Gustav III's practice of raising foreign loans when unable or unwilling to obtain additional supplies from Parliament.

Thus the separation of powers came into being, devised to give executive authority to the King and financial power to Parliament. However, though Parliament could check executive action, the King had no authority to interfere in taxation. On the other hand the balance of power was preserved in the most important legislative sphere, King and Parliament having joint responsibility.

The judiciary had no place in this scheme: once appointed by the King it was to be independent but was not to be a separate power which could check or balance the other two. Unlike the American Supreme Court, the Swedish Supreme Court had no authority to declare acts of the Legislature unconstitutional. Article 88 stated:

> The interpretation of civil, criminal and ecclesiastical laws shall be dealt with in the same manner as the enactment of such laws. The interpretation which the King gives through the Supreme Court when Parliament is not in session in answer to questions regarding the true meaning of the law may be overruled by Parliament at its next session. . . . Such interpretations as have thus been overruled shall no longer be valid and shall not be observed or invoked by the Courts.

This meant that the constitutionality of laws depended upon agreement between the King and Parliament, although the Supreme Court could be asked to interpret the law by the King. The court which was to try impeachment cases was not to be a regular court of the judiciary but a special body of high officials and judges (A. 102). Among the law officers, the King appointed the Attorney-General (*Justitiekansler*), and Parliament the Officer of Justice (*Justitieombudsman*), to watch over the judiciary on their behalf. Persons occupying judicial positions could only be removed from office after trial and sentence, with one exception: a parliamentary commission (*opinionsnämnden*) had the right to request the King to discharge Supreme Court judges who forfeited the confidence of Parliament (A. 103). This right was never in fact exercised.

According to the Constitution, changes in the law could be made in four ways. First, in matters affecting the general economy of the realm, the King could act alone (A. 89). Secondly, in agreeing to the imposition of taxation, Parliament had sole authority (A. 57). Thirdly, in ordinary legislation the assent of the King and three Estates was required (A. 87). Lastly, in matters affecting the fundamental laws or the privileges of the Estates, the assent of the King and all four Estates was necessary (A. 114).

There has been some controversy in Sweden over the relative influence of Swedish tradition and foreign theory and practice upon the form which the Constitution took. According to a conservative historian: 'The 1809 Constitution is simply the old ordinary Swedish type, standardised.'[1] Even the liberal Herbert Tingsten has written: 'The Swedish Constitution is based on a constitutional tradition with which only the English can compare.'[2] Influenced as they were by the current theory of the separation of powers, the authors of the 1809 Constitution nevertheless made use of old-established Swedish institutions.[3] For example, they revived the old Council (*riksråd*) and transformed it into a Council of Ministers (*statsråd*) which was to be a check upon the King's actions. Yet they did not alter the law whereby the appointment and dismissal of Ministers lay entirely at the King's discretion. Or again, they emphasized the importance of parliamentary committees, giving the Constitution Committee the task of reviewing the minutes of the King-in-Council, but they did not revive the practice of the Era of Liberty in the previous century when Parliament could actually revoke acts of the Crown.

Some provisions appear to be compatible with both Swedish tradition and foreign theory and practice. Amongst these is the right of the legislature to determine taxation. Other provisions are not so easily reconcilable. Financial practice in Sweden differs from Montesquieu's teaching and from American and British procedure, finance bills being the province not of a lower house but of all four Estates, before 1866, and of both

---

[1] Lagerroth, F., 'Beskattningsmakten i 1809 års RF', *Statsvetenskaplig Tidskrift*, 1938, p. 16.

[2] *Demokratiens seger och kris*, p. 570.

[3] In his *Studier öfver 1809 års författningskris*, Brusewitz stressed its foreign origin.

chambers since. In legislative practice, Montesquieu's theory that 'the executive ought to be given a share in legislation' coincides with the principle followed in Sweden as well as in the United States and Great Britain. 'The mutual privilege of veto' of which Montesquieu speaks exists, by implication at least, in the Swedish Constitution. In contrast, the United States Constitution explicitly provides for a Presidential veto, which is still used, and a veto-overriding authority in the form of a two-thirds majority in both houses of Congress. The last use of the royal veto in Sweden occurred in 1913, about 200 years after it was last exercised in England. Thus in the 1809 Constitution, and in practice for a century or more to come, there was no overriding legislative authority such as existed in the United States, where the legislature could pass laws despite the opposition of the President.

11. *The separation of powers in practice*

Whatever might be stated in the Articles of the Constitution, it remained to be seen whether they would operate in practice as their framers intended. There was soon evidence that not all of the elaborate checks upon the royal Executive would be enforceable.

Although Marshal Bernadotte did not succeed Charles XIII as Charles XIV until 1818, he virtually ruled the country from the time he became Regent in 1810. The Regency Act itself, the Freedom of the Press Act of 1812, and the 1815 Act of Union with Norway, were all passed by extraordinary sessions of Parliament and thereafter became law. Yet constitutionally extraordinary sessions had no authority over matters of fundamental law, and, moreover, the assent of two successive ordinary sessions of Parliament was necessary for any revision of the fundamental laws. But Bernadotte, as a marshal of Napoleon, was treated with great respect, and was allowed considerable latitude. He pursued his own foreign policy, much to Sweden's advantage, and acquired Norway in recompense for the loss of Finland, thus creating a united Scandinavian power which faced both the Atlantic and the Baltic. In domestic affairs in general, however, he was hampered by his inability to speak Swedish, and it was not until his later years that he became involved in serious controversy. Compared with his Gustavian predecessors, Bernadotte ruled constitutionally as Charles XIV, and for a long time there was no serious opposition to him in Parliament. The checks might seem insufficient, but not all of them were fully tested.

The King's Council (*statsråd*), which was the immediate check upon royal policy, was comparatively ineffective. Counter-signature was never refused. If Ministers disagreed with the King they 'made a reservation' in the Council minutes and, in extreme cases, resigned. On one occasion the whole Ministry made a reservation and stayed in office.[1] Ministers were appointed personally, and usually singly, by the King, and resigned individually. There was no instance of the resignation of a whole Council of Ministers. The Council met formally in the presence of the King. As early as 1816 there had begun the practice of holding preliminary meetings in his absence, and at one time Crown Prince Oscar presided at these meetings. There was no development of a Cabinet similar to that which characterized English government during the reign of the German-speaking George I. The connexion between the Council and Parliament was too tenuous, and there was, moreover, no Walpole in Sweden. The Council consisted largely of senior members of the Civil Service, rather than of members of Parliament. Until the appointment in 1828 of the first commoner, H. N. Schwan, head of Stockholm's largest business house, it was entirely composed of members of the nobility. In describing the Council as it was between 1809 and 1860, Kihlberg has remarked:

> The main impression remains that the Council seems to have been organized and recruited rather as the highest executive department, placed in immediate conjunction to the King, rather than as an organ for political co-operation and independent activity.[2]

It was not only the Council which was ineffective in the exercise of its constitutional duties. Parliament itself did not succeed in its assigned task of controlling the activities of the King-in-Council. Partly this was because the organization of Parliament in four Estates meant that the Constitution Committee had to obtain the support of at least three separate

---

[1] Edén, N., *Den svenska riksdagen under 500 år*, p. 234.
[2] Kihlberg, L., *Den svenska ministären*, p. 13.

bodies before requesting the King to dismiss a Minister according to Article 107 of the Constitution. None were in fact
dismissed under the terms of this Article. However, the Constitution Committee was also entitled, according to Article 106, to
impeach Ministers without recourse to the Estates, and on five
occasions, the last being in 1854, it did so. Each time, however,
the special court of impeachment (*riksrätt*) declared the accused
innocent. So long as the King, aided by the bureaucracy and
conservative nobility, dominated the political scene, Parliament
could not make its control over the Council effective.

Nevertheless, although juridically neither the Council nor
Parliament was able to act as the 'safeguard and restraint'
which Järta and the framers of the Constitution took to be implied by the interdependence of the legislative, judicial, and
executive powers, there were certain political developments
which affected the responsibilities of both bodies, and these
were to have repercussions in the future.

The changes affecting the Council came about in 1840 as the
result of the temporary control of the Constitution Committee
by a new generation of liberals. Supported by a general feeling
of dissatisfaction with the ageing Charles XIV's policy, the
Committee gave the King to understand that Parliament would
not tolerate Ministers whom it disliked. This did not mean that
the Council henceforth had to receive a vote of confidence from
the Estates, but it did cause the King to exercise discretion in
his appointments.[1] His successors were remarkably successful in
choosing Ministers in whom Parliament had reasonable confidence, and this was one reason for the comparatively slow
evolution of a Cabinet-type Ministry.

At the same time Charles XIV was compelled to reorganize
the administration, and in such a way as to give the Council
more direct responsibility. Seven Government Departments
were created: Justice, Foreign Affairs, Army, Navy, Interior,
Finance and, lastly, Church and Education, each being placed
under a Minister. To the seven Departmental Ministers were
added three others without portfolio. Two at least of these
'Consultative' Ministers were required by Article 6 of the
amended Constitution to have had administrative experience in
the State service. The existing Civil Service of Colleges and

---

[1] Kihlberg, op. cit., pp. 31–32.

similar Agencies (*verk*) successfully retained its position of independence, being responsible directly to the King-in-Council and not to any individual Minister and his Department. As a result, the Departments remained comparatively small organizations.

Unlike the Council, Parliament was in a position to increase its authority in its own peculiar sphere, which was that of finance. According to Article 57 of the Constitution, Parliament was solely responsible for the levying of taxation. Moreover, it had sundry other sources of income such as stamp duties and postage rates. Parliament also controlled Customs and Excise duties and this tended to restrict the freedom of the King-in-Council in contracting commercial treaties with foreign governments. In 1855 a further important source of revenue was placed in parliamentary hands by a law regulating and taxing the distillation of spirits. It was intended in 1809 that the Crown would have its own 'ordinary' income, and would approach Parliament for 'extraordinary' income, in which, at this time, taxation was included. However, as the industrial and commercial activity of the country expanded, and the cost of the civil and military administration rose, the Crown became increasingly dependent upon 'extraordinary' sources of supply, and therefore upon parliamentary goodwill. By the end of the nineteenth century, according to Pontus Fahlbeck, over three-quarters of the total revenue of 163 million crowns came from extraordinary sources.[1]

Parliament not only increased its responsibility for the income which the Crown received, but also demanded more detailed control over expenditure. In the earlier years of Charles XIV's reign the King was able to transfer moneys from one Estimate to another, but this practice was stopped (though the King never formally complied) when Parliament requested in 1841 that its appropriations should be used for the purpose specified and that alone. During Oscar I's reign scrutiny became closer until by the 1850's Parliament expected detailed Estimates before consenting to grant appropriations. It was aided in its task by the Parliamentary Auditors, who were given authority to examine all public accounts in 1830. In 1857 this examination became annual. Civil Service salaries also came under

[1] *Sveriges författning och den moderna parlamentarism*, p. 187, n. 1.

parliamentary scrutiny. (It is tempting to speculate upon the influence of this change upon the loyalty of servants of the Crown to the King when, as members of the Estates, they debated parliamentary reform in the 1860's.) It was in the 1850's that the construction of a system of trunk railway lines was begun by the State. Constitutionally it came within the Crown's power of economic legislation, but the project required State loans, which Parliament alone, through the National Debt Office, could authorize.

Neither the departmental reorganization nor the increasing importance of finance in parliamentary affairs seems to have caused any significant change in the relations of King, Ministry, and Parliament before the 1860's. The King retained his predominant position and the Council remained a group of Civil Service advisers. It was to be a long time before individual Ministers considered that their work was of concern to their colleagues, a prerequisite of Cabinet government. Although Oscar I (1844–59) was in some respects a liberal at his accession, and was expected to favour reform, he did not encourage the development of a Council dependent upon parliamentary support. It is true that younger men, not always drawn from the Civil Service, were appointed as Ministers, and that the.King introduced several reforms such as the improvement of the penal code, the abolition of the old system of craftsmen's guilds, and the improvement of the poor law. Nevertheless, during his reign the Ministry remained in principle unpolitical. There was an outcry from the bureaucracy because some of his younger Ministers had not served an administrative apprenticeship. (Two of Oscar's most criticized appointments, Nordenfalk and Waern, were ironmasters, a class small in numbers but of increasing importance.) After 1848, the King discontinued the appointments of certain counsellors from the world of business and politics, and the bureaucracy regained its ascendancy. He still occasionally took members of the Estates into his Council, but those few who were members of the Clergy or Burgher Estates (none were from the Farmers) usually resigned their membership of Parliament on their appointment. Ministers who were nobles continued to attend the debates in the *Riddarhus* as private members and usually defended Government policy. Nevertheless, it was Oscar I who was the first to invite

Gripenstedt and Louis De Geer to enter the Ministry, the two men who were most responsible for the Parliament Act of 1866.

Just as the Ministry failed to make use of the opportunities afforded by the 1840 reorganization, leaving executive power in the hands of the King, so Parliament seems to have been reluctant to exploit its growing financial power to achieve other legislative aims. To a great extent, of course, this was due to the divisions within the legislature. Yet although, according to Herlitz, Anckarswärd suggested in 1833 that the opposition should refuse all appropriations in order to put pressure on the Government, he was in a minority. A more common view was that of Schwerin, who in 1829 denied that 'the giving and withholding of supplies is the exercise of a power which the Estates possess'.[1] Commenting on the opposition, at times severe, to Charles XIV in his last Parliament, Herlitz remarks: 'As a weapon against the royal power, the finance power has not played any part.' For instance, the 1840 debates did not establish any right of the Estates to dictate the composition of the Council, despite their power over finance. Instead there continued the old custom of treating every financial question on its own merits rather than making the examination one of political principle. The King, for his part, did not try to rule without Parliament, or attempt to raise money without consulting it. Although the precise reasons for ministerial resignations and appointments in the nineteenth century seem still somewhat obscure, financial pressure from Parliament does not appear to have been one of them. One writer has gone so far as to describe Parliament as a body called together at intervals to dispatch Government business, rather than an assembly of representatives debating Government policy.[2] This curious weakness of Parliament was due to several circumstances, not the least important of which was the fact that it was unreformed.

[1] *Sveriges riksdag*, xii. 405 ff.
[2] Reuterskiöld, C. A., *Sveriges riksdag*, x. 9-10.

CHAPTER II

The Unreformed Parliament, 1809–1866

AT first sight it may seem surprising that despite the events of 1809 and the opportunity for a complete constitutional change, the Estates remained in being for nearly another sixty years. Even then, by agreeing to their own abolition, their fate was very different from that of the States General in France, where, however, the Estates were perhaps less representative and authoritative.

The word 'Estate' is ambiguous. It means on the one hand those of the Nobles, Clergy, Burghers, and Farmers who met as parliamentary representatives, and on the other the social classes of nobility, clergy, burghers, and farmers throughout the country. The parliamentary Estates will therefore be distinguished from the national estates by the use of capital letters. An examination of both Estates and estates is illuminating. The former were by no means unrepresentative of the latter, though these comprised only 70 per cent. of the population, of whom two-thirds were farmers. A division of the population according to estate was made in 1855 as follows:[1]

	per cent.		per cent.
Nobles	0·32	Ståndspersoner	2·18
Clergy	0·42	Foreigners/Jews	0·05
Burghers	2.24	Others	29·44
Farmers	65·35		
			100.00

The *ståndspersoner* were people of education who for one reason or another were excluded from membership of the estates.

Between 1809 and 1866 several attempts were made to widen the ranks of the Estates in order to offset the effects of the incipient industrial revolution and the increase in population. There was hardly time for some of the later reforms to take

[1] Sveriges Officiella Statistik. Litt. A., *Befolkningsstatistik för åren 1851–55, 3d afdelning,* Table No. 4. See also Wohlin, N., *Den jordbruksidkande befolkningen i Sverige 1751–1900,* p. 50.

effect before the movement for a far-reaching reform had succeeded in abolishing the Estate system altogether.

In this chapter will be discussed in turn the social classes
comprising the estates, their representatives in the parliamentary Estates, the reforms of the Estates brought into effect before
1866, and finally the proposals for the creation of a completely
new type of legislature.

1. The estates as social classes

The nobility included counts, barons, and gentry, a total of
about 3,500. Through the centuries no fewer than 2,788 families
had been ennobled, but by 1809 only 1,126 of these still
existed and by 1866 the number was reduced to 958.[1] Although
the last instance of ennoblement was in 1902 (Sven Hedin, the
explorer) the practice had virtually died out by the middle of
the nineteenth century.[2] The division which was politically important within the estate was not of rank but of function. For
example, there were landowners and bureaucrats, and their
interests were often not identical. The following table attempts
to indicate the professions of those nobles who attended four of
the Parliaments between 1809 and 1866.[3]

	1809–10	1828–30	1853–4	1865–6
Military Service	473	384	282	293
Civil Service.	143	165	129	174
Judges	64	56	38	48
Intellectuals.	7	15	12	25
Former civil servants . . .	101	44	23	19
Landowners/Ironmasters . .	195	140	136	243
Industry and Commerce . .	1	6	6	9
Others	7	4	10	16
	991	814	636	827

It is impossible to draw any but the most general conclusions
from these figures, since many nobles served at some time in
their life in the armed forces or Civil Service before retiring to
manage their estates. In view of the later importance of the
ironmasters it is a pity that they are not separated from the

[1] *Studier över den svenska riksdagens sociala sammansättning*, Table I, p. 54.

[2] Fahlbeck, E., *Sveriges riksdag*, viii. 456; Andrén, G., *Sveriges riksdag*, ix. 10. In
1946 there were 52 counts, 129 barons, and 482 other heads of noble families.
An Assembly of Nobles is held every three years in the *Riddarhus*.

[3] *Studier*, &c., Tables II–V, pp. 60–62.

landowners. One reason for their conjunction is the difficulty of classifying the landowners who owned iron-mines and iron-works situated on their estates. The size of the two groups 'Military Service' and 'Civil Service' is worth noting. The Swed-ish nobility had ceased to consist in the main of a landed aris-tocracy, a large number of nobles living on their salaries alone. Although the eldest frequently inherited the estate, each child retained his or her parents' rank.

The nobles held a position in the service of the Crown which was only gradually encroached upon. Senior servants of the Crown, such as Provincial Governors and the Governor of Stockholm, continued to be recruited almost entirely from the nobility, and it was 1845 before the constitutional stipulation that half the High Court judges should be nobles was re-scinded (A. 17).

It has been suggested that the economic position of the nobles worsened during the period, the argument being based on figures which show that between 1845 and 1863 the landowning nobility sold land exceeding the value of land which they bought by 45 million *riksdaler* (a *riksdaler* being worth just over a shilling).[1] According to a table prepared for King Oscar I, how-ever, land worth 15,462,142 *riksdaler* was sold by nobles in 1835, of which land disposed of by forced sale amounted to only 389,165 *riksdaler*. The writer comments that one reason for the sale was the need of industry for more capital each year. The large amounts sold in the years 1835 and 1836 he explains as due to the creation of mortgage banks (*hypotekskassa*).[2] It therefore seems doubtful whether the mortgaging of land by the nobles necessarily indicates their declining prosperity. Admittedly there was a gradual transfer of land to the farmers throughout the nineteenth century, but many nobles mortgaged their land in order to buy shares in joint-stock companies where there was a better and quicker return. If anything, the nobles who belonged to the landowning-entrepreneur class appear to have increased their political influence, while the large number who lived on salaries in State service in Stockholm declined in prestige and power.

The clergy of the State Church formed a separate estate. The

[1] Andrén, G., op. cit., p. 10, and Fahlbeck, E., op. cit., p. 456.
[2] *Oskar I:s och drottning Josephinas arkiv*, vol. xlix.

Lutheran faith became established during the reign of Gustavus Vasa, the first of Sweden's modern national kings. His successors, John III and Sigismund, tried for a time to re-establish Roman Catholicism, but the Uppsala Synod in 1593 accepted the Augsburg Confession, since when all Swedish kings have had to be of the 'true Evangelical faith, as adopted and explained in the unaltered Augsburg Confession and in the Resolution of the Uppsala Synod of the year 1593' (Article 2 of the Constitution). The victory of Protestantism was illustrated by Sweden's entry into the Thirty Years' War, and a special prayer is offered in all churches on Gustavus Adolphus's Day to the hero and champion of freedom and Protestantism. No other Swedish king is so honoured.

The Church acquired many of the characteristics associated with the Church of Scotland rather than the Church of England—with the severe John Knox rather than the tolerant Bishop Hooker. Roman Catholicism was stamped out, and as late as 1853 six women were sentenced to transportation for having been converted to the Roman religion. The Methodist minister George Scott was forbidden in 1842 to preach in Swedish, although he was able to continue his work in the English tongue under a law which permitted foreigners to practise their own religion. Both these decrees were the result of the machinations of Pastor Ekdahl, a fanatical Lutheran clergyman who insisted on appealing to ancient laws, much to the discomfiture of the Government. As it stood, the law was harsh, and the importance of being Lutheran was emphasized by the stipulation that loss of rights of inheritance should accompany withdrawal from the State Church.

In practice, the application of many of the laws was rarely severe in the period after 1809. There was little anticlericalism in Sweden despite the attitude of the Church at the time of the 1860 Toleration Act and the 1866 Reform Bill, which aroused some hostility. The leaders of the Church were on the whole willing to compromise on political matters, even though many of them had forceful personalities. They had to take into account the fact that many of the upper class had been influenced by the Enlightenment and were more or less freethinkers. Though some of the clergy opposed the introduction of the various Nonconformist bodies into a country uniformly Lutheran, the opposition was negligible in comparison with that in England in previous centuries. The explanation of the religious restrictions lay in the long deep-rooted fear of Roman Catholicism and they were removed only because the rise of other Protestant denominations made this necessary. The laws had the sanction of tradition and in most cases had ceased to be the symbol of intolerance. The number of non-Lutherans is still small. In 1950 there were about 300,000 Nonconformists, nearly 7,000 Jews, and less than 6,000 Catholics.

Traditionally the clergy were the learned estate and were recruited from all social classes. It was the ambition of many a poor father to send his cleverest son to the university (Uppsala or Lund) and then into Holy Orders. In the absence of an equivalent of the Justice of the Peace, the clergy had many civil duties to perform. They were the spiritual and intellectual heads of their parishes and their social standing was high. It had long ceased to be the custom to expect a newly appointed priest to save the parish from pension expenses by marrying his predecessor's widow, but his remuneration still consisted of glebe land rather than money. If he was of farming stock he looked after it himself, otherwise the estate was leased and he lived on the rent. Because they also depended on a good seed-time and harvest, the clergy shared in the lives of their congregations, and this may explain why they did not suffer undue unpopularity when in the 1860's they opposed the reform bill.

Like the nobles, the parish clergy tended to be conservative. They, too, depended to some extent on the goodwill of the Crown, for although many were nominated to their living by their congregation they were members of a State Church and ultimately appointed by the King, whilst over a third of the parishes were the gift of the Crown.

The towns were governed by the burghers, all of whom were members of a guild, had paid the necessary dues, and were registered in the Burgher Book. They alone were allowed to carry on handicrafts and commerce in the towns, and they levied tolls at the gates. The estate included all traders, wholesalers and retailers, manufacturers, and craftsmen, who formed rather less than a quarter of the inhabitants. Election of parliamentary representatives was carried out according to a scale whereby votes were allotted on the basis of wealth. Few of the burghers seem to have voted in parliamentary elections, and in Gothenburg, for example, only 114 votes were recorded in the election for the 1856–8 Parliament.[1] Each of the towns, which numbered over 80, was entitled to send at least one member, but the smaller towns shared the representation and services of a single member. One town was fortunate enough on one occasion to obtain the services of a sea-captain whose boat was laid up in Stockholm for repairs, thereby saving itself the considerable expense of travel and lodging.[2] The Constitution of 1634 was the first formal recognition of the right of the estate to be represented in Parliament. It was decreed that a town's representative should be some prominent citizen, and usually the burghers sent the Burgomaster, since besides being a trained lawyer he knew most about the town's needs. The disadvantage of the procedure was that because the Burgomaster was appointed by the King to his office, it was possible for the Crown to bring influence to bear upon a considerable part of the Burgher Estate.

The fourth estate consisted of the farmers, supposedly representing the *menige allmoge*, or common people, who composed the vast majority of Sweden's population. In 1855 only 15 per cent of the population were engaged in trade or industry. But in fact farmers only formed a third of the agricultural population, the remaining two-thirds, cottagers and landless labourers, having no representation. The farmers had the privilege of being represented as a separate Estate because they were landowners. They had always had a greater degree of independence than the peasantry in countries which had possessed a feudal system, and in status they perhaps corresponded to the English yeoman rather than to the continental peasant. One reason for the favour with which the King looked upon the farmers was that their chief loyalty was to the Crown, and they provided a traditional counterbalance to the influence of the nobility. Owing to the system of land taxes, the farmers were the country's chief taxpayers, and in time of war it was they who raised supplies for the army and sent their sons as soldiers. On being admitted to Parliament together with the Burghers as a parliamentary Estate, the Farmers were given equal voting rights with

[1] *Studier, &c.*, p. 83.
[2] Borell, B., *De svenska liberalerna och representationsfrågan, på 1840 talet*, p. 130.

the other Estates, and although on many issues they could be
outvoted, on matters of constitutional importance their assent
was vital.

Nevertheless, the farmers were regarded as an inferior class
and it took many years for their social standing to improve.
After about 1830 there was a gradual betterment in their
political and economic situation and in their personal capacity.
Instead of listening to Government agents, they began to
read Lars Hierta's *Aftonbladet*, the first popular and influential
newspaper, founded in 1830. Many farmers who came under
Hierta's guidance called themselves radicals. Economically
their position improved with the growing demand for corn in
western Europe. In 1846, the year in which Peel abolished
the English Corn Laws, the guild system was abolished by
Oscar I and the farmers were able to make use of the cheap
surplus labour in the countryside. The labourers lived mainly
on potatoes, thus enabling the maximum amount of corn to
be exported.[1]

Gradually the farmers raised their status to that of a rural
middle class and, though their sense of inferiority was by no
means removed, they came to regard themselves as the backbone
of the nation. The radical propagandists who aimed at securing
their support for parliamentary reform characterized them as
the representatives of nine-tenths of the population, which was
a gross exaggeration, but it was true enough that the farmers
more than the other Estates could claim to have the broad mass
of the people behind them. The Estate more and more supported parliamentary reform from 1840 onwards; the farmers
certainly intended that they themselves should be adequately
represented. The reformers had to decide how to introduce a
system of government which would not give excessive power to
the farmers. One simple solution was to restrict the suffrage, but
it would have been impossible to obtain the support of the
farmers for a bill which tended to disfranchise them.

One of the main objections to the four estates was that in
the nineteenth century they were becoming unrepresentative.
Sweden's population, which was about 1,750,000 in 1750,
doubled in the next hundred years and in 1865 was 4,100,000.
The greatest increase was among the poorer agricultural classes

---

[1] Gasslander, O., *J. A. Gripenstedt*, p. 85.

whose number, though unknown with precision, was at least a million in 1850. They were not an important factor politically and the debates on parliamentary reform were not affected by any consideration of their rights. (The servant class was often referred to by the neuter gender.) Theirs was a social problem and was solved by emigration to the United States and the movement to new industrial centres which sprang up as the industrialization of the country spread in the latter half of the century. The agricultural population doubled between 1750 and 1860, but whereas the number of *bönder* (farmers) increased by only a quarter (to about 230,000), the number of crofters and cottagers (*jordtorpare, backstugusittare, inhysesklasser,* and *statare*) quadrupled and in 1860 these were nearly as numerous as the farmers.[1]

Comparatively little is known of the life of the proletariat of this time since there was no Disraeli or Dickens to describe their condition.[2] The farmers wanted a more equitable distribution of taxation and the franchise for their own class: they had no particular interest in the rural poor.

Of far greater significance than the agricultural proletariat were the 70,000 or so unrepresented and often influential property-owning members of the middle class (*ofrälse ståndspersoner*) who really wanted a share in the franchise. The estate system permitted mobility chiefly to the clergy or nobility; usually a man who changed his station in life ceased to qualify as a burgher or farmer. There had grown up an important middle class who were not members of any estate, among whom was an increasing number of civil servants who were not of noble birth, and men of independent means such as doctors, schoolmasters, technicians, and many landowners. One of the two authors of the 1830 motion for reform, Richert, was an able lawyer denied access to Parliament. The estate system was not yet overwhelmed by an industrial revolution of magnitude, but it was affected by railway construction, which was beginning to assist the movement of population, making society less static and encouraging

---

[1] However, between 1860 and 1900 when the agricultural population remained stationary, the farmers continued to increase in numbers while the cottagers tended to show a decline. (See Wohlin, N., *Den jordbruksidkande befolkningen i Sverige 1751–1900*, pp. 1–51.)

[2] Fahlbeck, F., op. cit., p. 466.

sons to think of other occupations than their fathers'.[1] It was difficult to absorb members of new professions and occupations, and to ensure the representation of people who had moved their homes, and in the end the system of estates broke down under the strain.

11. *The parliamentary Estates*

The meetings of the Estates had a certain old-world pageantry and added colour to the nation's life. It was customary until 1830 for the Nobles to meet in the *Riddarhus* (House of the Nobles), the Clergy in the consistory of *Storkyrkan* (the Great Church), the Burghers in the Bourse and the Farmers in the Town Hall. In 1830 the three lower Estates acquired their own building. At the beginning of each session Parliament assembled at the Royal Palace in the Hall of State (*Rikssal*), where after an Address welcoming members and outlining Government policy, the King formally opened Parliament. Outside in the Square the Heralds were gathered in bright uniforms, the State Trumpeters blew a salute and the kettle-drums rolled. Inside the Palace, members of Parliament were dressed in the appropriate formal attire of their respective Estates. On business days they met at 8 a.m. and dispatched deputations or memoranda to keep the other Estates informed as to the progress of their discussions. Matters were debated concurrently,[2] partly to save time and partly to prevent the proceedings in one Estate from influencing another.[3] Despite this provision, sessions tended to be long, and when added to the extraordinary sessions called by the King they made the interval between sessions average three years instead of the five permitted by the Constitution. After 1845 the statutory limit was lowered to three and the average

[1] Railway construction began in the 1850's and increased as follows:

Year	Kilometres of track in use	Year	Kilometres of track in use
1856	66	1880	5,876
1860	527	1890	8,018
1865	1,305	1900	11,303
1870	1,727	1910	13,829
1875	3,679	1950	16,640

(*Statistisk Årsbok, 1914 and 1951*)

[2] Riksdage Ordning A. 46.   [3] Fahlbeck, E., op cit., p. 170.

interval became only two. Members were allowed unlimited time for discussion and there was little attempt to curb debate. It was estimated by Löwenhielm that an important bill on which the Estates disagreed and returned to committee could be discussed on no fewer than forty-two occasions.[1] A bill which was presented to the Estates, referred to committee and referred back again by the Estates before a final decision, would be discussed fourteen times.

Their privileges were carefully guarded. No quorum was stipulated for plena or committees, and there was complete freedom of speech. The minimum age for members in any Estate was twenty-five (*Riksdags Ordning* A.18). If a member persisted in straying from the subject of debate he could be restrained by the Speaker, who could himself be overruled by the Constitution Committee. Members were immune from indictment so long as they acted constitutionally. The constituencies who elected the members of the three lower Estates paid their salaries, and the desire of the electorate to shorten sessions had some effect on the behaviour of their representatives. Corruption was rare, partly on account of the strict election rules of secret ballot supervised by Provincial Governors and judges, and partly because all members except the Nobles were paid. Financial independence made members less susceptible to bribery. Infringement of the Electoral Law was punishable by from 8 to 16 days' imprisonment on bread and water.[2] Even more severe was the sentence for the use, or attempted use, of force against a member of Parliament, the Estates or their committees, to restrain them from performing their duty. It was high treason even if done at the command of a Minister on behalf of the executive power, and was to be punished according to the law.[3] The framers of the 1809 Constitution did not delete the traditional punishment for treason whereby the accused's right hand was cut off, after which he was broken on the wheel and then executed. All his property was surrendered to the Crown. Needless to say, the punishment was not applied after 1809. There was some embarrassment in 1834, when the editor of the newspaper *Stockholmsposten* was accused of 'high treason' against the King, on the grounds that he had referred to the deposition of

[1] Fahlbeck, E., op cit., p. 435.
[2] Ibid., p. 170.   [3] RF A. 110, iii.

Gustavus IV Adolf with the implication that another such revolution might be necessary. He received the legal sentence of death by execution, which was mitigated to three years' imprisonment. The editor refused to have his sentence mitigated, and in the end the Government was forced to extend a general amnesty to 'all political prisoners awaiting execution'. He was the only one.[1]

Partly because of the longevity of the Estate system, and partly because Sweden had never experienced the feudal hierarchy of King–baron–knight–yeoman, there was no opportunity for a parliamentary alliance such as that between landowners and merchants which had given strength to the British House of Commons. The King played the lower Estates off against the Nobles and encouraged division between them. During the so-called Era of Liberty in the eighteenth century when the Estates had been in the ascendancy, the Nobles had dominated Parliament and the Council of Ministers. Gustav III was able to reduce their power by persuading the other Estates to accept an amendment to the Constitution in 1789. This, while seeming to aim at the Nobles, undermined the authority of Parliament as a whole, and thereafter he governed with neither Council nor Parliament.

After 1809, when the Estates regained their proper legislative authority, the Nobles once more predominated. The senior member of each family (*huvudmannen*) was given authority to attend debates and on important occasions, such as the debates in 1809 and 1865, over 700 presented themselves. It was a long-established custom that nobles should be chairmen of each of the six parliamentary joint standing committees, on which the Estates were proportionately represented. Members of the most senior families were nominated ex-officio. Fortunately it was often possible to transfer the chairmanship to a man of ability who was prepared to give his time to the service of the committee. The nomination of nobles as chairmen did not necessarily mean domination of the committees by the Nobles Estate. Decisions were made by the whole committee, which jealously guarded its authority as the representative in equal numbers of all four Estates. There was no system of *rapporteurs*. In fact the committees had a corporate sense long before Parliament or the

[1] Hovde, B. J., *The Scandinavian Countries 1720–1865*, ii. 524.

Ministry. One concession by the Nobles in 1809 was a reduction in their number on committees to the same as that of the other Estates. Previously they had had double representation.

The Nobles were often careless about attendance at debates, and on one occasion there were only three present. To attend regularly required either independent means or State employment in Stockholm. It was comparatively easy for the bureaucratic nobles to be present, but difficult for country landowners who had estates to manage to afford town houses in Stockholm as well. Parliamentary sessions frequently lasted a year or more, and extraordinary sessions took place almost as often as ordinary ones (seven compared with ten in the period 1809–66). It is hardly surprising that attendance was sometimes low. But about 100 nobles were fairly regular attenders and in the more important votes each session between 200 and 400 took part.

The Estate retained its intellectual pre-eminence over the others through devices such as the transfer of chairmanships already mentioned. Membership of the *Riddarhus* could be transferred by the senior member of a family to someone else.[1] There were always seats to be bought for a price, provided the name of the purchaser was in the Peerage Calendar (*Adelskalender*), and young men were able to enter the Estate and make their mark while serving in the Law Courts or Stockholm garrison. Louis De Geer entered Parliament this way and found himself temporary chairman of the Constitution Committee when still in his thirties.

The politics of the majority of the Estate were conservative. For instance, it was here that the old guard Gustavians under Count de la Gardie formed the last opposition to the new liberal régime in 1810, whereupon the Government formed a secret police to watch their movements. The bureaucratic nature of the Estate, two-thirds of whom were in the civil or defence services, tended to make it subservient to the executive power, in other words to the King, upon whose favour depended the careers of many of the nobles and their sons. When the Government feared defeat in Parliament, clerks were sent round to the Colleges of the Civil Service and to the garrisons asking all good servants of the King to come and 'vote for the uniform'. The quartering of troops near the capital on occasion increased the number of

[1] Riddarhus Ordning A. 6.

such votes upon which the Government could rely. In the time of Gustav IV Adolf, the nobles had proved capable of rising against the King, but after 1809 the constitutional government of the Bernadottes and the fear that the days of their ascendancy as a class were numbered caused the majority to stand by their protector, the Crown. But they did not ask or want active personal intervention, as Charles XV discovered when in an enterprising moment as Crown Prince he took sides over an important railway bill.[1] The nobles were content to remain unorganized and leaderless, and to be attached to coteries rather than to become members of parties.

The opposition in the *Riddarhus* never became formidable in numbers but from its ranks came parliamentarians like Count Schwerin, dean of the diocese of Sala (who wanted a Parliament on the British model in 1815), Count Spens (who proposed the creation of Provincial Councils in 1834), and Baron Anckarswärd (who produced a motion for parliamentary reform in 1830). The Estate valued its reputation as a forum of ideas, and partly in order to leave its members entirely free it rebuffed all attempts to change its composition by the introduction of an electoral system. Its members could fairly claim in 1865 that they were sacrificing a great institution by passing the reform bill, and that they had no need to be ashamed of the part they had played in the discussion of the issue.

The Church's political position was much stronger than that of the Church of England, whose lower clergy had dropped out of Parliament at the time when the bishops and abbots drew together and became incorporated in the House of Lords. The suppression of the monasteries by Henry VIII reduced the representation of the English Church to the bench of bishops in the House of Lords, this number becoming proportionately smaller as more temporal peerages were created in the following centuries. In Sweden the Clergy Estate remained together and all the Clergy were represented in Parliament. The Archbishop of Uppsala, the eleven bishops, and the pastor primarius of Stockholm, not then a diocese, were members ex officio; the other members were elected by the diocesan clergy.

The number of vicars (*kyrkoherde*) who could be elected was forty-four. Curates could, if they chose, elect a representative

[1] Hallendorff, C., *Från Karl XV:s dagar*, pp. 35–45.

for each diocese, but seldom did so. The maximum number of clergy who could be elected was therefore seventy.[1] In the 1809 debates forty-five members of the Clergy Estate voted; in 1865 fifty-seven (including representatives of the Universities and Academy of Science) did so.

The conservatism and intolerance of many of the clergy was made manifest in the debates on the extension of the franchise to the Jews. Whereas the other Estates duly noted the admission of Jews to the British House of Commons in 1858, the Clergy Estate resolutely refused to give its assent when the question arose in 1862. The franchise was not extended to them until 1865, complete emancipation following five years later. (It was enacted in 1809 that only Christians could vote, and even then the Constitution Committee recommended the exclusion of Catholics on the ground that theirs was an intolerant religion.) The English and French press expressed their surprise over the state of affairs in Sweden. In an effort to explain the Government's attitude, one of the Ministers (Hamilton) asked a woman friend visiting France to insert in *Le Siècle* an anonymous explanation of the Government's unwillingness to pass a law of religious toleration. Countess Stackelberg succeeded in getting the article published, but unfortunately it appeared signed 'Count H. Hamilton, President of the Estates'. It was reprinted in the Swedish press, much to the author's embarrassment. He attempted to deny authorship, arguing that he would hardly have used a title which did not exist.[2]

Before the Jews were granted the vote, a toleration law was passed in 1860 for the benefit of the nonconformist bodies which were establishing themselves in Sweden. Care was taken to see that the Church did not lose revenue by the permission for other churches to proselytize in Sweden. Under the law everyone was registered at birth by the parish priest and paid Church taxes thereafter. Withdrawal from the State Church was difficult and conditional upon entry into another recognized denomination.[3]

[1] Riksdags Ordning A. 13.   [2] Hallendorff, op. cit., pp. 56 ff.
[3] A law which came into force on 1 January 1952, permits withdrawal from the Church unconditionally upon a personal request being made to the clergyman in the parish where the applicant's birth was registered. In order to pay for expenses incurred by the parish priest as registrar a third to a half of the Church taxes are still payable. There are other important provisions in the new law: Free Church

In general, the clergy opposed the new tendencies of the nine-teenth century, many of which weakened their position as leaders of the parish. The education reform of 1842, for instance, which made schooling compulsory, was accompanied by a re-form in local government by which a lay parish council was set up side by side with the clerical body. Although the parish priest was ex-officio chairman also of the new board, he did not have such a commanding position, and his authority gradually diminished in lay affairs. The reform in the poor law, so dear to Oscar I, resulted in the transfer of further duties to lay shoulders, though, in this instance, there was a different motive. It was stated in the *Riddarhus* debates of 1850–1 that the farmers were afraid that the parish priest might be too liberal in his care for the poor.[1] The local government reform of 1862 still further re-duced the power of the clergy and the setting up of a Church Assembly in 1863 indicated that once the reform bill was passed they would have to confine their activity mainly to Church affairs.

Thus in the debates over reform, the Clergy Estate argued from weakness and not from strength. As the economic and social importance of the farmers increased, the influence of the clergy declined. It was not surprising that the response of their representatives to proposals advocating a parliamentary reform which would oust them from national as well as local influence should be negative. Many of the earlier reforms required the assent of only three Estates, and some could be introduced by the King as part of his power over economic legislation. In the case of parliamentary reform, the privileges of the Estates were threatened, and since their consent was necessary the attitude of the Clergy was to be an important factor.

In the Burgher Estate, the number of Burgomasters decreased until by 1850 they comprised only about a dozen of the sixty or so representatives in the Estate. Another eight or nine came into the category of 'other magistrates'.[2] It is true that over a third, and sometimes nearly half, of the Estate still consisted of 'magisterial members', but on the other hand the 'other magi-

ministers may solemnize marriages, Ministers of the Crown need no longer be of the 'true Evangelical faith', and the bar on monastic institutions is lifted.
[1] Heckscher, G., *Svensk konservatism före representationsreformen*, ii. 214.
[2] Borell, B., op. cit., Tables on pp. 76–77.

strates' were laymen appointed by the burghers to assist the Burgomaster. To describe the Burgher Estate as to a large extent Crown-appointed has been challenged on these grounds.[1] The Parliament Act of 1810 extended the field from which members of the Parliamentary Estate could be drawn. According to Article 14, citizens who were not members of any guild could be elected as magistrates registered as voters in the Burgher Book. The presence of these magistrates enabled a wider representation than that permitted by the guild system, and it may reasonably be assumed that the Burgher Estate was less under Crown influence in the period before 1866 than it was a century earlier.

The number of members of the Estate varied. In Stockholm the electors were divided into twenty-seven different classes who elected an Electoral College of fifty persons required in turn to elect the following ten representatives:

3 magistrates.
2 wholesale traders paying at least 20 riksdaler in taxes
1 retail trader   ,,   ,,   ,,   10   ,,   ,,   ,,
1 manufacturer   ,,   ,,   ,,   10   ,,   ,,   ,,
3 craftsmen   ,,   ,,   ,,   5   ,,   ,,   ,,

Gothenburg sent three representatives, ten other towns sent two, and the remainder one. In recognition of the part played long ago by the copper mines in bringing wealth to the country, the Falu mining district returned a member. As the number of *bergsmän* electors decreased to about a dozen, this seat came near to being a rotten borough: in the nineteenth century it was controlled most of the time by the Falhem family.[2] The total maximum number of members of the Estate, if all the towns sent members, was 106.[3] The minimum, assuming some shared representatives, was 46. In the 1865 debate, 65 voted.

The countryside was divided into nearly 300 hundreds (*härader*), each of which was entitled to send one representative to the Farmer Estate. In practice members were shared by two, three, or even more hundreds, and in the more important debates between 100 and 150 votes were recorded. Notification of an

[1] Review of Andrén's book, *Sveriges riksdag*, vol. ix, by Axel Brusewitz in *Statsvetenskaplig Tidskrift*, 1940, p. 330, n. 1.
[2] Söderberg, T., *Bergsmän och brukspatroner i svenskt samhällsliv*, p. 64.
[3] Riksdags Ordning A14.

election was given in all parish churches after Divine Service and on the following Sunday the farmers of the parish gathered in the church to nominate an elector. He then proceeded to a central location in the hundred, where election of the representative took place under the supervision of the district (or assize) judge (*häradshövding*). No one was allowed to represent the farmers in Parliament if he was elegible for election to another Estate or held office under the Crown.[1] This prevented the infiltration into the Estate of the clergy, nobles, civil servants, and anyone else who was not a farmer. The stipulation had its advantages but also its drawbacks and helps to explain why, although theoretically equal to the others, the Farmer Estate tended to be treated as inferior.

The farmers were by no means unschooled—the introduction of compulsory education in 1842 did not imply its absence before that date—and several of their number were men of ability like Anders Danielsson and Nils Månsson of Skumparp, respected by the other Estates. The diary of Per Nilsson of Espö records many pertinent observations on parliamentary life in the mid-nineteenth century. The diarist seems to have attended the theatre and opera, and dined with the King and leading members of the *Riddarhus*, as though this was part of the normal routine of the leading members of the Estate. Yet it must be admitted that indulgence in spirits was common among the farmers in the first half of the century. Pope remarked of Queen Anne that 'she doth sometimes counsel take and sometimes tea': of some of the farmers it could be asserted that they were more addicted to alcohol than to committee work.

In many matters the Government could ensure the Farmers' acquiescence through pressure applied by the Speaker (whom they addressed as Father Speaker), and the Secretary, both of whom were appointed by the Crown. The Secretary, especially, was a man on whom the King could rely and whose guidance in matters of law and privilege was necessary to the Farmers. In 1809 the Constitution Committee rejected the Farmers' request to elect their own Speaker, but in 1863 they were permitted to elect their own Secretary. Pressure was less necessary after 1809 than before, and in view of the wording of the Constitution had to be used with discretion. On one memorable occasion, the

[1] Riksdags Ordning A. 15.

signing of the Constitution itself, intimidation had to be used. The Farmers refused to let their Speaker sign it until their grievances were redressed, particularly the burden of taxation. The deadlock was ended after some three weeks by a summons to the whole Estate to attend at the Palace where, in front of the Council of Ministers, the King, Charles XIII, harangued them on their duty to their country. He then asked all those who had forbidden their Speaker to sign to step forward. None did so, and the Speaker thereupon signed the document in the King's presence.[1] After 1809 bribery was occasionally used. An extraordinary session of Parliament was called in 1817 to deal with the financial crisis, and certain misgivings in the minds of the Farmers were calmed by Government-sponsored entertainments and certain gifts of money.[2] Anders Danielsson's great task as leader was to make the Farmers withstand this pressure. To some extent he succeeded, but there were still cases of bribery in the sixties when the railways were being built.

Nevertheless there was a gradual rise in the status of the Farmers and this was not altogether favoured by the other Estates. The fear of farmer-domination (*bondevälde*) in a reorganized Parliament was increased in 1851 when the Farmer Estate refused to support the Burghers in the final debate on the 1848 reform bill because it was not radical enough for their interests. If the farmers were to increase their political power, they might even succeed in redistributing the burden of taxation.

III. *Reforms in the composition of the Estates, 1809–1866*

In 1809 the Estate system was becoming outmoded. Moreover, the abolition of the French Estates had turned liberal opinion against this form of parliamentary organization. However, the Swedish Estates still served a useful purpose, and to describe them as a piece of 'ramshackle, antiquated and cumbrous machinery . . . on the medieval pattern',[3] though it represents general opinion about them, is probably too harsh. In 1809 the Estates did not appear so absurd as fifty years later, despite the fact that the actual machinery was less cumbrous than before.[4]

[1] Fahlbeck, E., op. cit., p. 52. [2] Ibid., pp. 288–9.
[3] Elder, N. C. M., 'The Parliamentary Role of Joint Standing Committees in Sweden', *Am. Pol. Sci. Review*, June 1951.
[4] Heckscher, G., op. cit., ii. 126.

For example, one of the main difficulties of the four-chamber system was resolved in 1857 by the introduction of joint sessions of the whole Parliament, and in 1860 Ministers were permitted to attend debates and address them in their capacity as Ministers of the Crown. Had the reforms in the latter part of the period been given time to have their effect, the unfavourable verdict on the Estates even as late as 1866 would have had to be modified.

Of the Estates, the Nobles alone remained unchanged. In the 1820's the Clergy underwent a liberal period and in 1823 it was the first Estate to open its doors to new members after the new Constitution came into force. The theology faculties of the two universities were already represented; now two representatives from each faculty were admitted, and two from the Swedish Academy of Science. These men included important figures like E. G. Geijer, F. F. Carlson, J. J. Nordström, and C. A. Agardh, who played a prominent part in the debates. The conversion of Geijer to liberalism in 1838 strengthened the liberal forces in the Estate, though it was hardly sufficient to offset its general conservative character.

The most important change in the composition of the Burgher Estate was the admission of ironmasters in 1830, despite the opposition of the craftsmen. The six representatives whom the ironmasters returned from 1834 onwards played a considerable part on committees, especially the Constitution Committee. Between them they owned half as much property as the rest of the Estate put together. Nor were all ironmasters represented as such. Half the country's ironworks were in the possession of landowner nobles and it is interesting to observe that several of these (e.g. the Anckarswärd brothers and Gripenstedt) were eager for political and economic reform, like their colleagues in the Burgher Estate.

The number of craftsmen in the Estate declined, so few towns sending craftsmen as representatives that had it not been for Stockholm's statutory three members from this group there would not have been more than two or three of them in any of the four Parliaments between 1840 and 1851. They were unable to put up much resistance to the decree of Oscar I abolishing the guild system in favour of free enterprise in 1846. Although it was to be a long time before Swedish industry was based on factories rather than on crafts, the political power of the crafts-men was already rapidly declining. Presumably the size of a social or economic group is not necessarily in proportion to its political power. Otherwise, the relative strength of the iron-masters and craftsmen would be inexplicable.[1]

There was an important reform of the franchise of the Estate in 1858; henceforth all who possessed a certain amount of pro-perty (in practice most householders) were enfranchised. The graded scale whereby the richer voters had more votes than the poor was retained despite energetic protests by the Burghers to the new Chancellor, Louis De Geer (who was not yet an advo-cate of parliamentary reform). In the Parliaments of 1862–3 and 1865–6 the Estate represented a considerable proportion of the urban middle class and its influence upon the attitude of the Clergy and Nobles to the reform bill was correspondingly greater.

There was a reform of the Farmer Estate in 1845 when farmers owning tax-exempted land (*frälsehemmansägare*) were admitted. Other minor alterations in the franchise affected small groups of farmers. The most important reform of the franchise did not come into effect until 1863, too late to affect the outcome of the reform bill, when at long last the property-owning rural middle class, the *ståndspersoner*, were admitted to Parliament. By placing its members in the Farmer Estate, Parliament gave final proof that the fourfold division was outmoded.

These changes in the composition of the Clergy, Burgher, and Farmer Estates show that some attempts were made to adapt Parliament to modern requirements. After the learned pro-fessions had obtained admittance to the Clergy Estate there were several unsuccessful requests for the admission of secondary school teachers. In 1830, at the time when the Burgher Estate was opened to ironmasters, the parliamentary debates were made public.

During the period there were also indications of a departure from the Estate principle. In 1828 it was agreed to allow voting in committees to take place *per capita*, i.e. according to the

---

[1] Thus the Free Churchmen and the Temperance enthusiasts were not pro-portionately much more numerous in 1900 than 1950, but their influence was far greater at the turn of the century.

individual's decision and not according to the majority opinion of the representatives of each Estate (A. 38). The widened franchise to the Burgher Estate meant the abandonment of profession as a qualification, and the substitution of property, while the admission of *ståndspersoner* to the Farmer Estate was hardly in accordance with the historic tradition of that chamber. Yet these innovations and the creation of an entirely new franchise for local government in 1862 did not arouse opposition on grounds of principle.[1] Moreover, in their different ways the abolition of the guilds, the law of religious toleration in 1860, the inauguration of the Church Assembly in 1863, and the Free Trade decree of 1864 did not conform to the Estate principle.

IV. *Proposals for a new Parliament, 1830–1860*

There was no steady progress towards an inevitable and complete reform of Parliament. By 1848 a clear majority of Burghers and Farmers favoured the abolition of the Estates, but among the Nobles and Clergy the anti-reform faction remained in the ascendancy until the very last days of the 1865 debates. It is difficult to measure the changing opinions quantitatively because political parties had been somewhat in disrepute since the Era of Liberty, and were not advocated by the reformers even in the older sense of groups of members in the legislature generally recognized by the electorate as having a certain political point of view, and elected because of their policy. Because there were coteries rather than organized groups, discussion took place in the various parliamentary clubs after the session opened. It frequently happened that a committee proved to be more conservative or liberal than was thought likely when it was formed, the views of members often being ascertainable only by a reading of their speeches and scrutiny of their voting. Occasionally a man was elected because he favoured reform (the practice in Gothenburg in the 1840's) but this was not always so. Those towns who appointed their Burgomaster as representative usually paid little regard to his political persuasion.

The reform discussions during the period 1830–60 have generally been regarded as a controversy between liberals and conservatives. In the absence of an agreed definition of a

---

[1] Andrén, G., op. cit., p. 29.

Swedish liberal or conservative at this time, the nomenclature is somewhat vague. The 'men of 1809' were 'liberals' in the sense that they wanted the legislature to have a greater share in government, but they and their successors became more conservative and after 1830 there were few people who would not have supported their view of the importance of Parliament.

There were at least three different types of liberal. First there were the radical-liberals such as Anckarswärd who wanted an immediate abolition of the Estates and the creation of a single-chamber legislature. This group drew its inspiration from Norway and was especially influential in the early stages of the agitation in the 1840's. Although the junior partner in the Dual Monarchy, Norway had already acquired a modern legislature in 1814, and in many ways the Norwegians were held to be an example to the more conservative Swedes by the liberal members of the Swedish Parliament. Free Trade was adopted in Norway, Jews admitted to full rights of citizenship, and a law of religious toleration passed, long before the Swedes followed suit.

Another group of liberals were the economic-liberals, who favoured Free Trade and increased foreign commerce, and amongst them could be numbered King Oscar I and his Finance Minister Gripenstedt. These men were often of a different type from the radical-liberals like C. H. Anckarswärd; indeed, many who were economic-liberals in their business life were conservative in their attitude towards parliamentary reform. A third group consisted of moderate-liberals who believed that political change was necessary, and that the Estate system should be abolished, though not by any radical solution of the problem. Thus a man like Louis De Geer, a judge and servant of the Crown imbued with a sense of Swedish parliamentary traditions, may be called a moderate-liberal. Of course the difference between these points of view was not always clearly understood, and the references in some Swedish writings to the 'Opposition' in Parliament (a vogue word of the time culled from British parliamentary practice) do not always distinguish the various types of liberal. However, this analysis becomes important when assessing the reasons for the success of the 1866 bill after so many failures.[1]

[1] In his posthumous *History of Economic Analysis*, pp. 393 ff, J. A. Schumpeter appears to have attempted a somewhat similar analysis. His broader approach led

Those liberals, usually radicals, who were active in the early stages of the reform agitation do not seem to have derived much inspiration from Britain, contact being largely confined to Gothenburg business men such as C. F. Waern. The unreformed British Parliament was notorious among Swedish liberals for its corruption and dependence on the royal power, its few admirers being men like Count Schwerin, who would have liked Sweden to have possessed a House of Lords on the British model, representing the landed interest. To the liberals, on the other hand, intent on devising a more suitable upper chamber than the *Riddarhus*, an imitation House of Lords appeared 'an empty charade of pomp and circumstance'.[1] Some Stockholm radicals read Bentham and had connexions with his disciple George Grote, but they were few in number. Bentham did not have much direct influence in Sweden. Even the 1832 Reform Bill seems to have played little part in stimulating Swedish interest in parliamentary reform.

The generic term 'conservative' has been used to describe all those who supported the Crown above everything else, or who defended the Estate principle, or who opposed the liberal motions for reform. Some conservatives were most afraid of the possibility of control of Parliament by the farmers; others distrusted most of all the radicals, or middle-class industrialists. Leadership of the conservatives after 1840 passed to von Hartmansdorff, a civil servant who rallied his colleagues and the die-hard conservatives to his side. But his views were too conservative in social and economic questions for the King, and the absence of support from the Court weakened the effectiveness of the group in the *Riddarhus*. After 1848 a new group became important, consisting of aristocratic landowners such as C. O. Palmstierna and Henning Hamilton. Known as the *Junker* party, they disliked the viewpoint of the bureaucrats and of von Hartmansdorff in particular.

The inspiration for conservative thinkers was provided by German Idealism. C. J. Boström, said to be Sweden's greatest philosopher in the nineteenth century, was a Hegelian who championed the Swedish system of King, Estates, and Civil

him to make a general distinction between the liberalism of the earlier political economists and that of later social reformers.

[1] Quoted in Fahlbeck, E., op. cit., p. 322.

Service as conforming to the idea of the organic state. However, his lectures at Uppsala and his speeches in the Clergy Estate proved of little avail. As a nation the Swedes were not interested in metaphysics and the practical results of their own 'organic' system were proving it to be out of date as the era of *laissez-faire* and industrialism opened.[1] Moreover, Sweden's long history as a single nation was very different from Germany's, whose scholars were seeking a theme of unity. In the latter part of the century the rise of Germany did prove to be an important outside influence upon Sweden, but then it was the practice of Socialism and the doctrine of a strong monarchy which attracted the Left and Right respectively: German Idealist political theory was not important.

Representatives of the main groups, whether liberal or conservative, were to be found in the *Riddarhus*, from which much of the inspiration of the other Estates came. One or two Burghers were important members of the liberal groups, the bulk of the support of the moderate-liberals coming from the towns. Similarly, though the Clergy Estate was thoroughly conservative, the leadership of the conservative opposition was in the *Riddarhus*. The Nobles' debates were therefore of the greatest importance from the point of view of opposition to parliamentary reform.

Shortly after the end of the 1830 Parliament, C. H. Anckarsward and J. G. Richert, the one a noble and the other a lawyer, published their plan for parliamentary reform, the most important proposal since 1810. They left no one in doubt of their radical views: 'Our constitutional system is a deceit and our representation insufferable beyond description.'[2] The 1830 motion differed from later ones in proposing a single chamber. Anckarsward was impressed by the structure of the unicameral Norwegian Parliament (*Storting*). Like Richert he favoured a Parliament controlled by educated men, and in Norway in 1830 a large number of middle-class representatives, including civil servants and clergymen, were returned by an electorate of farmers and fishermen, who themselves formed only one-fifth of the legislature. Consequently the Swedish radicals did not share the fear that a reform of the legislature would lead to domination

[1] Heckscher, G., op. cit., i. 88.
[2] Fahlbeck, E., op. cit., p. 320.

by the farmers. Anckarswärd's single chamber was a little deceptive since it was to consist, like the *Storting*, of a chamber within a chamber. Seventy-five of the 175 members were, on occasion, to form a separate body. The franchise was weighted in favour of the rich, who were to appoint nearly a third of the members.

By 1840 with the aid of the enthusiastic ironmasters in the Burgher Estate and the journalism of Lars Hierta, editor of *Aftonbladet*, the reformers had succeeded in enlisting the support of a majority in the two lower Estates. In that year anti-Government feeling was running high in the *Riddarhus* and the Government had not made sure that the nobles who were appointed to the Constitution Committee were its loyal supporters. The liberals obtained control of the Committee and then produced their own motion for reform.

The Constitution Committee's bill outlined provision for two chambers, the upper being elected by the lower. The qualifications required from the electorate voting for the lower chamber were higher than those in the 1830 motion. One reason for this alteration was a decline in admiration for the *Storting* after the 1832 elections had increased the proportion of farmers in the Norwegian Parliament from 21 per cent. to 45 per cent. There was no longer assurance that, if given the vote, the Swedish farmers would nominate members of the middle class. Instead of the vote being given to all who paid 5 *riksdaler* in taxation, as in 1830, the minimum requirement was 10 *riksdaler*, and gave a man only 1/100 of a vote. There was plural voting in the form of a graded scale whereby a rich man who paid 1,000 *riksdaler* was awarded the maximum of 6 votes. It was difficult to regard this as a radical measure.

Nevertheless, the motion proved too revolutionary for the Nobles and Clergy Estates and was rejected by them in 1844. Two years later Oscar I set up a Representation Committee, which appeared to indicate interest in a liberal measure of reform, until it was learned that the King himself wished to appoint one-third of the members of the upper chamber. Two Ministers (Jonas Waern and Faxe) were against this proposal and Schartau argued that were it put into effect part of the legislature would presumably consist of the King's friends and this would undoubtedly conflict with the principle that the people alone had the right to determine their taxation.[1] Before the issue became controversial the revolution in 1848 swept across Europe and the Government thought it advisable to introduce a bill itself, and this proved to be a rather radical measure of reform. It embodied Count Spens's idea of an upper chamber elected by provincial councils of electors, and proved to be the solution adopted in 1865 when a graded scale, the Swedish form of plural voting, was applied to the First (upper) Chamber.

The Government bill was defeated by all except the Burgher Estate in 1851 at its second appearance before Parliament. The Nobles and Clergy again found it too radical, while the Farmers did not think it radical enough. The King had not encouraged his supporters in Parliament to vote for the bill, and this ensured its defeat. No further important proposal was made until after his death in 1859. Sweden, like western Europe and the United States, underwent periods of reaction, and the 1850's were years of withdrawal from political reform.[2]

By 1851, twenty-one years had passed between the presentation of the Anckarswärd motion and the defeat of the Government bill, and little progress would seem to have been made. However, by Swedish standards, matters were proceeding as the Constitution intended, since the proposals involved changing a fundamental law. Private motions such as Anckarswärd's could not be moved in the Estates but went directly to the Constitution Committee (according to A. 81) which decided whether or not to propose to the Estates that the motion be accepted with or without amendments. Such a motion, and motions prepared by the committee itself, could be discussed in general terms but could not be voted upon by the Parliament then sitting. They had to lie (vila) until the next Parliament met. A private member whose motion was rejected by the Constitution Committee could require of the Committee its reasons and could then publish his motion and the Committee's reply. Government bills (propositions) were also sent to the committee first and not discussed by the Estates until the following Parliament.[3] But the

---

[1] Borell, op. cit., p. 207.
[2] Cf. the Third Empire in France, the Derby and Aberdeen Ministries in Britain, and the presidencies of Fillmore, Pierce, and Buchanan in the United States.
[3] Government bills were called *propositions*; other proposals were termed motions.

committee could either accept or reject these: it had no power to amend. If the *proposition* was accepted it lay until the following Parliament; if it was rejected, Parliament could debate the matter at once. If the vote was in favour of the bill, or if two Estates supported it, the bill then lay until the next Parliament. In this way the Constitution Committee was prevented from having an absolute veto over legislation affecting the fundamental laws.[1] Moreover, until a *proposition* accepted by the Constitution Committee was rejected by the Estates it was not possible for it to consider further proposals on the same subject.

Hence, in accordance with this procedure, the 1830 motion of Anckarswärd and Richert, which was presented too late for discussion by the 1830 Parliament, was examined by the Constitution Committee in the next Parliament of 1834–5. In the following Parliament, 1840, the Constitution Committee produced its own motion which was debated and rejected by the Parliament of 1844–5. The next Parliament met in 1848, when the Government *proposition* was presented to the Constitution Committee, to be rejected by the Estates which met in 1851. Parliaments met infrequently and lasted for only one session— long enough to deal with business which had accumulated in the intervening period and was ready for debate at the beginning of the session. In the course of twenty-one years the private-member's motion had been succeeded by a Constitution Committee motion and finally a Government *proposition*. Consequently when reform was taken up once more, by De Geer in 1861, the ground had been prepared. He even felt he needed no committee to draft a proposal for him, and presented his own bill to the Constitution Committee, which accepted it in the session 1862–3. It was therefore debated by the Estates in the next session, 1865–6.

The failure of the early movement for reform can be attributed to three main factors: the effect of 1848, the Year of Revolutions, the policy of Oscar I, and the diversion of interest to economic affairs.

[1] A. 81. In 1856–8 Parliament after a long battle secured the right to immediate discussion and rejection of a bill reported out by the Constitution Committee amending the Constitution, although, 'if approved, the bill would still lie, as previously, until the next Parliament. See Fahlbeck, op. cit., p. 176. These rules had their origin in the Era of Liberty rules of 1766.

. The year 1848 revealed the fundamental disunity of the reform movement. The landowning aristocracy had hoped for a
reform which would reduce the influence of the multitude of civil
servants and army officers who outvoted them in the *Riddarhus*.
The ironmasters and business men resented being confined
to a limited representation in a junior Estate. The farmers and
urban middle class believed that they deserved a much larger
share in Parliament. Some of the support in the *Riddarhus* in
1840 stemmed merely from a desire to express dissatisfaction
with the bureaucratic Council of Ministers. But the European
revolutions caused many liberal groups to think more cautiously
about the effect of reform. It became apparent that the aims
of the landowners, townsmen, and farmers did not coincide.
The Estates drew apart from one another and the possibility of a
united front in favour of an agreed measure of reform faded.

Oscar's policy, or, perhaps, the lack of it, contributed to the
failure of the reform movement to survive the year of revolutions. Had he wanted a reform of Parliament, he could have
ensured the passage of the 1844 bill. For a long time it was
thought that in his early years at least Oscar was interested in
replacing the Estates by a bicameral legislature. His occasional
leanings in that direction have, however, been recently explained as tactics to win support for the social measures with
which he was more concerned.[1] By choosing younger men like
Gripenstedt who were interested in social and economic reform,
the King was able to adopt an intermediate position between
the large conservative group in the upper Estates and the
radicals in the lower. In this way, though he lacked the forceful
character of his father, Oscar managed to retain much of the
power of the monarch. He was a trimmer whose aim was to
secure sufficient support for his policy, no matter from which
parliamentary quarter it came. Thus the 1848 bill was presented
in order to draw the teeth of the opposition: it later became
clear that the King had no intention of persuading the conservative majority in the *Riddarhus* or Clergy Estate to accept it.
In 1850 and 1851, with the help of the Chief of Police in Stockholm, he bought out two newspapers of radical-socialist leanings
in order to muzzle their propaganda.[2] That he was able to do so

[1] See Borell, B., op. cit., pp. 153 ff., 203 ff., and Gasslander, op. cit., pp. 31.-32.
[2] Borell, p. 283. They were *Folkets Röst* and *Söndagsbladet*.

not only indicates the weakness of the socialist movement, but also suggests that it was the reaction after the year 1848 which made this step possible.

Lastly, interest now turned to business matters in which Oscar's support of Free Trade enabled him to be politically successful. Even in the early years of his reign he had enlisted the services of liberals for the Council of Ministers by his economic policy. Jonas Waern was a liberal chosen for the Ministry for his economic and not his political views. An iron-master who favoured parliamentary reform and was said to be the most radical of the Ministers in office before 1848, Waern helped to bring about the Free Trade reform of 1846. Disillusioned over Oscar's attitude towards the abolition of the Estates he at last resigned in 1848. Yet he did so only when the King's Free Trade policy aroused his misgivings.

Many of those who had espoused the cause of parliamentary reform in the 1830's and 1840's—landowners, business men, and ironmasters—began to reap the reward of Free Trade in the 1850's. The construction of railways began, the iron and timber industries expanded, and the export of corn continued. The total value of foreign trade, which had averaged nearly 55 million *riksdaler* in the years 1836–40, gradually increased in the next five years to 58 million and in 1846–51 to 71 million. But in the next period, 1851–5, the average annual total of exports and imports was nearly 114 million *riksdaler*.[2] Parliament's interests may be gauged from the 1854 session, which included debates resulting in votes which reduced Customs duties, permitted the building of railways, forbade the domestic distillation of spirits (much to many farmers' annoyance); simplified the land tax, improved the postal services, and introduced the decimal system.[3] So many proposals involved the Crown's economic legislation that it was essential to have Oscar's support. In return, perhaps, Parliament did not press parliamentary reform.

[1] See Lindgren, J., *Från Per Götrek till Per Albin*, chap. 2.
[2] Montgomery, A. *The Rise of Modern Industry in Sweden*, p. 119.
[3] Fahlbeck, E., op. cit., p. 396.

CHAPTER III

The Preparation
of the Parliament Act of 1866

1. *The appointment of Louis De Geer as Chancellor*

IN 1858 the Crown Prince Regent appointed an apparently harmless bureaucrat, Louis de Geer, as Minister of Justice and Chancellor. The following year Oscar I died and Charles became King. In 1860, Charles XV met his first major political setback, and dismissed the Minister 'responsible', Count Henning Hamilton. These three events were of some importance in preparing the way for another attempt at parliamentary reform.

The appointment of De Geer did not seem to imply any change in the traditional order. His rejection of the plea of the towns to abolish plural voting to the Burgher Estate convinced the liberals that he was no more in favour of a new type of legislature than his predecessors.

Moreover, though a member of the landowning nobility by birth, De Geer was a bureaucratic noble himself, having served the Crown most of his life. At thirty-seven he had been made President of the Göta Court of Appeal, a distinguished judicial appointment. Charles's intention seems to have been to appoint a man whom he knew and trusted, popular with the *Riddarhus* and yet without a definite policy of his own. He meant to dictate policy himself and appointed as his *aide* his former tutor, Hamilton, a competent senior conservative. To this end, Hamilton was made Consultative Minister (i.e. without portfolio) and the Ministry was known as the Hamilton–Manderström Ministry, Manderström being the Minister of State for Foreign Affairs. The Chancellor as such had not yet been recognized as the leader of the Ministry. This was, however, to be the last occasion when the Council was known by its strongest personalities and not by the name of the Chancellor. At first De Geer did not shape policy and indeed looked upon Hamilton as his senior colleague and mentor.

Charles XV (1859–72), a monarch who lacked his father's subtlety and his grandfather's masterfulness, but imagined he possessed both, hoped at the beginning of his reign that with Hamilton's aid he would exercise his full constitutional power and 'alone govern the realm' as Charles XIV had attempted to do. To make the Council a more serviceable instrument for his policy he took an active part in making it more homogeneous in its composition and methods of carrying on business, but he was unable to give it the firm and stable leadership it required. The serviceable instrument soon proved to be the master, and, by his over-confidence in himself, Charles contributed to the rise of the Ministry as the real repository of executive power.

Charles's disposition showed itself in the sort of close companions he chose. Fond of drinking bouts and occasionally even inviting members of the Farmer Estate to spend an evening at the Palace, he established a reputation of camaraderie among the ordinary people. He was a big man physically, of fine military bearing, and once he told the radical leader, August Blanche: 'You are the mob's king, but I am the people's king.' Admired by men and adored by women, he was sometimes called by a later generation the 'Father of Sweden' for much the same reason as England's Charles II was called 'the pattern of his people'. His incursions into politics were irregular, and a cartoon of the time showed him standing in front of his easel—he claimed to be a painter as well as a poet—while the Council waited for his presence. In public, the Ministry played up to Charles's ambition to be a strong King; in private, they knew that he lived in a world of his own imagination. Louis De Geer, who cannot be said to have borne him ill will, wrote shortly after his death in 1872 a private letter in which he said:

Everything of significance that happened during his reign took place against his will, e.g. in foreign policy, parliamentary reform, promotions etc. He certainly did not give in to his people's will from a good heart but intrigued against [everything]. But he never had strength even to fight for (hardly even to retain) a principle. So it is difficult to know where his greatness lay.[1]

He added later in his Memoirs: 'It was, as a matter of fact,

[1] Louis De Geer's *Brevsamling*, p. 47.

like that of his celebrated friend Frederick VII [of Denmark], only weakness.'[1]

His failure to prevent parliamentary reform was the most outstanding of several reverses suffered by Charles, the first of which followed his promise to the Norwegians that he would abolish the office of Governor of Norway, without having first ascertained the opinion of the Ministry and Parliament. There was an outcry in Sweden and he had to retract under pressure from De Geer, who thereby helped to establish his position as chief Minister. Hamilton, who was partly to blame for the King's pledge, was forced to resign as scapegoat for the King and outwardly the reputation of the monarchy was preserved. The next setback was in 1863 when Charles wanted to fulfil his promise to Frederick VII of Denmark that in the event of a Prussian attack on Denmark he would support him with 20,000 troops. The Ministers, largely guided by Gripenstedt, insisted that the promise had no validity because they knew nothing of it, and forced Charles once more to go back on his word. Later he tried to excuse himself on the grounds that he had made the promise personally to Frederick, whose death in 1863 absolved him from any responsibility.

It is true that once he realized that the Ministry was bent on reform, Charles half attempted to replace it, but Hamilton was now Minister to Denmark and none of the conservatives approached wanted to take on the responsibility of government. The presentation of the reform *proposition* to Parliament in 1863 so increased the popularity of the Ministry that thereafter no one dared to upset it. This was an important reason for Charles's resigned attitude.

The departure of Hamilton from the Ministry in 1860, though necessitated by his support of the King's Norwegian volte-face, enabled the Ministry to act more in concert. That Hamilton himself was aware that his landowner-conservatism was not in accord with the general opinion of his colleagues was made clear in a letter he wrote on 1 December: '...my departure was for the general good. I consider not only that the Department for Church and Education[2] has come into better hands but

[1] De Geer, L. *Minnen*, ii. 137. Nisbet Bain accepted the fiction of Charles XV as the author of the reform bill in his book *Scandinavia* published in 1905 (pp. 433-4), and does not appear to have read the De Geer *Memoirs*, which were published in 1892.   [2] He accepted this post in 1859.

that the present Council can longer and more easily hold together without me.'[1] If Hamilton had not resigned when he
did, he might have felt impelled to do so later, because in a
letter to Manderström on 8 August 1860, De Geer disclosed his
new interest in parliamentary reform. As it was, during the
early stages of the reform bill, the man who was recognized as
the leading conservative, and who was to be its most eloquent
opponent, was out of the country.

It has been remarked that when De Geer entered the Council
of Ministers in 1858 he was not regarded as a supporter of
parliamentary reform. It was not long, however, before he felt
impelled to change his mind, though the precise reasons for
his altered opinions in 1860–1 are still obscure.[2] The petitions
for reform he received from the Burgher and Farmer Estates
in 1860 at the close of the parliamentary session may have
convinced him that the reform of Parliament could no longer be
delayed, and his success in handling the Norwegian question
may have suggested to him that he alone could bridge the gap
between the conservative and reformer's points of view. As a
moderate-liberal he refused to commit himself to the Friends
of Reform movement founded in 1859, or to decry the conservative opposition. Later on he became particularly anxious
to retain his influence with the King, whose threat of veto might
rally the conservatives against reform and secure its defeat.

, De Geer's decision to introduce a reform bill dates from an
audience with the King to whom he offered the customary
'Humble Pro Memoria' of 16 July 1861, beginning:

As a more rational system of representation has been adopted by
the whole of the rest of Europe with the exception of England (whose
aristocracy with all its wealth has succeeded in remaining in its
Upper House only at the cost of renouncing all real influence, above
all in financial issues), it seems time to bring about a reform in
Sweden where the injustice of leaving the right to levy taxes with
four Estates, two of which are privileged, may in troublous times
lead to the gravest consequences.[3]

The reference to the British[4] Upper House was a warning that
an 'Upper Chamber based on nobility was not feasible.

[1] Hallendorff, op. cit., p. 81.
[2] Thermaenius, E., in *Svenskt biografiskt lexikon*, vol. x: 'Louis De Geer', p. 527.
[3] De Geer papers, Litt. A.
[4] In Sweden, reference is usually made to 'England'.

His reason for insisting upon the need for reform was the weakness of the Estate system, and 'the impossibility of having strong government'. Whether he meant strong government by the King or by Parliament and Ministry was not clear. De Geer was so impressed by the need to replace the Estates by a bicameral legislature based on a general franchise that he wrote:

... fundamentally my opinion is so determined that I find myself as Chancellor in duty bound to regard the introduction of reform as my most important task, and to try to make those preparations which are the Government's responsibility; as a consequence thereof I must resign my office if the Government is unwilling to put its moral weight into the scale on the side of reform, and is not prepared to act as soon as a favourable opportunity presents itself.

It was an ultimatum—but from De Geer, not from the Ministry. Although in a sense the King was the 'Government' and the Council of Ministers without independent status, his references to the 'Government' in the context might well have included his colleagues as well as the King. He had not told the other Ministers, at least officially, of his intentions and so his threat of resignation would not have involved them or the King in a crisis. He offered to remain silent on the subject for six months in order that the King would have time to make up his mind whether to dismiss him or not. As yet the country knew nothing of De Geer's intentions and so in a sense the threat of resignation was not so serious as it might seem. Had he been a typical bureaucrat he would, no doubt, have resigned forthwith, but such a course would have struck De Geer as contrary to the best interests of the country. The six months' silence was offered instead.

The King did not take the obvious course, dismissal, but tried to dissuade him and to delay bringing the issue to a head. At the time of the Pro Memoria he was about to set off on his summer vacation to France and Norway, and told De Geer that he would consider the matter on his return in the autumn. On reaching Norrköping on the way south, however, he sent Hamilton back to Stockholm to try and deter him. The mission proved unsuccessful and Hamilton proceeded to Copenhagen, the King travelling on through Växjo. De Geer had suggested that if he was asked to resign, the King might grant him the

Provincial Governorship of Växjo when its present occupant, Count Mörner, retired. Charles persuaded Mörner to postpone his retirement.

On his return from France, Charles was more favourably inclined to De Geer's plans now that he had heard from Napoleon III of the advantage of associating domestic reform with a forceful foreign policy. (Napoleon was not averse to a strong Scandinavia to the north of Prussia.) Without much diplomacy the King informed De Geer outright that he would support a reform bill on condition that the Ministry supported his Scandinavian policy. However, under no circumstances would De Geer accept · such a bargain and the matter went no further.

The autumn of 1861 passed into winter and still the King showed no sign of dismissing De Geer, being naturally reluctant to take decisions and still hoping that the matter would be dropped. In January 1862, a deputation waited on De Geer with a request for Government action in the reform question. He responded prudently but positively and his speech was recorded in the official gazette. To his surprise he noted that neither the King nor his colleagues made any comment. He did not realize that to no one but himself had the occasion much significance; but the six months had expired and the words he used were by no means the usual ministerial platitudes.

Now, when it was too late, Charles began to think of dismissing him. Between 1862 and 1864 there were several ministerial 'crises' which De Geer and his colleagues weathered successfully, for by this time they were supported by a public opinion showing an interest in political affairs rarely apparent since 1809. Some conservatives began to fear that a change might be a change for the worse and that a new Ministry would have to resort to more radical measures. De Geer now knew that he was indispensable to moderate opinion. As for the King, he had been unable to forestall De Geer, to bargain with him, or to dismiss him.

De Geer's method of preparing the Government bill (*proposition*) illustrated his moderation. He examined the proposals and debates which had already taken place and tried to discern what were the minimum demands of the lower Estates, and the maximum concessions of the nobles and clergy. By basing his bill on the 1848 proposal, then considered rather radical, he showed that he realized that much had happened in the past fourteen years. It was now generally accepted that the farmers and urban middle class would control the lower or Second Chamber, though it was still uncertain who would sit in the upper house or First Chamber. Oscar had wanted to appoint some members himself and some conservatives had thought that there should be ex-officio representation of nobles and bishops. However, in 1862 Provincial Councils were created, and De Geer made these the electoral colleges for his upper chamber. By now, even in conservative circles, hopes of some small relic of the Estate era in the upper chamber had receded.

De Geer was presented with three major difficulties: first, the construction of a lower chamber which would represent the farmers and the middle class, but not the uneducated masses; second, the formation of an upper chamber which would meet liberal demands and yet restrict membership to the upper classes; third, the delineation of the respective authority of the chambers.

The exclusion of the uneducated was secured by the award of the franchise only to those who possessed certain income and property qualifications, the middle class being favoured by the construction of special urban constituencies often much smaller than those in the country. In this way De Geer hoped to have a Second Chamber somewhat similar in composition to the combined Burgher and Farmer Estates as they were after the recent reforms.

The election of the First Chamber by twenty-four Provincial Councils and a special Council representing Stockholm conformed to liberal ideas. The 1862 decree which inaugurated these Councils did not, however, affect the status of the Provincial Governors who were appointed by the Crown and whose offices carried on provincial administration. Popular local government remained confined to towns and villages. Apart from the hospital service which was placed in their hands, the new Councils (*landstingen*) were given little responsibility and were to meet once a year in September. According to De Geer's bill the Provincial Councils were to have a new, strictly political, function: the election of members of the First Chamber. Another liberal reform was the extension of the franchise to the Provincial Council electorate. Both men and women who paid taxes to their commune and were at least twenty-three years of age were given the vote.

Nevertheless there were certain 'guarantees' which were to reduce the liberal element of the First Chamber franchise to insignificant proportions. The graded scale (plural vote) was introduced whereby a rich man or business enterprise might possess as many as 5,000 votes in the country or 100 in the towns. The new Provincial Councils were not representative of the common people.

Finally there was the problem of the respective authority of the chambers. To prevent both liberals and conservatives from opposing the bill he made the chambers exactly equal in competence and authority. This principle, to some extent followed in the Estate system, was to remain the cornerstone of Swedish parliamentary practice.

In the summer of 1862 De Geer rented a villa in Djurgården, where he prepared his bill. Having informed Charles in Kristiania of his activities he received a reply dated 10 August addressed to 'My dear friend' and saying that De Geer's letter 'certainly gave me a headache'. The King went on to make an important concession: he was now 'convinced of the necessity for a change in the representation, and one not based on the Estates'.[1] But he warned De Geer that the bill must be one which he and all four Estates could accept. Oscar had made a similar condition in 1844 and had not meant, as some liberals had hoped, that he would use his influence with the Estates to persuade them to accept reform. Until the King openly declared himself in favour of a reform bill, the chances of the Nobles and Clergy Estates agreeing to it were very slight. As if to confirm De Geer's worst suspicions, Charles added that in his Speech from the Throne at the opening of Parliament in October, 1862, he would say nothing about the reform lest the Nobles should be alarmed.

II. *The contents of the bill*

With few alterations the bill which De Geer prepared in the summer of 1862 became the new Parliament Act (*1866 års Riksdagsordning*). Some of its eighty-two articles were inherited from previous Acts, but a completely new document was made

[1] De Geer papers, Litt. B.

necessary owing to the abolition of the Estates. Together with the 1809 Constitution it forms the second major fundamental law in force today, the reform bills of 1907–9 and 1918–21 merely involving the amendment of certain articles.

The first article established the 'equal competence and authority' of the two chambers. In a commentary De Geer explained that this meant that all matters which could be raised and discussed in one chamber could be raised and discussed in the other (A. 55), that all the Crown's communications and *propositions* should go to both chambers (A. 54), that all committee reports should be presented to both chambers so that simultaneous debate could take place (A. 59), and that the regulations for the consideration of business should be the same for both chambers.[1] In the same article it was stated that members of Parliament were bound only by the Constitution. This was amplified by De Geer to mean that members 'need not render account of their actions to the electorate', which accorded with his distaste for political parties. Both the provisions were inherited from the Estate system.

Articles 2–5 were of a general nature. Parliament was to meet annually on 15 January, extraordinary sessions being summoned for special purposes at the request of the King (A. 2). Members were elected for a certain period, but before this time had elapsed the King could dissolve one or both chambers and order a new election (A. 3). Members were not to be hindered in the performance of their duties (A. 4). Except at its own request for dissolution, Parliament was to continue in session for four months unless the King ordered a new election to one or both Chambers. The new Parliament was to meet within three months of the dissolution of the old, and could not be dissolved by the King under any circumstances until it had sat four months. Extraordinary sessions could, on the other hand, be dissolved by the King at his pleasure (A. 5).

Previously there had been no specific date for meetings of Parliament and the length of ordinary sessions had been three months, extension to four being possible if three Estates desired it. The most important innovation was the introduction of annual sessions.

[1] De Geer papers: *Kommentär till Riksdagsordingen.* The articles are numbered according to the 1866 *Riksdagsordning.*

Articles 6–12 were concerned with the election of the First Chamber, the term 'first' being preferred to 'upper' because the chambers were to be of equal status. Election of members was indirect, Provincial Councils and large towns which did not form part of Provinces electing one member for every 30,000 inhabitants. Members were elected for a period of nine years (A. 6), and were to be men over thirty-five years of age who for at least three years previous to the election had either owned real estate of at least 80,000 *riksdaler* taxable value or had earned an annual income of at least 4,000 *riksdaler* taxable value.[1] A member lost his seat if at any time after the election he was 'no longer eligible for membership of the chamber', that is, for instance, if for any reason within or beyond his control, the value of his estate fell below the minimum laid down in this article. Members did not receive any remuneration for their services or even travelling expenses; they were, however, at liberty to resign provided they did so between sessions (A. 12).

The provisions affecting the Second Chamber were contained in Articles 13–25. The chamber was elected for three years (A. 13, i). Judicial districts (*domsagor*) formed county constituencies on the basis of one member for every 40,000 inhabitants. Towns could form their own constituencies, but were divided into two types: those which had a population of 10,000 or more and elected a member for every 10,000 inhabitants; and those with less than 10,000 but which, possessing their own jurisdiction, could join together in groups and form separate constituencies, electing a member for every 6,000 inhabitants. The latter arrangement was to be sanctioned in the first place by the Crown, and afterwards by Parliament which was to review the position every ten years (A. 13, iii). This provision was to be of considerable importance in the 1890's when the Farmer's party decided that the smaller towns were over-represented.

The electorate for the Second Chamber was to consist of men entitled to vote in local elections and who, in addition, either owned real estate of a taxable value of at least 1,000 *riksdaler*, or for at least five years had leased farm property of taxable value of 6,000 *riksdaler* or more, or paid taxes on an income of at

---

[1] In 1875 the name of the *riksdaler* was changed to *krona*, the value remaining the same. Until the Second World War the rate of exchange was a little over 18 crowns to the £, falling to 14·50 in 1947.

least 800 *riksdaler* a year (A. 14). In the explanation attached to
the bill presented to Parliament in 1863, De Geer adhered to
the theory that the ownership of real estate gave a man more of
a stake in the country than income from other sources.[1] At the
same time he could not raise the qualifications much above
1,000 *riksdaler* without excluding many farmers who had been
members of the Farmer Estate.[2] The use of the term 'taxable
value' excluded those whose income was unknown to the revenue
authorities.

Elections were to take place in September every three years,
even if in the meantime Parliament was dissolved by the King
(A. 15). Hence although Parliament was dissolved early in
1887 the triennial elections took place as usual a few months
later. The election of members was to be direct in those towns
which returned members of their own. It was to be indirect
where a large constituency was formed by a group of communes
or small towns. These each returned one elector, and an additional elector for every 1,000 residents in communes and every
500 in towns. Each elector had one vote in the election of the
member of the Second Chamber. If they chose, the communes
and small towns could, however, elect members directly (A. 16–
17). There was to be no plural voting, in contrast to Provincial
Council elections.

Members of the Second Chamber were required to be at
least twenty-five years old (the age qualification of the Estates),
and to have been entitled to vote in the local constituency for
which they stood as parliamentary candidate for at least a year
(A. 19). There were thus residential qualifications for Second
Chamber members, but no mention of property qualifications
other than those affecting the electorate. Members were not
allowed to resign unconditionally as in the First Chamber, but
only if they became legally disqualified, or reached the age of
sixty, or had already attended three parliaments (A. 21). They
were to receive a salary of 1,200 *riksdaler* and travelling expenses,
and an additional expense allowance of 10 *riksdaler* a day during
extraordinary sessions. Anyone absent from Parliament was to
have 10 *riksdaler* a day deducted from his salary (A. 23).

Articles 24–30 were of a general nature. There was to be a

[1] *Kong. Maj:ts Nåd. Proposition*, no. 61, p. 41.
[2] Thermaenius, E., *Lantmannapartiet*, p. 35.

secret ballot and the election of a candidate or list of candidates
found to be in some way ineligible was to be invalid (A. 25).
Members were to be Swedish citizens of the Protestant religion.
A candidate was disqualified if he:

  (a) stood under guardianship;[1]
  (b) had put all his estate into the hands of his creditors;
  (c) was indicted for a criminal offence;
  (d) had lost his rights of citizenship or been declared unfit
      to represent the wishes of others;
  (e) had been guilty of bribery or corruption or threats at an
      election or had disturbed the freedom of election (A. 26).

Fines were imposed by both chambers on members who were
absent without permission (A. 30).

There followed six Articles (31–36) of a rather detailed nature
on the assembly and dissolution of Parliament. Under the title
'The Preparation of Matters', Articles 37–50 dealt with the
appointment and composition of committees.

It has already been pointed out that the joint standing committee system had long played an important part in Swedish
parliamentary life. The Secret Committee of the Era of Liberty
had been the most powerful in Swedish history. In 1809 six
joint standing committees were set up on a permanent basis.
The 1866 bill reduced the number of these from six to five, the
General Purposes Committee (*Allmänna ekonomi och besvärs
utskottet*) being dropped. The committees remaining were:

  The Constitution Committee of 20 members
  The Supply or Appropriations Committee of 24 members
  The Committee on Ways and Means of 20 members
  The Bank Committee of 16 members
  The Law Committee of 16 members

Each chamber elected half the members of each committee
(A. 37, i), an equal number of deputies being also elected
(A. 37, ii). Two other types of committee were permitted:
special committees, the appointment of which might be considered preferable to the submission of a matter to one or more
of the joint standing committees, and temporary committees of
either chamber to deal with matters not belonging to the standing committee (A. 37, iii). In extraordinary sessions only those

---

[1] This referred to persons who were of age but who had been placed under
guardianship by a court of law.

committees required for the particular matter in hand were to be appointed (A. 37, iv).

The Constitution Committee continued to examine the minutes of the King-in-Council (A. 38). The most important committee was the Committee of Supply, which examined the public finances and could report to Parliament the misdemeanours of Ministers who in financial matters had countersigned measures contrary to Parliament's decision (A. 39). Ministers were still excluded from committees (A. 43), which elected their own chairmen and vice-chairmen and appointed their secretary and staff from the Civil Service (A. 44). If a committee required information from the Civil Service, its chairman was entitled to request the appropriate Minister to obtain the King's permission to get the information needed (A. 46). Committees could hold joint meetings if necessary (A. 47). When voting took place by secret ballot, one voting slip was taken out and sealed, to be used only in the event of a tie (A. 48). This had been the procedure before 1866, made necessary by the equal representation of Estates on committees; after 1866 the equal representation of chambers made it equally essential. Confidential information on foreign affairs could be given by the King to a 'deputation' of six members from each chamber (A. 50). This, like its predecessor, was commonly called the 'Secret Committee', a rather confusing title for a body which was not recognized as such in the Constitution.

Articles 51–78 contained rules for debate in the chambers. The Speaker was empowered to declare the expressed opinion of Parliament according to the Constitution, but was not permitted to take part in debates or bring them to a close without the assent of the chamber (A. 51). Freedom of speech, the immediate closing of debate if the King were present, and other provisions in the 1809 Constitution, were repeated in the 1866 Act. Government requests and bills were presented to the chamber by a Minister (A. 54).

Motions by private members, with the exception of constitutional amendments, were to be presented within ten days of the session's opening (A. 55), and were permitted on all questions in which Parliament could make a decision. Parliament was not allowed to discuss petitions by private persons.[1] If a

[1] Malmgren, R., *Sveriges grundlagar*, 5th ed., p. 163, A. 55, n. 1.

matter fell within the competence of a joint standing committee, it could not be voted upon in the chambers until it had first been submitted to the appropriate committee (A. 56). These two articles signified that the four months' session was intended to deal with a known total amount of business, and at the beginning of the session, motions and *propositions* were to be divided between the appropriate committees. Before a motion was referred to a committee, members could usually debate it in general terms, but since no decision could be reached, and submission to the committee not delayed (A. 58), these *remiss* debates tended often to have little importance. The two main stages in the discussion of a *proposition* were the committee discussion and the final debate in the chambers. When all business reported from committees had been debated, the session of Parliament ended.[1]

In the final voting, the Speaker first of all asked the chamber whether it agreed to close the debate. If the answer was in the affirmative he asked the chamber if it was willing to accept the *proposition*. Frequently the chamber wished to amend bills and there was thus employed the sytem of *proposition* and *kontra-proposition* (A. 60). For example, the Speaker would ask, 'Those who desire the House to accept the committee's proposal vote "Yes". Those who do not wish this, vote "No". If the Noes have it, the House has accepted N. N.'s amendment.'[2] This enabled the House to decide its general preference for the original bill or the committee bill (if it differed from the original proposal). It could then go on to vote for amendments to the bill as proposed by members of the committee or chamber.

The Speaker was obliged to reject propositions which he found to be unconstitutional. If the chamber disagreed with his ruling, it could submit the matter to the Constitution Committee, whose judgement was final (A. 61).

The decision of one chamber was submitted to the other, members being given the opportunity to express their dissent from the vote at the end of the minutes (A. 62). A bill on which the chambers failed to agree was sent back to the committee (A. 63), a very important provision. Before 1866 the bill would have been sent to a 'strengthened' committee, i.e. the

---

[1] For discussion of the committee system, see Elder, loc. cit.
[2] Malmgren, op. cit., p. 169, A. 60, n. 13.

original committee specially increased in numbers to 120, in order to assist the Estates to reach agreement. Under the new law, the committee which had handled the *proposition* was not augmented, but was expected to review the original *proposition*, the committee's own decision, and the debates in both chambers, and if possible produce a solution acceptable to both. This process was known as arbitration (*sammanjämkning*). If and when both chambers accepted the same *proposition* it became law. As previously, constitutional amendments required the assent of successive sessions (A. 64). These were the only matters on which final decision could be postponed from one session to another.

Unless the chambers finally came to the same conclusion, a bill was killed (A. 63). The only exceptions to this rule were financial measures (A. 63). If, for example, in the Budget the two chambers could not agree, and the arbitration of the Committee of Supply failed, then each chamber voted on the two different bills accepted by the chambers. The bill which received most votes was accepted as Parliament's decision. This was called the Joint Vote although in fact the vote was taken by each body in its own chamber.

Parliament was given authority to designate the successor to the Throne if ever that became necessary (A. 66) and to appoint the guardians of a King who was a minor (A. 67). It still appointed an official (*Justitieombudsman*, known popularly as the JO) empowered to ensure that the law was obeyed by officials of the Crown and Judges (A. 68). There also remained the commission of forty-eight members of Parliament who could recommend that one or even all of the Judges of the Supreme Court should be 'excluded from the confidence of Parliament' (A. 69). An official was appointed to assist the JO in checking the observance of press freedom (A. 70).

A parliamentary electoral college of forty-eight appointed six parliamentary Commissioners to supervise the Bank of Sweden, and another seven Commissioners to be in charge of the National Debt Office. Parliament appointed twelve of its members to be parliamentary auditors of the public service, the Bank of Sweden and the National Debt Office (A. 71–72). Its functions were in some ways analogous to those of the British Public Accounts Committee.

The last four articles of the bill explained how parliamentary decisions were to be put in force. Since the King enjoyed the power of initiative and veto, most bills passed by Parliament did not become law until he also had signed them (A. 79). They were then issued in his name (A. 81) and finally published (A. 82).

III. *The views of the King*

De Geer sent his draft of the bill to the King, who in his private capacity could influence the members of the Estates when they came to discuss the measure. As chief Executive he could refuse to present the proposal as a Government *proposition*. The King's answers were in some instances officially inspired by influential conservative nobles at Court, and on one of his replies there is written the pencilled note *Lagerbjelke?* in De Geer's handwriting. The correspondence thus has considerably more significance than if the indolent Charles had been a minor and solitary figure in the preparation for reform.

The King's arguments in his correspondence with De Geer were in favour of a more conservative bill. In particular he felt that the 'guarantee' of its conservative nature needed strengthening. While accepting the basic property-qualifications for the Second Chamber franchise, the King proposed that here too there should be a graded scale of votes since it was 'an old Swedish custom to vote according to the taxes one paid'. To this, De Geer retorted: 'It seems to me to be making the whole Parliament based on plutocracy to allow money alone to be the deciding factor in the Second Chamber also.' Nor was it, he added, 'an old Swedish custom' to vote according to the taxes one paid. 'Taxation', he added, was not 'the only or most important of parliamentary issues', and the interests of others besides the rich must be safeguarded. He declined to make indirect elections to the Second Chamber compulsory instead of optional.[1] The King preferred a longer term for the Second Chamber, saying that three years was too short and less satisfactory than the French five-year and British seven-year terms. De Geer defended his original suggestion and alleged that the British term remained so long only because of the high cost of elections.

As De Geer expected, the King attacked the use of untried

---

[1] There is an alternative draft containing compulsory indirect election among the De Geer papers, Litt. E, no. 5.

Provincial Councils as electoral colleges for the First Chamber. But the alternative he proposed consisted of ex-officio membership for certain nobles and possibly bishops, and perhaps certain royal nominations (as in Denmark). De Geer replied in the same vein as the Council did to Oscar in 1846: the chamber was designed to represent the people and not to be a coterie of royal advisers.

He justified the greater size of the Second Chamber by saying that as the more popular house it should have a greater voice in financial matters—the only business for which the Joint Vote was to be used. At first he offered to exclude the youngest members of the Second Chamber from the Joint Vote, making the numbers taking part equal. The King thought it would be simpler to construct two chambers of the same size from the beginning. Nothing was done, and the chambers remained unequal in numbers. In presenting the bill to the *Riddarhus* on 5 January 1863, De Geer remarked that the homogeneity of the First Chamber would more than outweigh its inferiority in numbers.

The King not only commented on the composition of each chamber and their mutual relations, but questioned the tendency of the bill to increase the authority of the legislature at the expense of the royal executive power. He was particularly afraid lest by permitting Parliament to meet annually, it would 'land us head over heels in parliamentary government'.[1] De Geer assured him that nothing was expected beyond cooperation between the two sources of political power.

In the matters so far discussed, De Geer was unmoved by the King's remonstrances. In three others he changed his mind and altered his draft. He had proposed that the new chambers should elect their own Speakers on the grounds that 'the Government draws displeasure upon itself if it makes a bad appointment but receives no credit for a good one'.[2] The King replied that an unfriendly Speaker could do a lot of damage,[3] and De Geer then withdrew his suggestion. The appointment of Speakers did not, however, arouse much parliamentary controversy in Sweden and the Crown continued to nominate them.

His second concession was in the question of salaries to members

[1] De Geer papers, Litt. D, 1, no. 1.
[2] De Geer papers, Litt. E, 3, no. 11.   [3] De Geer papers, Litt. F.

of the First Chamber to whom, he considered, ought to be paid due recompense for willingness to spend nine years in the service of Parliament. However, the King decided it would be an additional guarantee of the conservatism of the First Chamber if its members were unpaid, as it certainly was. An interesting proposal made by De Geer which was rejected by Charles was that civil servants should be excluded from Parliament. It is curious that a former civil servant should produce such a suggestion, which accorded with the ideas of the economic-liberals but hardly with those of a judge and servant of the Crown. The King feared that their exclusion would lead to parliamentary government as in England.[1] Had the proposal been put into effect, the chambers would have been deprived of many of their leading men. It has been suggested that a poor, sparsely populated country could not have afforded to dispense with its highly educated public servants as members of Parliament.[2]

The result of the correspondence was to leave the *proposition* very much as De Geer intended it. The King was not entirely pleased, but he was at a loss to know what he could do to prevent De Geer from carrying out his plans.

Besides dealing with the King's objections, De Geer asked for the advice of various friends. A. W. Björck, a magistrate in Gothenburg and a leading liberal member of the Burgher Estate, persuaded him to modify the property qualifications for the Second Chamber electorate lest many of the poorer people who owned small plots of land should have the vote. It was at this stage that De Geer raised the property qualification to a minimum of 1,000 (taxable) *riksdaler*. This excluded many whose stake in the country was tiny, but the requirement was still low in comparison with the annual income qualification of at least ʹ800 (taxable) *riksdaler* for urban wage-earners. R. T. Carlén, a lawyer and a liberal, thought the property qualifications for membership of the First Chamber were to the disadvantage of the educated but less well-to-do middle class. De Geer did not,

---

[1] Kihlberg, op. cit., p. 113.

[2] Thermaenius, op. cit., p. 88. According to a later Liberal Prime Minister (Staaff) who reviewed this question, it was traditional in Scandinavia and Germany, though not in England and France, to permit civil servants to enter Parliament (Staaff, K., *Det demokratiska statsskicket*, ii. 379).

however, adopt his proposal that schoolteachers and others should be enabled to sit in the First Chamber by, for instance, exempting from property qualifications senior members of the Second Chamber who might want to transfer membership.[1] Count Gösta Posse, a landowner, was responsible for the insertion of a clause permitting leaseholders of property worth 6,000 (taxable) *riksdaler* to vote for members of the Second Chamber, by remarking that unless this was done he would be the sole voter in his own parish. He also thought the 1,000 *riksdaler* minimum was too low for property which was owned and the 800 *riksdaler* income qualification too high.[2]

The summer of 1862 ended and Charles returned to Stockholm. Parliament was to meet in October. De Geer had to make sure that the King and Ministry were acquainted with the draft he proposed to place before the Estates for submission to the Constitution Committee. There was not much difficulty with the Ministry since Manderström, Carlson, and Gripenstedt were in favour of the bill and the others knew that they must either accept it or resign. The King, however, proved more amenable than De Geer had expected. At first he did not seem pleased with the whole of it, but later he even agreed to mention the bill in his Speech and to use his influence to exclude ultra-conservatives from the Constitution Committee. In January 1863 Malmsten, one of De Geer's less enthusiastic colleagues in the Ministry, wrote to Hamilton:

De Geer's observations are rather well put together and are more impressive each time one reads through them. The change in the King has been noteworthy. For example, on Tuesday he declares that he does not want to talk about reform before the eleventh hour of Parliament, and then two days later De Geer is called to him to receive a command that the bill shall be produced as quickly as possible. The King has determined no longer to insist on the points that he previously unconditionally demanded (e.g. that he should elect some members of the First Chamber and that the members should hold their seats ex-officio). . . . The King has seriously devoted himself to work at the meetings. . . . Not once has the dashing, agile, wild (sit venia verbo) [personality] broken through.[3]

---

[1] De Geer papers, Appendix H. See also Andrén, op. cit., pp. 39–40.
[2] De Geer papers, Appendix I.
[3] Carlquist, G. *Ur Henning Hamiltons brevsamling*, pp. 85–86.

Unfortunately Malmsten does not explain why the King should have suddenly shown interest in reform. However, the decision, impulsive though it probably was, secured the presentation of the proposal as a Government bill.[1] It was referred to the Constitution Committee by the Estates on 5 January 1863. After some weeks' discussion it was adopted unchanged, and in the committee's report of 27 February, only eight of the twenty-four members added reservations.[2] It may be presumed that the voting was something in the nature of sixteen for the bill and eight against. Only two of these eight were nobles; the other four nobles on the committee supported the *proposition*.

The remaining six opponents were the six clerical representatives led by Bishops Anjou and Sundberg. They all subscribed to the same reservation, which was long, denunciatory, and in many ways perspicacious. Like the two nobles who opposed the bill, they were distrustful of the Provincial Councils, which they thought would unduly favour the agricultural interest. The property qualifications might make attendance impossible for anyone but 'Stockholm capitalists, civil servants and other citizens', and if it so happened that the Provincial Councils chose the road of 'capitalist conservatism' it might be simplest to remove the window-dressing and let the First Chamber appear 'as a plutocratic element where one may possibly find wealth but where one has no right, according to the Parliament Act, to look for anything else'.[3]

The qualifications for the Second Chamber franchise were described as 'arbitrary' by the Clergy. Particular attention was paid to the representation of the towns. As the law stood, only two, Stockholm and Gothenburg, were entitled by the new Parliament Act to send their own representatives; the remaining eighty-three could combine to return members from what would often be grotesque constituencies.[4] The number of such constituencies, moreover, was not finally established and could be restricted at some future date.

In making both these comments the Clergy were justified. The Provincial Councils did in fact often make their choice of

[1] Three weeks later Charles's Civil List was increased by Parliament at the Ministry's request (Andrén, op. cit., pp. 42–43). See also Oscar II and the 1906 reform *proposition*, *infra* pp. 153–4.

[2] *Konstitutions-Utskottets Memorial*, no. 7, pp. 14–38, 1862–3.

[3] *K.U. Mem.*, no. 7, p. 27.   [4] Ibid., p. 30.

members of the First Chamber largely on grounds of capitalist conservatism, and the smaller towns were to find their representation restricted by an Act of 1894 (though only after urban representation had increased from 50 to 80 seats in twenty-five years). However, the Clergy were wrong in imagining that the Second Chamber would prove dominant by reason of its greater numbers.

Moreover, the alternative reform proposed by the Clergy was somewhat unrealistic. To escape the 'Scylla and Charybdis' of money qualifications and the perils of democracy, they could only suggest a partial change in the representation based in the beginning on classes instead of Estates.[1] It was perhaps implicit in this suggestion that the clergy formed a class. They realized that most of them would be too poor to qualify for admission to the First Chamber, and too much of a different class to be chosen as representatives in the Second Chamber by the farmers, who would want their own interests represented. They therefore examined the bill more critically than anyone. To add to their annoyance, they had been set apart from politics by the creation of the Church Assembly which would, moreover, have to obtain the concordance of Parliament and King in matters of Church law. Their representatives on the Constitution Committee expressed dismay at the prospect of parliamentary control—a Parliament to which Jews would have the vote, and to which would be eligible so-called 'Protestant-Christians', a nomenclature which, they maintained, comprised apparently even the most anti-Church dissenting sect. The reservation ended with a plea that the Church laws might, like economic legislation, be placed directly under the King: Sweden's history might no longer be the history of her Kings, but the royal power was still one of the strongest bastions of the Swedish people's freedom.[2]

Episcopal dismay over the proposition was most vividly expressed in a letter from the archbishop to De Geer:

Rather than accept it, the Church and its devoted followers will let themselves be exiled from the State [disestablished?]—contenting themselves with the tolerance enjoyed by Jews and heathens, and leave to the State the supreme happiness of existing without a

---

[1] Ibid., p. 23.   [2] Ibid., p. 37.

Church and thus also without Christianity, inasmuch as the one is inseparable from the other.[1]

In fact, the new arrangement gave the clergy more independence. Whereas an Estate could be overruled by the other three Estates in all matters which did not affect the fundamental laws, under the new dispensation the assent of the new Church Assembly was necessary for every measure affecting the Church and neither Parliament nor King could override it. But this consideration did not deter the Clergy in their opposition to the bill.

De Geer was not goaded into making a retort to the criticism he received. Instead he told some petitioners for reform: 'Let us always remember that the nation's thanks are due in the first place to those who make, not to those who demand, the greatest sacrifice on the altar of the Fatherland.'

In March the bill was returned by the Constitution Committee to the Estates, where its opponents had not yet gathered their forces. The Clergy Estate critically discussed the *proposition* for some time; the Burghers and Farmers welcomed it. The nobles said very little, W. F. Dalman, the old liberal of the 1840's, taking the opportunity to be somewhat Delphic in his ambiguity:

England, for example, in the course of 600 years, yes, even 800, has increased more and more in political power, prestige, and wealth with an aristocratic administration and a monstrous legal system which in any other land or with any other people would surely have led to the most awful results and long since plunged the country into ruin.[2]

Yet, he went on, the United States was a democracy, and at that very moment was involved in a terrible civil war.

The debates were unimportant at this stage; what mattered was the support of the King and the acceptance of the *proposition* by the Constitution Committee. Parliament ended, members went home, and it was to be two and a half years before the matter was discussed in the Estates again. It remained to be seen whether the conservatives would muster their strength in

[1] De Geer papers, Litt. L.
[2] *Ridderskapet och adelns protokoll*, 18 March 1863, iii. 223.

the *Riddarhus* against the reform. If the King changed his mind again the bill might be defeated and the Ministry knew that he hoped in the intervening years the matter might lose its popular support. There had been a period of reaction after 1848: there might also be one after the liberal victories in Europe in the years 1860–2.

CHAPTER IV

The Passing of the 1866 Parliament Act

1. *Before the debates*

As the King had hoped, there was a decrease of interest in reform in 1863 and 1864, but in 1865, as the time for the next Parliament drew near (it met in the autumn), there was a revival of activity on both sides. Meetings were held throughout the country and pamphlets were written by the leading protagonists. The pamphlets are of interest because they express the views of De Geer, Hamilton, and others more clearly than the *Riddarhus* debates in December 1865. By that time the arguments had become well worn, and appeal was made to the emotions rather than to the reason of members of the *Riddarhus.*

The conservative pamphleteers failed to present a good case for themselves. The pamphlet produced by Boström, the Hegelian professor of philosophy at Uppsala, was entitled, 'Are the Estates competent to decide to accept the so-called reform *proposition* on behalf of the Swedish people?'[1] To this question he replied in the negative, arguing that the State was a family, the governing of which was a moral responsibility. The Estates had been given this responsibility, from which they were no more entitled to withdraw than a father from his duty to care for his children. As if to illustrate the paucity of the conservatives' ideas, the pamphlet was not straight from his pen, but merely a revised edition of his *Aphorisms* written in 1850 in criticism of the 1848 reform *proposition.*[2] Such a defence of the Estates could hardly win support in the country for the conservative cause, and yet there was no sign of a new policy to meet the needs of the times.

The most popular conservative argument was that the Estates supported the Crown and were a necessary adjunct to the royal power. This was not likely to attract the liberals, but their

---

[1] Boström, C. J., *Äro Rikets Ständer, &c.*, Uppsala, 1865.
[2] Heckscher, G., op. cit., ii. 193.

conversion was not to be expected; it was, however, possible that the King might take notice and withdraw his support of the Ministry. On his return from Copenhagen in 1864, Hamilton once again entered the discussion, and he also defended the Estate system on the grounds that it was an important support of the Crown.[1] By suggesting that the new bicameral legislature would challenge the authority of the monarch the conservatives hoped that Charles would follow his father's example when the time came for a final decision, and bring his influence down on the side of the Clergy and conservative Nobles.

De Geer did not remain silent. He had spent the intervening years reading De Tocqueville, Guizot, and J. S. Mill, and though in his memoirs he said he had been guided by his 'practical instinct' when framing the bill,[2] it was with arguments drawn from these writers that he put the case for reform in a series of articles in the journal *Wäktaren* published later as a booklet, entitled *Några ord till försvar för det hvilande representationsförslaget.*

The first problem, he suggested, was that of the First Chamber. Birth, he said, no longer established the right to political privilege and therefore not even one chamber could be restricted to the aristocracy: 'We see how even in England the upper house has lost a great deal of its former influence in that land where tradition is respected more than anywhere else and where the members [of the House of Lords] still possess both hereditary nobility and large estates.'[3] His aim was to secure not a conservative legislature but a balance of conservative and liberal forces in the two chambers, and he argued that the conservatism of the First Chamber could best be secured by a system of indirect election. Believing that the Provincial Councils would elect able men he prophesied that Sweden's experience would be as heartening, as that of the United States where the Senate, according to De Tocqueville, had an unrivalled reputation.[4]

---

[1] Hamilton, H., *Bidrag till granskningen, &c.*, Stockholm, 1865.
[2] De Geer, *Några ord till försvar, &c.*, Stockholm, 1865, p. 10.
[3] De Geer, *Minnen*, i. 238.
[4] Admittedly De Tocqueville wrote in the years 1835–40 but after the Missouri Compromise of 1820–1, 'for the next forty years, down to the Civil War, the Senate enjoyed a much greater prestige than the House'. (Nevins, A., *Ordeal of the Union*, i. 164).

Another problem was the extent of the franchise for the more liberal Second Chamber. 'To govern in our time means that one must guide public opinion: but to guide it one must know what it is.' This was the view of the same liberal Louis De Geer who later declared: 'I am an optimist not only in the question of world government but in the question of the development of mankind.'[1] Optimist though he was, he did not think that the time was ripe for the introduction of universal suffrage, maintaining that those who had material worries and anxieties would not have time to devote themselves seriously to politics, and ought'not to be given the vote. He countered the old radical demand for a single chamber with Guizot's observation that if there was only one chamber, however elected, there would be despotism. He thought, too, that the new idea of proportional representation sponsored by Hare and Mill, whereby the whole country formed one constituency, was unsuitable for a large and sparsely populated country like Sweden.

De Geer dismissed Hamilton's assumption that the Nobles were the King's chief support, suggesting that the King could assure himself of their support only if he was able to dominate them, which he was manifestly unable to do. The creation of extra nobles to swamp the Estate was impracticable in view of its large size, and he wondered if Hamilton was suggesting that it was the duty of a noble never to oppose. Moreover, he thought it was unfair to say that the introduction of a bicameral legislature would imply a challenge to the Executive's authority by the legislature; such had certainly not been the case in either France or Prussia. The Emperor Napoleon III, argued De Geer, ruled France as he pleased because of the affection in which he was held by the people, while the power of the King of Prussia lay in the army he commanded: it should be unnecessary to point out that the King of Sweden had both the affection of the people and control of the army.

In answer to the objection of the Clergy to the bill's property qualifications, which they had described as the victory of plutocracy, he said that they were not ends in themselves but rough indications of a man's status. His aim was to separate the educated from the uneducated, not to exclude voters merely on grounds of lack of means. This might, in fact, occur, but he

[1] De Geer, *Minnen*, i. 177.

could think of no suitable alternative to a property qualification. The old class election, he suggested, had been a satisfactory alternative so long as there was agreement as to which class should have power.

The articles showed De Geer to be a moderate-liberal who wanted to abolish the Estates but who was unwilling to extend the franchise to the lower classes or to extend the power of the legislature. Although he believed that the Ministry should exercise its authority he did not consider that this constitutional duty involved parliamentary government.

It was another Uppsala professor, H. L. Rydin, at this time still a liberal, who put the argument against the Estate system in its most concrete form.[1] In his pamphlet he pointed out that in the eighteenth century and indeed in 1809, it was the nobility who formed the chief opposition to the royal power. He thus refuted Hamilton's contention that the nobles were the bastion of the monarchy. He defended the introduction of property qualifications (which previously had not applied to the Clergy and Nobles Estates) by bluntly stating that men were no longer divided into four Estates representing the nation's public, spiritual, and economic life, but merely into rich and poor (cf. Disraeli's two nations), who should not be organized in Estates, but allowed to form a multitude of free associations. Rydin voiced the feelings of the economic-liberals when he expressed the hope that the abolition of the Estates would encourage the development of manufacture and trade. Like the farmers the economic-liberals expected to gain from the reform, but preferred to say little about it. But even Rydin did not want ministerial government, which he said was suitable only for Great Britain. It was better to have a King who possessed certain executive powers.

Yet it was to be enthusiasm, not arguments, which secured the victory of the bill. Throughout the length and breadth of the country where reform meetings were held there could be no doubt whatsoever of the attitude of public opinion. In only one parish, that of a Dr. Runsten, who fiercely opposed the measure in the Clergy Estate, was there an anti-reform meeting. The Central Committee of the Friends of Reform, led by Baron

[1] Rydin, H. L., *Betraktelser i representationsfrdgan*, Uppsala, 1865.

Hugo Hamilton,[1] collected 60,000 signatures for the petition it forwarded to the Government. Over seventy members of Stockholm City Council, and thirty-nine members of the staff at Uppsala University wrote to express their support of the bill. Far from interest declining, it seemed to increase as 1865 drew to a close.

It has been suggested that the popular movement of opinion in 1865 was of far greater importance than some contemporary accounts, notably De Geer's, would suggest.[2] This particularly applies to the 'Storm Deputation' of November. On 11 November a call went out from a reform meeting in Gothenburg asking every district in the country to nominate a representative for a deputation which was to wait upon the Ministry on 28 November. No fewer than 270 representatives arrived, speedily conveyed by the new railway system, and De Geer addressed them. Although mindful of the King's undecided attitude, he was aware that as far as the general public was concerned, the King had initiated a reform bill which he had asked the Estates to accept. De Geer therefore spoke to the deputation in terms which cleverly compromised Charles, saying that their interest in the bill:

would gladden his royal heart. No King has placed such trust in his people. May the Swedish people show themselves worthy of that trust and may they never forget that it is due to him and to him alone that thanks are due for the highmindedness and magnanimity of the *proposition*. The responsibility for any defects lies with those who framed it, not him who granted it.[3]

He ended his speech with the hope that the Nobles and Clergy would vote for the bill and that their acceptance would be unanimous.

De Geer was loyal to his King, being partly responsible for the legend which grew up of Charles XV's 'happy days'. However, on this occasion, although he gave the King undeserved credit for originating the bill he also prevented him from expressing his opposition to it in the future. The 'Storm Deputation' may well have set the seal upon the King's support for the bill.

Charles was unwilling to receive the deputation formally, but

---

[1] Not related to Henning Hamilton except in common descent from Malcolm Hamilton, Archbishop of Cashel, Ireland (died 1629).

[2] Thermaenius, E., Article in *Svenska Dagbladet*, 20 December 1935.

[3] De Geer, *Minnen*, ii. 6–7.

as he did not want the representatives to leave Stockholm without his having spoken to them he saw as many as 186 privately on the following day. The artist and satirist Fritz von Dardel, a confidant of the King, noted in his diary a few days later, on 2 December, that a change had occurred in Charles and that he had given up hope of defeating the bill. He realized that to oppose it would mean that his popularity and his pride in being the 'people's King' would be destroyed, and his dreams of a strong Scandinavia for ever unfulfilled. The delegates had made a strong impression on him without realizing how necessary it was that he should be so impressed.

There was some fear of disturbance as the time of the debates drew near. The King-in-Council increased the Stockholm garrison and made efforts to keep the people calm. There was no such mob as in the great cities of Europe, but there was some apprehension of popular disturbance if the bill was rejected. August Blanche, the radical leader, had a certain number of sharpshooters among his supporters and it was uncertain whether his threats of direct action would be carried out or not. But since violence was unusual in Sweden, apart from occasional stone-throwing, the fears may have been exaggerated.[1]

When Parliament met on 16 October De Geer estimated that over two-thirds of the Nobles opposed the bill. Moreover, a predominantly conservative Constitution Committee was appointed. Since the views of the other Estates were not in doubt, interest centred on the *Riddarhus*. Before the debates began, some conservative Nobles asked De Geer to address them on the subject of reform, and a week later another group in favour of the bill arranged a meeting. There was some surprise that the invitations to this meeting were sent out by two courtiers, Bildt and Björnstjerna. Bildt was reputed to be the King's mouthpiece in Parliament and Björnstjerna was a man with considerable influence among the army officers. It certainly appeared as though the King was at least not working actively against De Geer.

ii. *The debates, December 1865*

Parliament met to debate the reform bill on Monday 4 December. As expected, the lower Estates passed it with little debate.

[1] Cf. the tension in 1918, chap. XI.

The vote in the Farmer Estate was unanimous; in the Burghers it was 60 in favour and only 5 against.

The Clergy Estate was in a dilemma. According to the Constitution, bills were as far as possible to be debated simultaneously. If the Clergy were to debate the bill forthwith, it would not take them very long to reject it; but if the Nobles were to have a drawn-out debate ending in acceptance of the measure, this would leave the Clergy in the unhappy position of being the only Estate against it. However, if the Nobles rejected the bill, the Clergy wanted to support them. The question of the Clergy's best course of action was raised by Dr. Sandberg, an indefatigable speaker who had already that day spoken four times on matters ranging from railway building and pensions for elementary schoolteachers to the method of publicizing official announcements: 'Why should seven hundred gentlemen and knights of arms push a tiny flock of unarmed clergymen into the heat of battle as the *avant-garde* to receive the first shot?'[1] Professor Selander reminded the house that Article 47 of the Parliament Act prescribed concurrent debate in the chambers[2] but he was overruled by Archbishop Reuterdahl (the Speaker) who somewhat casuistically declared that the Article was for the guidance (*mål*) of the house and not a direct order (*bud*) which must be obeyed.[3] The house thereupon voted for an adjournment by 35 to 20, the radical newspaper *Aftonbladet* describing their action, on 6 December, as 'magnificent proof of their complete political nullity'. The Clergy did not meet again until 8 December, when the four-day debate in the *Riddarhus* was over.

Over 700 Nobles met in the *Riddarhus*, and their chamber was as crowded as in 1809 when Gustav IV Adolf was deposed. De Geer and Gripenstedt each spoke twice during the debate and until the final count the issue was still in doubt. The occasion was memorable for many reasons and throughout the atmosphere was tense with uncertainty, even though the level of debate was not always high.

On the first day Count Erik Sparre remarked that decades were as minutes in the life of a nation. In England the movement for reform which culminated in 1832 had begun, he said, in 1738.

---

[1] *Preste-stånds protokoll 1865-6*, p. 189.   [2] Ibid., p. 192.
[3] Ibid., p. 193.

There had been little agitation in Sweden before 1840 and ten of the twenty-five years which had passed since then had been spent by Parliament in the debate of railway matters.[1] It was therefore, he suggested, still too soon to pass the bill.

In general the opposition speeches showed no more originality than the conservative pamphleteers. A noticeable characteristic was melancholy. Partly it was a relic of the 'pathetic rhetoric' which had been fashionable in the Gustavian era, but it also expressed the natural feelings of men who feared that the long glory of the Nobles Estate was ending. It was difficult for them to resist recalling the glories of their ancestors, men who in many cases had fought their way across Europe under Gustavus Adolphus or Charles XII and who had often received their title of nobility (*ridderskap*) for gallantry in the field. Now the venerable *Ridderhus* was to be abolished and its place was to be taken by an electoral system which would, as Klinckowström remarked, result in gentlemen being outvoted by their servants.

Baron Klinckowström's contribution was a little confused. He told his colleagues that Americans had asked him whether Sweden still loved its King, and that the French had said they repented the abolition of their Estates. He disliked the idea of a Church Assembly, which would be a power independent and indeed above King and Parliament—the seed of a Protestant popery. He did, however, make one important comment on the *proposition*. The financial and property qualifications which seemed so secure a bulwark for conservatism would be no barrier if the currency depreciated, as had happened recently to the American dollar in the Southern states. He added that since the bill referred to 'taxable' income, Parliament could, by raising or lowering taxation, alter the taxable value of income and thus influence the size of the electorate and number of eligible members of Parliament.[2]

Gripenstedt replied to the last point by pointing out that the application of Parliament's taxation requirements rested with local boards and any misuse of the power could be remedied in the courts.[3] Addressing the general body of the opposition he

---

[1] *Ridderskapet och adelns protokoll 1863–6*, i. 292.
[2] *R. o. a. prot.*, pp. 226 ff.
[3] Yet the authorities are said to have manipulated the taxpayers' list in Stockholm during the election year 1887 so that the number with taxable income of

asked them to believe that others besides the nobility possessed the qualities of commonsense, patriotism, and honesty, adding somewhat tartly that it was a general principle that no man should be a witness in his own case.[1]

The 'Lucifer of the debate' was undoubtedly Herr Curry Treffenberg. His speech may seem in print to be pointless bombast, signifying nothing, but when he rose to speak in the debate his commanding presence, burning passion, and declamatory manner turned the chamber for a moment into a theatre in which a great tragedy was being enacted. Remarking that he had listened to the Government speakers with much awe and enchantment, he placed one hand on the lectern, and waved the other, saying:

> Even I had been on the point of leaving behind me all the traditional beliefs implanted in my childhood, all the memories of the Boström view of society from my time at the University, and all the warning testimony of our own and other countries' history, in order to join the friends who supported the Government's *proposition* and step on board this merry pleasure yacht decked with roses and pennants, and which with music in the bows and wafted by a following wind, would immediately lead the whole nation to the island of the blessed.[2]

Like Hamilton he objected to the diminution of the royal power which the bill entailed, and said that Sweden did not need the measure. The Swedish people were the 'happiest and freest in the world'. The success of the idea of reform was due merely to the reiteration of the cry that the times required a change.[3] He referred to Burke's doctrine that the State was an organism which he had said should be treated, like a doctor healing his sick father, 'with a slow and respectful hand'. He quoted De Tocqueville back at De Geer and reminded him of the discomfiture of the French nobles in 1789 as they watched the people misusing power which rightly belonged to the King. But it was such extraordinary metaphors as these which pleased

---

between 800 and 900 crowns was 7869 compared with 13806 in 1886 and 13135 in 1888 (Lindgren, J. *Från, per Gotrek till Per Albin*, p. 67, quoting David Bergström's pamphlet '*Den politiska rösträtt*').

[1] *R. o. a. prot.*, pp. 267 ff.   [2] Ibid., p. 345.

[3] He referred to the cry 'Carthago est delenda' contained in an indiscreet letter from Richert to Hierta in 1845 explaining the need to keep the public interested in reform even though they might forget why it was necessary.

his hearers: 'This change of thought which, as was discovered, bore at birth its Jesuitical mark of Cain upon its brow . . . was with strong muscles climbing up the first steps to the throne and was reaching with its black hand to grip the throat of society.' Finally he warned the Government that they would not realize their hope of a willing acceptance of the *proposition* by the Nobles and Clergy. The bill would only be passed out of despair. At the end of the speech there was thunderous applause.

De Geer and Hamilton did not distinguish themselves, becoming involved in an analogy of a house containing four families which was burnt down.[1] At one stage in the debate De Geer suggested that Hamilton and his friends might like to take over the Government, but this was clearly not Hamilton's wish, for in his second speech he referred to the esteem in which the country held De Geer and argued that if there was to be reform it could not be in better hands. The absence of genuine fighting speeches by opponents of the bill is striking and suggests that not only were they resigned to the prospect of defeat but that their hearts were not in the battle. There may have been truth in Adolf Hedin's later assertion that the Nobles only pretended that they were losing by the reform.

Thursday, 7 December was the fourth day of the debate and still many Nobles wished to speak. But as the day wore on the cry of '*Proposition! Proposition!*' was increasingly heard until at last the Speaker asked the House if it wished to proceed to the vote. It was now afternoon and the crowd which had gathered outside the *Riddarhus* was becoming somewhat restive. No one knew whether it would get out of hand, but the Speaker felt it advisable to ask for the vote to be taken in time for members to go home before dark. On the question being put, there was a shout of 'Yes' and the vote was taken: 294 Nobles voted against the *proposition* and 361 in its favour. The Swedish House of Nobility had voted itself out of existence.

The House was not allowed to disperse on this note of excitement. The reform bill was only part of the day's proceedings and the House had next to agree to a proposal to raise the salary of an elementary schoolteacher and a bookkeeper in a village called Tumba of a few hundred souls. The business dispatched, the House adjourned at 3.30 p.m. The waiting

[1] Hamilton's speech, pp. 303 ff.: De Geer's, pp. 367 ff.

crowd called 'Hurrah' as the Ministers came out, and then. dispersed jubilantly and in an orderly fashion.

On Friday the Clergy met and passed the bill without a division. According to custom those who disliked a measure were entitled to register their 'reservation' in the minutes, even if there had been no division. It had taken some diplomacy on the part of the archbishop to persuade the Estate that they had no alternative but to accept the bill, and many of the Clergy were determined not to perjure themselves by making no protest. No fewer than 27 availed themselves of the power of reservation and the archbishop had to make strenuous efforts to prevent a majority of the 57 members present from doing so. Had 29 made a reservation it would have clearly indicated that in fact a majority of the Clergy had opposed the reform, and the unpopularity of the Church would have been almost as great as if they had voted against it.

De Geer's hope that the assent of the Estates might be unanimous was not fulfilled; on Saturday a long list of Nobles joined the Clergy and added their dissent to the *Riddarhus* minutes.

Without full knowledge of the conservatives' case it is not possible to say for certain why they waited until the Saturday before producing their own alternative proposal. They had been unable to persuade any Stockholm printer to print it, and had sent it to Uppsala 40 miles away, where there was a printing press owned by one of the five intrepid Burgher members who dared to vote against the bill. The students of the university heard about it and are said to have tried to prevent publication by threatening to burn the place down.[1] All this delayed the presentation of the motion until the voting had taken place. However, it has been maintained that the bill could have been presented without first having been printed, and so this excuse does not stand examination.[2]

Another suggestion is that the conservatives wanted to wait until De Geer's bill was defeated before introducing their own measure; one of the conservative leaders, Nils Tersmeden,

[1] When asked for instructions the Burgher member wired the manager of the press 'Släck, slit, slå, slynglingarna'—for which, alas, there is no alliterative translation.

[2] Andrén, op. cit., p. 198.

wrote to a friend L. F. Rääf on 7 November that they must avoid a split prematurely.[1] In any case the motion could not have been discussed by the Constitution Committee until the vote on the De Geer proposal had been taken.[2] The delay in the presentation of the conservative draft arouses the suspicion, nevertheless, that they were not serious, or they would have used the proposed motion as a debating point.

Even if the De Geer bill had been defeated, it is doubtful whether the conservative draft would have been more effective than previous conservative proposals. It was too radical to be an acceptable conservative document, and yet it differed from De Geer's in that the First Chamber was to be elected by various corporate bodies such as the nobles, clergy, universities, town councils, Provincial Councils, and wealthy taxpayers in town and country. The Second Chamber, which was to have equal power, was to be elected according to a much wider franchise than De Geer's, including all who paid commune or State taxes. However, there was to be a graded scale, although in contrast to De Geer's bill business companies were not given a vote. The conservatives' Parliament was intended in practice to have much less authority, as the provision that it should meet only once every three years unless called by the King clearly indicated. Like the Government bill it seems to have favoured 'capitalist conservatism'.

The withdrawal of royal support was perhaps the main cause of the defeat of the conservatives' plans, for it influenced the bureaucrats and army officers, who otherwise had no particular allegiance. Hamilton was not by nature a commander of men, able to lead a last forlorn defensive stand. Faced by a strong, firm united Council of Ministers supported by public opinion, the conservative opposition proved weak and undecided.

Among the 394 Nobles who voted in favour of the bill there may have been many who normally rarely attended: 191 more Nobles were present than during the session of 1853–4 which rejected the 1851 motion put forward by the conservatives. The increase was largely in the landowner/mineowner group which mustered 243 instead of 136.[3] It is not without significance that

---

[1] Quoted in *Statsvetenskaplig tidskrift*, 1949, p. 48.
[2] Heckscher, G., *Svensk konservatism före representationsreformen*, ii. 194.
[3] *Studier över den svenska riksdagens sociala sammansättning*, p. 60.

the victory of the bill made this social group the largest in the new First Chamber and reduced the representation of the Civil Service and army, which in the *Riddarhus* numbered over half the House, to barely a dozen in the next twenty years. It may also be noted that, according to a leading member of the Farmer Estate, plans were afoot in November 1865 for distributing lists of opponents of the *proposition* throughout the country so that tenants of recalcitrant Nobles would know which way they had voted.[1]

The passing of the bill did not result in an immediate dissolution. The Estates decided to complete the business of the session and continued this work until June 1866, when the King finally signed the bill, which became the 1866 Parliament Act (*Riksdagsordningen*), referred to in Swedish documents as the 'RO 1866'. On 22 June the Estates gathered in the Hall of State in the Palace for the last time to hear the final speeches of the session. The *Lantmarshalk* described the occasion as 'a moment in the life of nations when the step of Time could almost be heard', and the King declared: 'We end today not only a memorable session but a whole era in the history of the Swedish people, an era which is measured in centuries.'[2] Some of the pomp and ceremony left Swedish life. The heralds and trumpeters appeared for the last time and Ministers ceased to ride in their colourful robes to the State opening of Parliament.

III. *The conditions of success*

While it is true to say that the reform movement expanded from a handful of enthusiasts in 1830 to a nationwide campaign in the 1860's, there was at the same time a qualitative change in the composition of the movement which deserves some notice. It has already been suggested (Chapter II) that the year 1848 was a watershed in the history of the reform movement, the period of reaction which followed the year of revolutions being characterized by an increasing interest in business matters. Before 1848 the liberals were frequently Utopian radicals of the middle and upper classes who admired the Norwegian Constitution and believed that the farmers possessed a sturdy common sense which entitled them to a greater share in the

---

[1] Per Nilsson i Espö's diary for November 1865.
[2] Fahlbeck, E., op. cit., p. 432.

legislature. After 1848, as it became evident that the Swedish farmers wanted a position of power in the new legislature, or at least in one of its chambers, this radical-liberalism, with its tendency to romanticize the farmers, declined. There were, to be sure, reform meetings held at Örebro in 1850 and 1851 but, after the rejection of the Government's reform bill by the Estates, the movement died away. The farmers and some of the middle class remained faithful to a reform which would reduce the power of the nobles, clergy, and bureaucracy, but lacking leaders they accomplished little.

During the 1850's the businessmen who might have led the lower Estates in a political campaign against the Church and the Civil Service found themselves working with conservatives in economic affairs, sharing the same views on such important matters as railway construction. It has been suggested that more ironworks were owned by the nobility than by the middle class, and so both groups were concerned with the development of an industry which trebled its production between 1830 and 1870 and exported no less than four-fifths of its production of 270,000 tons in the late 1860's.[1] Oscar I and the Crown Prince shared the general enthusiasm for industrial development, and the common interest which brought the Court and economic-liberals together weakened the bond between the civil servants and the Throne. The 'Junkers', who by 1854 had replaced the von Hartmansdorff group in the *Riddarhus*, had commercial and industrial interests, and by the 1860's many of the nobles and some Ministers were in favour of more efficient political machinery to accomplish their economic ends.[2]

The leading liberals in the 1860's were therefore more often a new type of economic-liberal rather than the radicals of the 1830's and 1840's. There was, admittedly, a revival of liberal ideas throughout Europe in the 1860's, but in Sweden at any rate this revival seems insufficient by itself to explain the course of events. Some at least of the Nobles in the *Riddarhus* who were conservative in politics were economic-liberals in their business outlook, and it was this coincidence which softened the blow of the Parliament Act for them.

No personality sums up the rise of this new generation of economic-liberals, able to wield influence far out of proportion

[1] Montgomery, op. cit., p. 82.   [2] Cf. Heckscher, G., op. cit., p. 203.

to their numbers in both the Ministry and the Estates, on domestic as well as foreign policy, so much as Johan August Gripenstedt, who held the key post of Finance Minister from 1856 to 1866. Gripenstedt started his career as a radical. Like De Geer he was the son of a landowner who was unable to do much more for him than secure his future career which was, in Gripenstedt's case, the army. As a cadet at the artillery school he took part in political debates with Henning Hamilton. At the age of twenty-seven he entered the *Riddarhus* where he joined the opposition led by C. H. Anckarswärd, and read De Tocqueville. He had already been impressed by the writings of Edward Lytton Bulwer. He declined to 'vote for the uniform' even when reprimanded by his Commanding Officer, General Lefrén, who was also a member of the *Riddarhus*. During his radical spell, Gripenstedt proposed a 5 per cent. death duty on the estates of those who 'had enjoyed all society's advantages'.

His marriage to Anckarswärd's eldest niece in 1842 led to a change in his political views and he became an economic-liberal. As manager of his father-in-law's Nynäs estates, which included a mining district as well as many farms, he received 4,000 *riksdaler* a year as salary. Now a member of the land-owner-ironmaster upper class, concerned with increasing corn production and iron exports, Gripenstedt's interests turned increasingly towards economic matters. He strongly supported Free Trade, and was drawn towards the Government when Oscar became King in 1844. When the King abandoned the cause of parliamentary reform, Gripenstedt did not withdraw his support for the Crown, nor do the Anckarswärds seem to have shown any displeasure at his retention of royal favour, possibly because they too were becoming more interested in their large estates than in the cause of parliamentary reform. On the defeat of the 1848 bill during the session of 1851, the Anckarswärd brothers retired from political life. The radical period was over.

Gripenstedt had received the flattering appointment of Consultative Minister in 1848, when he was only thirty-five, partly as a sop to radical opinion; but he remained in office until his resignation in 1866, and was therefore a Minister throughout the reactionary fifties. There seems little doubt that he was ambitious and eager for office, and must have been a rather unusual personality among the elderly civil servants who were the most frequent holders of ministerial positions. He realized soon after entering the Ministry that executive power lay in the hands of the King himself, and made that the starting-point of his policy. Oscar I was glad of his support in economic matters, especially in railway building, and retained his services to show he had not altogether abandoned liberal ideas. Gripenstedt, on his side, maintained his connexions with the liberal press, particularly with S. A. Hedlund, editor of *Göteborgs Handels-och Sjöfartstidningen*. However, in this earlier period as Consultative Minister from 1848 to 1856, Gripenstedt's authority in the Council does not seem to have been particularly marked.

It was from the time of his appointment as Finance Minister in 1856 that he demonstrated his power both as a personality and as the representative of the economic-liberals. This ministerial position, which Gripenstedt was to enhance during his ten years of office, was only awarded to those who possessed considerable independent means. Fortunately, Gripenstedt had recently purchased the Nynäs estate from his father-in-law for 300,000 *riksdaler*. Yet even before his appointment he showed, at least in private, a belief in the neutrality policy he was to support later in his career. Fearing that Oscar intended to join Britain and France against Russia during the Crimean War, he hinted to liberal newspapers that the King was planning to involve the country in the hostilities, and that he might even carry out a` *coup d'état*.[1] It is more probable, however, that Oscar's main intention was to break with Russia and to initiate an independent foreign policy by supporting the Western powers.[2]

Foreign affairs were not the only matters in which Gripenstedt accepted the views of the economic-liberals. In domestic economic policy he was the champion of the moneyed classes, making his greatest speech in 1857 when he defended the Government's policy of establishing trunk railways. He thereby established his reputation in financial and economic matters at the time when the depression after the Crimean War was arousing some criticism of his Free Trade policy. De Geer commented in his Memoirs that Free Trade had become an article of faith for him. When Charles XV formed his first Ministry in

[1] Gasslander, op. cit., p. 166.   [2] Lundh, H. L., *Skandinavism i Sverige*, pp. 38–39.

G

1858, Gripenstedt's career hung in the balance. The Crown Prince Regent's views were not even as liberal as his father's, and Gripenstedt feared that Hamilton might suggest his dismissal. He quickly changed his religious policy to suit Hamilton and opposed Gunther's Dissenter Law after previously letting it pass without reservation in the Council's discussion of the question. Hamilton came to regard him as his most useful ally among the old Ministers, and the King let him remain a free-trade Finance Minister in return for his help over religious issues. Charles and Hamilton were, moreover, both interested in railway construction, and this enabled them to come to terms with Gripenstedt. The appointment of De Geer made Gripenstedt's position easier, and in 1860, despite the King, the Toleration Act was passed.

In 1864 Gripenstedt made his most famous contribution to Swedish foreign policy by his insistence at Ulriksdal that the King should retract his promise to help the Danes with 20,000 men in the event of a Prussian attack. At this conference between the Ministry and the King, whereas De Geer adopted a compromise attitude and Hamilton, as Minister to Denmark, supported the King, Gripenstedt by force of will won his point. It is of interest that he was able to do so partly by threatening to resign unless the King changed his mind. Gripenstedt's cautious attitude to this aspect of the King's Pan-Scandinavian policy was shared by business circles who feared that trade would be damaged by involvement in war.

Nowhere is the change from idealism to realism as the dominant liberal viewpoint more evident than in the varying attitudes towards Pan-Scandinavianism (*Skandinavism*). In the 1840's this was largely an emotional student crusade for aid to Denmark in its efforts to retrieve Schleswig, but after the defeat of the Danes by Prussia in 1848 there was considerably more support in Sweden for some form of alliance with Denmark in order that a strong Scandinavia could defend the common interests of the two countries. Oscar I was no Pan-Scandinavian, but he was astute enough to realise that the radical-liberals who demanded a thorough reform of Parliament were in the forefront of the Pan-Scandinavian movement, and he appeased them by helping to apply pressure on Prussia in the conclusion of peace. In the 1850's he began to think of Pan-Scandinavianism

as a policy whereby Norway–Sweden could establish itself as a
northern power independent of Russian influence, and during
the Crimean War he entered into negotiations with Britain and
France. His successor, Charles XV, continued the policy of
aiding Denmark by his promise of Swedish troops in the event
of a Prussian attack.

The main opponents of both kings in their Pan-Scandinavian
policy were the economic-liberals, including men like Hedlund,
and it was their view which prevailed. Radicals such as Adolf
Hedin were to remain Pan-Scandinavians until the Franco-
Prussian war of 1870 ended the era.[1] It is interesting to note that
Louis De Geer did not share the radicals' sympathy for Norwegian nationalism, and indeed established his ascendancy
over Charles XV by opposing his plan to abolish the office of
Governor-General of Norway. In this matter he was attuned to
the feeling of Parliament which, though divided on the question
of parliamentary reform, was much in favour of a firm policy
towards the junior partner in the dual monarchy.

iv. *The role of Gripenstedt in the reform of Parliament*

If, as is here suggested, a necessary condition of De Geer's
success was the support of the economic-liberals, and if their
greatest parliamentary representative was Gripenstedt, the
question naturally arises whether the traditional view of De
Geer as the 'Lord Grey of the Reform Bill' requires some modi-
fication. For example, the success of the bill was to a considerable extent dependent upon the transformation of the Council
into a Ministry with a corporate sense, a new feature of Swedish
political life due in no small measure to the activities of Gripenstedt, as the Ulriksdal conference indicates. Moreover, the good
relations of the Ministry with the press and general public were
in some measure due to his good offices. He also had influence
with the Farmer Estate, haranguing them in 1863 over their
refusal to sanction the payment of a debt of a million *riksdaler*
owed by the King, and even suggesting that the reform bill
might not be passed unless they acquiesced.[2] Certainly no
account of the passing of the first reform bill can omit mention
of the part he played both before and during the debates.

[1] Lundh, H. L., op. cit., pp. 63–64.
[2] Per Nilsson i Espö's diary, 1 February 1863.

Whether Gripenstedt had greater influence over the Ministry than De Geer is more doubtful. The Chancellor had his own connexions with the public and the press, and was hardly unsympathetic to the 'capitalist conservatism' of the economic-liberals, since he advocated this policy himself. Both De Geer and Gripenstedt attended the reform banquet given by Gothenburg business-men in 1864. As for the Farmer Estate, the farmers' rejection of Gripenstedt as leader of their party in the new Parliament of 1867 suggests that they were not particularly devoted to him. Lastly, it is no doubt true that at Ulriksdal it was Gripenstedt who presented an ultimatum while De Geer acted as moderator, but in his private relations with the King De Geer may not have been so compromising as Gasslander suggests. In a letter to Charles on 16 May 1864, after the King had thought of replacing the Ministry, he informed the King in no uncertain terms that his inability to replace his ten Ministers was a sign that his foreign policy was impossible and ought to be changed: it destroyed confidence in the Ministry if the King gave a different account of Sweden's policy to private subjects of foreign states.[1] Moreover, it was De Geer and not Gripenstedt who fought Charles over the abolition of the Norwegian Governor-Generalship.

Gasslander rightly points out that Gripenstedt was, nevertheless, the only Minister who had taken part in the 1848 reform bill, and that therefore he had considerable acquaintance with the whole question.[2] Yet curiously enough there is little evidence that in the preparation of the bill he played an important part. De Geer makes no mention in his Memoirs of any collaboration at the time when he was himself examining the 1848 bill, though he says he valued Gripenstedt's contribution to the Ministry's discussions. It is possible that De Geer played down the importance of Gripenstedt, and there is no doubt that he was not quite so modest as his Memoirs suggest, but there is no evidence of joint authorship of the 1866 Parliament Act. Gripenstedt's lack of interest in reform in the 1850's, his easy acceptance of office in conservative as well as moderate-liberal Ministries, and his political intrigues, may be compared with the more principled, judicious, and moderate policy of De Geer, who, it must be remembered, was equally determined

[1] De Geer, *Minnen*, i. 268.   [2] Gasslander, op. cit., p. 277.

and resolute when he found his policy opposed by the King.

Undoubtedly the architect of victory was Louis De Geer. It was he who won the confidence of all those who favoured reform, whether radicals or economic-liberals, and as a moderate-liberal he was admirably suited to the task of steering the bill through the Estates. Even without his initiative, the reform of Parliament could not have been delayed much longer, but it might have taken a different form and would probably have been accomplished less smoothly.

v. *De Geer's intentions*

De Geer was able to stamp the new Parliament with his own beliefs, and there is still some controversy about his success in achieving the aims he had in mind—and even concerning what his aims were. His general intention seems to have been solely to remodel the legislature, the acquiescence of the King being contingent upon an assurance that he would not upset the traditional balance of power between the royal Executive and Parliament. The restriction of the reform to the legislature has been described as one of the two conservative successes in the reform debate.[1] Yet it is very doubtful whether De Geer wanted any form of parliamentary government. Since he disliked political parties he could not give Parliament the leadership which parliamentary government would have made essential, and as a civil servant, albeit a judge, he did not have the politician's point of view. By temperament and by conforming to the long Swedish tradition of some division of executive and legislative functions, he was unable to conceive of any marked weakening of the royal power. He therefore continued the peculiarly Swedish custom of equal chambers, merely reducing the number between which harmony and balance were expected to prevail from four to two. While he never expressed his intention so crudely, it was in fact to balance, and if possible to reconcile, Capital and Agriculture. Some of Mill's radical ideas may have provided inspiration for the Second Chamber, but the basis of the First was Bagehot's 'capitalist conservatism' which De Geer quoted with so much approval.

His particular intentions regarding each chamber also seem

[1] Heckscher, G., op. cit., ii. 196-7.

fairly clear. The farmers were to be given control over the Second, while the First would be dominated by the upper class *herrar*. The property qualifications restricting membership of the First Chamber are said to be the other conservative victory. Here again, however, the success was only partial. In their counter-proposition, the conservatives had proposed that half the seats should be given to the nobility. De Geer, on the other hand, introduced a system of elections by which a common bond of wealth would unite senior civil servants (often Provincial Governors), landowners, and industrialists. This replaced the aristocratic assortment of bureaucrats, army officers, landowners, bishops, and priests. Birth itself, in contrast to the conservative proposal, was no criterion of membership. A somewhat nebulous aristocracy was replaced by a rather strictly defined plutocracy.

By giving a wide franchise to the Second Chamber, De Geer acknowledged the impossibility of withstanding the second great interest, the farmers. The conservatives' plan for indirect election to the Second Chamber and a minimum age-limit of thirty-five would never have passed the scrutiny of the Farmer Estate. De Geer let the farmers dominate the Second Chamber, but he expected to counter their influence by overweighting the town representation. The Second Chamber would be divided between town and country, and in matters of moment the First Chamber would be able to seek allies in the Second sufficient to prevent policy from being dictated by the farmers.

The bicameral system was new to Sweden. Somewhat naturally there have been speculations about its origin and inspiration. It has been suggested that in theory De Geer wanted a First Chamber on the American pattern rather than the British, that is to say, composed according to the wishes of the electorate rather than by hereditary right of certain families; however, it is argued, by giving only the rich access to the Chamber and in this way distinguishing between the composition of the two houses he chose in practice the English system.[1]

Indeed, it is difficult to see the value of analogies of the

[1] See the Pro Memoria quoted on p. 46, and cf. Rexius, G., *Det svenska tvåkammarsystemets tillkomst och karaktär*, 1915, pp. 304 ff. Also Brusewitz, A., Review of Andrén's *Sveriges riksdag*, vol. ix in *Statsvetenskaplig tidskrift*, 1940, pp. 327 ff., and Hovde, B., *The Scandinavian Countries*, ii. 536–7.

upper houses of these three countries based solely on their composition. Moreover, in so far as their personnel *can* be compared, it would appear that in general the rich were more in evidence in all·three upper chambers than in the lower houses. Some reference should therefore be made to methods of selection. It is true that in Sweden, as in the United States, members were to be indirectly elected by the general public, but whereas the Swedish First Chamber was definitely intended to over-represent the richer classes of the population, the United States Senate was primarily intended to give the States of the Union equal representation in Congress. Moreover, although members of the First Chamber tended to represent the landed and moneyed classes, as did the House of Lords, the British upper house was primarily a chamber of hereditary nobility far more exclusive even than the *Riddarhus* which the elective First Chamber had replaced. Indeed there are so many important differences between the upper chambers of the three countries that comparisons on the basis of their few points of similarity are misleading. In rejecting the hereditary principle when considering the form of the First Chamber, De Geer did not necessarily show preference for the American Senate rather than the British House of Lords, as appears to be the implication of some of the comments on the 1866 Parliament Act. He was simply following his own choice of a 'capitalist conservatism'. This suggests that he had departed from the belief that birth or title alone gave a man the right to sit in Parliament, but had not reached the stage of thinking in American terms of popular, though indirect, electing. Using property as his criterion he conformed to the ideas underlying the economic-liberalism of the time.

It was the property qualifications affecting both chambers which were attacked when later reform bills were presented to Parliament; and it was due to them that there was to be a conflict between the public opinion represented in the Second Chamber, and the upper classes or *herrar* represented in the First. The fight over the Estate principle had been won and men of property given power: forty years later, they themselves were to be on the defensive.

CHAPTER V

Political and Social Developments, 1866–1905

THE intention of the 1866 Parliament Act was primarily political, namely, to change the system of representation. Parliament in its turn, however, was to be affected by the social changes which resulted from Sweden's industrial revolution.

1. *The new Parliament*

Though there can be no question of the importance of the year 1866 as a watershed in Swedish history, there was no social upheaval as, for instance, in France after 1789. In abolishing the Clergy Estate, the Parliament Act certainly reduced the authority of the Lutheran Church in political affairs, but it is more questionable whether the end of the Estates meant that: 'When in 1867 the *Riksdag* assembled under the new conditions it was evident that the preponderance of power lay—as De Geer intended it should—with the middle classes',[1] unless the term 'middle classes' signifies senior civil servants, landowners, and farmers as well as the still small urban bourgeoisie; in other words, unless representatives formerly belonging to other classes are now for convenience called members of the middle classes. At first there was little change in the type of members elected to Parliament, and the franchise had been drawn so as to be as little affected as possible by the abolition of the Estates; furthermore one consequence of the advent of a new class to political power—social reform—is noticeably absent.

The striking feature of the new Parliament was not its difference in composition from the old Estates but its similarity to them. The 190 seats in the Second Chamber were allotted on the basis of 135 to the provinces and 55 to the towns, figures rather similar to the membership of the two lower Estates. It was almost as if the two Estates had been joined together, since

[1] Svanström and Palmstierna, *A History of Sweden*, p. 415.

57 of the members of the new chamber had been in the Farmer Estate and 31 had been Burghers. Thirteen Nobles and 6 Clergy brought the total of former members of Estates to be elected to the Second Chamber to 107. The element of continuity was at least equally strong in the First Chamber where, of the 125 members, 64 had sat in the *Riddarhus*, 5 in the Clergy Estate, and 13 in the Burghers. Ten years were to elapse before the first farmer was elected to the First Chamber and twelve before the first manual worker was to sit in the Second. The strong representation of the *Riddarhus* may explain why opposition to the bill had never been very great: control of one chamber out of two was in some ways better than one Estate out of four.

Considering that the minimum age for membership of the First Chamber was 35, it was comparatively youthful, the average age in 1867 being 52. (It rose gradually, reaching 60 in 1906.) Its composition belied De Geer's hope that the gulf between the two chambers would not be too wide. He had doubled the property qualifications of the 1848 bill and had agreed to the withdrawal of his suggestion that members be paid, but he could hardly have expected that the average income of members would be as high as 7,470 *riksdaler*, or nearly double the minimum. Only 6,100 people were eligible for membership, of whom 4,350 lived in Stockholm. Since there was no residence qualification for the First Chamber, wealthy Stockholmers were able to stand for election in the provinces, and 40 per cent. of the members were from the capital. The prophecy of the Clergy had not been vain. The plutocratic character of the chamber was illustrated by the return of 28 ironmasters and factory owners, but more significant was the return of 95 members who had served the Crown in some capacity or other. Fifty-one were at present servants of the Crown, including the 10 Ministers and 24 senior civil servants (Provincial Governors, heads of administrative agencies and judges). Of the 17 junior State employees, 9 were judges, 3 civil servants, and only 1 an officer of the armed forces.[1] The bill had not reduced the number of servants of the Crown as such but only the junior army officers and civil servants. Yet no table of the

---

[1] *Studier över den svenska riksdagens sociala sammansättning*, p. 104.

chamber's composition can be accurate since many members · could be with equal justice designated army officers or land-owners or capitalists. Forty-six called themselves landowners. The fears of the Clergy were fully realized: they never returned more than six members after 1867, though towards the end of the period under review there was a slight increase in the number of professional men, some of whom might have been members of a Clergy Estate.

The Second Chamber was younger in composition, the average age varying from forty-seven in 1870 to fifty-three in 1900. Of the 190 members 107 had sat in the Estates. Despite the residence qualification civil servants were returned in con-siderable numbers and in 1876, by which time the chamber can be said to have settled down, there were 48 civil servants in a chamber of 198 members. The number of persons classifiable as business men was 33. Easily the largest group was the Farmers' bloc, which numbered 114, if 19 landowners are included. The first worker (*arbetare*) was elected in 1878 and in 1905 there were still only 10 workers in the whole of Parliament.

De Geer succeeded in leaving the farmers in a minority in the Joint Vote. Thus, as always, the farmers were under-represented in Parliament, occupying half the seats in one of the two cham-bers although forming three-quarters of the whole population. The scheme whereby small towns were able to return a member for every 6,000 inhabitants successfully prevented the rural constituencies, which returned one member for up to 40,000 inhabitants, from controlling more than two-thirds of the seats in the Second Chamber.

There was little change in the composition of the chambers in the next forty years. The First Chamber remained plutocratic, aristocratic and, above all, bureaucratic, the Second a mixture of about 100 farmers, 30 civil servants, 30 business men, and others. Comparisons are hard to make owing to the gradual increase in membership of both houses. This was finally limited in 1894 to 150 in the First Chamber and 230 in the Second. The Joint Vote thenceforth required a majority of the total of 380 members. Assuming everyone voted, this meant that the First Chamber required the support of twenty-one members of the Second Chamber to make its will effective.

11. *The franchise*

The franchise was still restricted to a small proportion of the population; only 5 per cent. of the 4 million inhabitants in 1870 possessed the vote[1] to the Second Chamber. Some members of the working class had the vote, particularly ironworkers, and some smallholders also engaged in industry or other occupations, but many preferred to abstain from voting rather than reveal that their incomes were taxable. In that year less than 100,000 went to the polls. Polling was more than twice as high among the 98,000 townspeople as in the country districts, but even in the towns it was low. Nor could the general apathy be attributed mainly to indirect elections, since by 1884 the number of constituencies which still employed this method had dropped to fifty-nine, whereas the percentage going to the polls had only increased by 6 per cent. Swedish writers do not seem to mention distance from polling-stations as contributing to the apparent apathy. For twenty years there was extremely little political interest in the country at large, partly because the period was comparatively uneventful and partly because a modern party system had not yet developed.

The franchise for electing the Provincial and City Councils which formed the electoral colleges for the First Chamber was double that of the Second Chamber electorate, including as it did all men and independent women who paid commune taxes. There was considerable variation between provinces, towns, and communes. In the island (and province) of Gotland 16 per cent. of the population were entitled to vote: in Södermanland 6.7 per cent. In 1904 no fewer than 42.5 per cent. of the whole population of the town of Sigtuna were enfranchised, with which may be compared Linköping's 16·7 per cent. The electorate in the communes varied between 36·5 per cent. at Träkumla in Gotland and 1·2 per cent. in Bollerup, a village in the province of Kristianstad. However, the graded scale and the admission of business firms to the voting register nullified the wide First Chamber franchise. In 1904, by which time the financial position of the working class had improved considerably, the franchise of nearly a tenth of the 2,386 communes was

[1] There is in Sweden a tendency to give the figures of the franchise in percentages of the whole population, thus making it seem remarkably low. Of adult males 20 per cent. could vote in 1870.

controlled by the votes of three voters or less. The growth of industrialization in the countryside and the consequent increase in the voting power of the owners of industry and their workers gradually altered the balance of power, making the opposition of the farmers progressively weaker, especially in the north.[1]

Comparisons between the franchise before and after 1866 are not possible, because before the Parliament Act each district regulated its own franchise and there was no national minimum qualification for the exercise of the franchise to the Burgher or Farmer Estates. There does not, however, appear to have been much change. Louis De Geer wrote in his Memoirs: 'In the passing of the Parliament Act the aim had chiefly been to abolish the Estates and prepare the entry of categories standing outside the Estates though they could be considered of similar rank, but any need to extend the franchise downwards was not then recognized.'[2] Thus the aim of securing representation of the 'categories of equal rank' was achieved and certain anomalies were removed. Many rich men who previously were denied access to the *Riddarhus* now sat in the First Chamber with the aristocracy.

III. *The weakness of liberalism*

To what extent the bill was a victory for liberalism may be argued. It certainly did not meet the demands of the radical-liberals. But the economic-liberals were satisfied and many would have agreed with the bank director A. O. Wallenberg, who as one of the Burghers had been eager to abolish the Estates, when he said that the reform was adequate enough and that he did not want to hear of any extension of the franchise.[3] During the period there was a change in the sympathies of the iron-masters. Before 1866 they had been radical reformers: by the turn of the century ironmasters like Lindman and Lundeberg were conservative leaders. In the Second Chamber the farmers were also content with the franchise as it stood in 1867.

Thus to call the Parliament Act a victory of the middle class or of liberalism is to give an impression of Swedish political development which is misleading. The age of liberalism in the

---

[1] Figures taken from Andrén, op. cit., with modifications according to *Studier*, &c.

[2] De Geer, *Minnen*, ii. 249. [3] Spångberg, V., *Karl Staaff*, p. 28.

political sense had not yet arrived, and the urban bourgeoisie upon which it depended was still small in numbers.[1] Since the Act was not followed by any liberal measures of social reform responsibility for inaction must rest with Louis De Geer, who admitted that he considered that the Government's duty lay not in giving Parliament the leadership it required but in withstanding any attacks that might be made upon the King's power.[2] (There was no Whig tradition in Sweden, which seems to make De Geer's appellation of Lord Grey of the Swedish Reform Act something of a misnomer.) He even secured the appointment of Bishop Sundberg, an opponent of the Act, as Speaker of the Second Chamber, despite the protests of the farmers. It would seem that in persuading De Geer that the position of the King might be threatened by the reform, the conservatives had placed the Ministry on the defensive once the bill was passed. As was his wont, De Geer remained aloof from parties, even from the 'Ministerial' party formed by friends of the reform in Parliament for the express purpose of defending the Ministry, and he remained convinced to the end that Government should be above all faction. Notwithstanding his expressed opinion that civil servants like himself should not sit in Parliament, he and five of his colleagues accepted election to the First Chamber. One figure, however, was missing; through ill health Gripenstedt resigned from the Ministry in 1866. Lacking his energy and willpower it soon relapsed into the weak Council which it had been before the era of reform began in the sixties.

The Ministry was a spent force. Whether this was due to the resignation of Gripenstedt or to the victory of the bill which united it, it is hard to say, but most probably from the combination of the two. There was nothing now to unite radicals, moderates, and economic-liberals. Nor were other causes of failure lacking. A new Parliament has energy because it has new men, but in Sweden the Ministry and many members of Parliament were the same. Moreover, by continuing to exist for another six months (until June 1866) in order to dispatch

---

[1] Note Hovde's title of Chapter XIII (op. cit.): 'The Social Struggle for Political Power, 1815–1865: The Victory of Liberalism (i) The Period of Reaction 1815–30. (ii) Liberalism Victorious 1830–65. (He is writing of the three Scandinavian countries.)

[2] De Geer, *Minnen*, ii. 58.

the remaining business of the session, the Estates weakened the psychological effect of the reform and made it appear less dramatic than if they had been abolished early in December 1865.

Moreover, the year of the new Parliament was not propitious. Both 1867 and the following year were times of bad harvest, and as an agricultural country, Sweden was seriously affected. The Government had no desire or opportunity at such a time to embark on any expensive social reforms.

In this respect it is questionable whether comparisons between England after 1832 and Sweden after 1866 are possible. Answering criticisms of the Government's lack of initiative, De Geer complained that he could not think of any reforms which were necessary. Indeed in Sweden parliamentary reform was the climax of a series of reforms, in contrast to Great Britain where the 1832 Reform Act preceded a spate of Acts of Parliament including the Poor Law Amendment Act and the overhaul of municipal government. Whereas after the English 1867 reform bill it was necessary 'to educate our masters' by introducing the Elementary Education Bill, compulsory education had been introduced in Sweden in 1842. The establishment of a Church Assembly (1863), the reform of local government (1817, 1842, and most of all 1862), and the introduction of Free Trade (1846, 1864) all preceded the 1866 Parliament Act. There was some truth in De Geer's assertion that members could only echo Wallenberg's remark: 'It is very difficult to say *what* ought to be done, but *something* must be done.'[1] One difficulty was that the sort of reforms which remained unaccomplished were distasteful to economic-liberals like Wallenberg and his friends.

iv. *Adolf Hedin*

However, there was one man who had a programme of reform, and who helped to found a party in the Second Chamber to press for its accomplishment. His name was Adol Hedin, a man who spent his parliamentary career from 1869 to 1905 preaching liberal doctrines in a Second Chamber for the most part unsympathetic to his views. Publicist and literary critic, this 'Father of Swedish liberalism' lived long enough to

[1] *Minnen*, ii. 58.

see the rise of a modern Liberal party. As the writer and Parliamentarian who most influenced the younger generation of
liberals, he was very much responsible for many of the ideas
which dominated the Liberal party formed in 1900. Greatly
influenced by French culture and closely aware of political
developments in Britain and the United States, he looked west-
wards rather than to Sweden's nearest southern neighbour,
Germany. Much as he disliked British imperialism, he disapproved even more strongly of the policy of the German
Government.

Hedin's *Fifteen Letters*, published in 1868, formed the basis of his
creed. His theme was the 1866 Act. Though he agreed that it owed
much to liberal principles, he denied that it was a victory for
democracy, insisting that the reform required completion. He
argued that the conservatives had merely pretended that they
were making a sacrifice when they passed the bill, in that they
must have known that it would bring them advantages. Why,
he asked, was it necessary to add such high property qualifications to all the other precautions taken to secure the First
Chamber's difference in character from the Second? Differentia-
tion could have been achieved without the property qualification, and as things stood, the chamber contained too many
Stockholmers and civil servants. The effects of plural voting
were harmful: in one constituency a business firm had more
votes than half the population and as a result only 172 voters
thought it worth while going to the polls. He criticized the
system of allotting votes according to the direct taxes paid by
the familiar radical argument that the poor who carried a heavy
burden of indirect taxation were unrepresented. There should
be no fear that working men would elect unsuitable representatives. Among the reforms of Parliament he suggested was the
limiting of the term of office for First Chamber members from
nine years to six.

While advocating a crusade for a further reform of Parliament, he claimed that he could not find a party to lead it. He
maintained that those who thought there was already a suitable
body of leaders in the Farmers' party were mistaken, since these
men, though they had supported the reform of Parliament, had
done so for their own reasons. They had opposed compulsory
education and local government reform and now their party

was a body from which the soul had flown. He pleaded for a new liberal party dedicated to the fight against bureaucracy and possessing above all things a conscience. On occasion its members would have to be prepared to submit their individual wills to the necessity of uniting in the common cause.

In stressing social conscience Hedin was a good example of the nineteenth-century radical. He constantly attacked the harsh laws which applied to the poor and destitute, particularly the threat of imprisonment which hung over those who no longer had enough to keep themselves (*lösdrivare*) and resorted to begging for alms. The lack of self-respect in the lower classes was ascribed by him to undue servility. In 1887 he supported Free Trade on social grounds (the need for cheap food for the poor) when the Prime Minister and his colleagues based their arguments on its economic effects.

Perhaps his greatest legacy to the future Liberal party was the belief that the royal executive power should be more closely controlled by the elected representatives of the people in Parliament. He preferred the British system of parliamentary government to the Swedish separation of powers. In particular he opposed the article of the Constitution which stated that economic legislation was the prerogative of the Crown, maintaining with great force throughout his parliamentary career the belief expressed in the *Fifteen Letters* that economic legislation ought, like civil legislation, to be enacted by King and Parliament jointly and not by the King alone. Other signs of royal power which he disliked were the nomination of the Speakers by the King and examination by the Executive of the competence of members to take their seats in Parliament. He believed that the Provincial Councils ought to be given greater power and have a status above and not below the Provincial Governors appointed by the Crown. In Stockholm the Governor held too much authority, especially over the police.

It is not surprising to find Hedin attacking two institutions which traditionally supported the Monarchy: the Church, and the army. Of the Church he remarked that according to the Constitution: 'no one's conscience ought to be forced, but each should be protected in the free exercise of his religion so long as he does not disturb the public peace or arouse popular anger thereby' (A. 16). But there were still in force other laws which limited the freedom of religion. All servants of the Crown had to be of the 'true evangelical faith'. The decision to change one's religion involved a personal appearance before the parish priest who was entitled to warn the dissenter of the perils of leaving the established Church. All nonconformist bodies were under police supervision; no one was allowed to abandon religion altogether. Only Russia and Spain, he argued, had harsher religious laws, and England ('prejudice's promised land') had admitted the Jews to Parliament in 1858 and permitted a Mohammedan to obtain a post in the public service.

In attacking army organization he pleaded for a less anti-quated system of recruitment and supply, and suggested the replacement of land taxes, &c., by conscription. In this way a 'people's army' might be created instead of one where country lads provided the cannon fodder and the nobility the officers—twenty-eight of the army's thirty generals were of noble birth. Hedin's interest in a strong army, which distinguishes him from the pacific English radicals, stemmed from the fear of Russia which he shared with many of his countrymen. The growth of Germany was a counterpoise to Russia, and many conservatives came to look upon Germany as Sweden's natural protector and ally. But to Hedin the choice between two illiberal powers was unattractive and he preferred to see a strong Scandinavia under Swedish leadership. He differed from Charles XV by maintain-ing that Norway ought to be treated as an equal partner in the Union, and he rightly recognized that the failure of the Swedish Crown to treat Norway as an equal in diplomatic affairs was the chief source of friction between the two countries. Given the right policy of co-operation, a strong and independent Northern power was possible. The dream of everlasting peace he dis-missed as a 'childish fantasy'.

One letter (the fourth) contained a prophecy of the future role of the United States in European affairs somewhat reminiscent of Rousseau's on Corsica. The time would come, Hedin observed, when Europe would have to make the choice between being Americanized or being taken over by Asian barbarism. There was no doubt which choice Hedin preferred. Popular education had made America 'the most civilized country in the world'. How great a difference there seemed to be between this free nation of independent people and the rigorous life of Sweden where only the Bible and catechism were read at school![1] Was the aim of Swedish education, he asked, to produce Churchmen or citizens?

Even before large-scale migration made the United States political system familiar to many Swedes, radicals like Hedin looked to the New World and not to Britain for their political ideals. England's parliamentary government aroused their interest but the country's notorious social conditions received their denunciation. At heart Hedin was a child of the French Revolution and he found the aristocratic way of life among the governing classes of Britain more appropriate to the *ancien régime* than to the liberal era. The reputation of Britain may have suffered at this time from the hands of her own critics. Hedin knew England from the writings of Mill and those who complained of the industrial evils of economic *laissez-faire*; his knowledge of the United States on the other hand sprang from the out-of-date eulogies of De Tocqueville. He therefore praised America and American institutions and denounced the policies of Britain.

v. *The New Liberal party, 1868*

In the middle of 1867 Hedin founded the New Liberal Association and at the beginning of the 1868 session a Liberal party was formed in the Second Chamber, about twenty members of the Chamber showing interest. Under the parliamentary leadership of A. V. Uhr (Hedin was not yet a member of Parliament for a Stockholm constituency), the New Liberal party proposed universal suffrage for men and women over twenty-one and many other innovations which shocked both chambers. All were defeated without debate. There was a brief revival, but a year or two later the party disintegrated. Its failure, like that of the Chartists in England, was partly due to its premature existence, for there was not the foundation for a large body of radical-liberal opinion in the country. The proportion of university students, doctors, journalists, and the professional middle classes in general, was lower in Sweden than in Denmark and Norway.[2] Partly, however, failure was also due to Hedin's temperament.

[1] Unlike the author of *Martin Chuzzlewit*, Hedin had not visited the United States.
[2] Tingsten, H., *Den svenska socialdemokratiens idéutveckling*, i. 21–23.

Destined to play an important part as the chief critic of the
Government for over thirty years ('more feared even than the
Constitution Committee') he was unable to work with others,
least of all to lead a political party.

Still, if the time had been ripe, someone else would have
taken over the leadership of the New Liberal party. De Geer had
been mistaken in thinking that there would be a balance of his
capitalist conservatism by more liberal forces. The economic-
liberals were by no means equally concerned with political
liberalism and lost much of their interest in politics once the bill
was passed. The farmers who had been dubbed 'radicals' during
the agitation proved to be staunchly conservative once they
had obtained their share of power. The policies of the two
chambers after 1866 are evidence of the slight impact of liberal
social ideas on either of them. Hedin's small group of radicals
was ineffective; liberals like Hedlund and Key believed their
future lay with the Farmers' party of the Second Chamber;
others like Wallenberg, Rydin, and Waern found themselves in
alignment with the First Chamber's conservatism. The Ministerial party, formed to defend the reform, changed its name to
the Intelligentsia and later the Centre, but did not prove a
powerful force.

Perhaps as serious as the absence of a liberal leaven, was the
friction which soon developed between the chambers. The
harmony foretold by De Geer when he made them equal in
authority and competence failed to materialize. Instead there
was a constant difference of opinion over financial and economic
policy, the majority in the First Chamber opposing the Farmers'
party in the Second.

VI. *The Farmers' party: its grievances*

The Farmers' party of the Second Chamber, which took shape
during the 1867 session, was the only real parliamentary party.
Strengthened by the return of as many as fifty-seven members
of the Farmer Estate it was able to enforce a discipline as strong
as that which the old Estate wielded over its members. It
became customary for members who agreed to its thirteen-
point programme to register with the party at the beginning
of the session. Among the demands of the party were: reform
of the militia system, economy in the public finances and

removal of the taxes which lay particularly upon the farmers, abolition of the old road transport regulations, school reforms, and the alteration of the communal franchise. Its author was Emil Key, and some of the points tended to reflect his personal opinion more than the general view of the farmers. Policy was determined by a nine-man committee of senior members of the party (*förtroenderåd*), an institution which was to be an integral part of later parliamentary parties.

Leadership of the Farmers in 1867 was a prize sought after by several who had not been members of the Farmer Estate. The party was formed around Count Arvid Posse, a landowner of ancient lineage from Scania, who had bitterly opposed the reform of Parliament. He was now regarded as a traitor to his class and was commonly thought to be using the Farmers' party to achieve his ambitions of personal political power and revenge on De Geer. A leader of a different type was Emil Key, the landowner and writer, who was main author of the party's programme.

For the first twenty years or more of the new Parliament's existence, the main bone of contention was the policy of the Farmers' party in continuing the traditional opposition of the farmers to Government expenditure, especially on defence (except when a malicious member of the First Chamber proposed that the salaries of members of Parliament should be reduced). This policy was to some extent understandable, because the farmers had believed that after the reform of Parliament a more equitable system of taxation would be devised. However, so long had controversy raged over the public finances that it was to take many years before agreement was finally reached upon their reform.

In the remote past, owners of land had been required to do service for the Crown if they were of the nobility owning free land (*frälsejord*), and to provide supplies if they were farmers cultivating what was called 'taxable land' (*skattejord*). As compensation for the services they rendered, the nobility were exempt from taxation of their land. As time went on, however, they were not always called upon to serve, and what had been compensation became a privilege. In contrast, the land taxes (*grundskatter*) and other impositions continued, much to the annoyance of the farmers. It has been said of one such tax, the

Landtågsgården to support the war against Sigismund, King of Poland, in 1617: 'The war ended, Sigismund's line died out, the Polish kingdom ceased to exist, but the *Landtågsgården* remained.'[1]

It is true that once levied these land taxes remained fixed once and for all, which meant that in the course of time many obligations became less onerous, especially as new cultivation was undertaken.[2] But the inequalities of the arrangement were unfair, and, moreover, the division of land into different categories had far-reaching social as well as financial implications. Taxable land was not so easily disposable as free land, chiefly because the Crown's anxiety to ensure that taxes would be paid involved restrictions upon its sale.[3] Gustavus Vasa had introduced the notion that Crown and farmers shared in the ownership of the land, a semi-feudal theory which led to the growth of social distinctions based on the type of land owned.[4] In addition, the Crown demanded payment in kind, asserted the right to confiscate land on which taxes had not been paid for three years, and forbade farmers to buy free land.[5]

In the eighteenth century there was some improvement and in 1789 farmers were allowed to buy free land. (It was farmers who owned this type of land, *frälsehemmansägare*, who were admitted to the Farmer Estate in 1845.) Grievances over the land taxes were responsible for the Estate's unwillingness to agree to the 1809 Constitution, in which these taxes were specifically placed under Crown authority as part of its 'ordinary income', but it was noticeable that the Nobles no longer based their opposition upon the argument of class privilege.[6] By 1809 there was some acceptance of Adam Smith's argument that taxes should be levied according to capacity to pay and not on the assumption that, because everyone received equal protection from the State, taxation should affect everyone equally. It was the argument of 'fairness' which was used, the Nobles maintaining that free land was more expensive to buy than taxable land (because it was untaxed) and therefore any proposal to 'equalize' the burden of land taxes by extending them to all land was manifestly unjust.[7]

[1] Spångberg, op. cit., p. 10.
[2] Thomson, A., *Grundskatterna i den politiska diskussionen 1809–1866*, p. 331.
[3] Ibid., p. 51.   [4] Ibid., p. 331.
[5] Ibid., p. 327.   [6] Ibid., pp. 328–9.   [7] Ibid., p. 128.

The farmers were unsuccessful in their pleas, and no real changes were made before 1866. To their disappointment, the Farmers' party then discovered that many of their proposed reforms could be blocked by a refusal of the King-in-Council to give its assent, and even where Parliament was in a position to exercise its own jurisdiction, the homogeneous First Chamber, aided by the Second Chamber minority, was often able to defeat it in the Joint Vote. Nevertheless, the transformation of the national economy was exposing the anomalies and shortcomings of the old fiscal system. A start was made in 1869 when it was agreed that henceforth payments should be in money instead of in kind.

It was in 1873 that the first important step was taken to change the system, a 'compromise' being agreed to by both Chambers, according to which the land taxes would gradually be written off. However, owing to differences of interpretation the Compromise did not immediately become effective. In 1885 it was decided that 30 per cent. of the taxes should be rescinded, and seven years later that they should be completely abolished, the system of land taxes finally ending in 1904.

The land taxes were not the only grievances which were redressed during this period. The *Indelningsverk*, a system of land allocation whereby the army, Civil Service, and clergy received remuneration direct from the taxpayer in the form of houses, land, and provisions, was abolished at the same time as the land taxes, State servants henceforth receiving salaries from the Exchequer (*statsverket*). The First Chamber succeeded in protecting the Civil Service from Second Chamber attacks by persuading the Speakers of both chambers to enunciate, in 1874, the principle that the 'ordinary income' of the Crown could not be reduced without the consent of the King. This was in contrast to the tendency of Parliament in general to claim the exercise of financial powers constitutionally pertaining to the Crown. In 1876 it was decided that this convention should apply to whatever succeeded the *Indelningsverk*.

Certain duties (*besvär*) such as the upkeep of the Church, the poor law and communications, were also made less burdensome or abolished. The *skjutsstadga* whereby farmers provided horses, transport, and accommodation for travellers on official business was one of the most burdensome responsibilities, especially as the facility was often abused by the *herrar*. In 1878 it was virtually abolished, the last vestiges disappearing in 1911. The ancient system of providing troops (*rustning* and *rotering*) was abandoned at the same time as the land taxes and *Indelningsverk*. In its place conscription was extended, the period of forty-eight days agreed to in 1885 being extended to ninety in 1892.

At first sight the Farmers' party appears to have been an obdurate group of men acting in their own interests. Closer examination, however, reveals that these men were fighting against an unjust and antiquated institution, which was not altered until a modern system of conscription and income tax replaced the *Indelningsverk*, *grundskatter*, and similar traditional sources of men and materials.

In 1880 the Farmers' party defeated the second De Geer ministry and many in the First Chamber thought it was appropriate that it should be given its first opportunity to govern. Oscar II, who had succeeded his brother in 1872, took the advice of several members of the First Chamber and called upon Count Posse, whose Farmers' party had been responsible for the failure of so many of the weak bureaucratic Ministries which had been in office since 1867, to head one himself. He did so, but without receiving the full support of his party. They were unwilling to take office because they said that they did not want to bind themselves to supporting the Government and thus be no longer free to exercise power without the responsibility of office. Partly too, of course, the farmers were unused to government and did not want their failure to make them a laughing-stock. 'Imagine a farmer in gold trousers!' exclaimed Carl Ifvarsson. They had wanted parliamentary reform because it gave them power to restrain the Government: they did not want to have to form the Government. Many of them were still obsessed by a sense of inferiority, and their more able leaders were afraid of being thought traitors to the party by accepting office. Finally Posse formed a government which had the highest proportion of nobles of any during this period—seven out of ten Ministers. However, he made the innovation of asking a committee of parliamentary members to formulate defence policy, and this was strongly weighted with farmers. Thirteen of its nineteen members were from the Second Chamber and of them twelve were farmers and six others on the Farmers' party committee (*förtroenderåd*). But in presenting his defence *proposition* in 1883 he neglected to keep in close touch with the party and was defeated in his own chamber by 153 votes to 144. As leader of the Farmers' party he should have realized how much he depended on its support as chief Minister of the Crown, especially as he was not a man in whom the First Chamber had confidence.

Thus the farmers, by holding to the doctrine of division of powers, let pass their one opportunity in this period of shaping a Ministry. Never again were they to form such an important part of the Second Chamber. Their timidity cost Posse dear, the immediate result of his defeat in both chambers being his resignation and the ending of his public career, of which this Ministry was to have been the climax. There was once again a return to bureaucratic Ministries, with the First Chamber *herrar* opposing the Second Chamber farmers.

VII. *Social changes*

Before a real development in politics could come about, a social as well as an industrial revolution had to take place. Much remained to be done to educate the expanding population, socially as well as politically. If the future Liberal party owed much of its political inspiration to Adolf Hedin, it owed many of its principles to two other movements which helped to change the social character of Sweden—Nonconformity and Temperance. These prepared the ground for the political awakening which took place after 1887.

The first important change in habits concerned liquor consumption, spirit-drinking being the great curse of Sweden in the nineteenth century as of some other countries. A correspondent of the newspaper *Fram* (directed by young Socialists) commented on the 'deplorable boorishness and demoralization' of the youth in one province:

> They drink at home, they drink on their way to Church, or meeting house, on the way home: wherever young people gather for an evening a bottle of spirits is in the middle of them. A person taking to the road on a Saturday or Sunday evening is in danger of being set upon by drunken farmhands and labourers and risks his life if he tries to talk sense with them. The general opinion amongst young

people here in Småland as in so many provinces, is that one cannot have a jolly time without spirits.[1]

Conditions had improved since the worst period of spirit drinking—the early and middle nineteenth century—but they were still bad. Liquor consumption was particularly serious in northern Europe because it involved not the sometimes innocuous wine or beer but crude spirits which excited men's passions and in the long run damaged health. The writer of a play or novel in nineteenth-century Sweden frequently introduced drunkenness into his plot as a major influence on the life of at least one character.

The Temperance movement, led by Peter Wieselgren, a Lutheran clergyman, started in the 1830's. In 1855 Parliament checked the unlicensed domestic distillation of spirits, in the face of heavy opposition from the Farmer Estate. (Had the reform been proposed some years later, the Second Chamber might have successfully opposed it.) The introduction of the Good Templars in 1869 and several other American temperance organizations in the following years gave a new impetus to the Temperance movement, which began to assume large proportions. By 1890, 85,000 people were members of the four Temperance societies, and in the 1890's the advocates of temperance became increasingly influential in politics.

Although the Englishman George Scott had preached Methodism in Sweden in the early 1840's, it was after 1866 that the Nonconformist movement grew. The Baptists were the first group of Dissenters to become established (1857), followed by the Methodists (1863), and the Salvation Army (1886). Within the State Church itself P. P. Waldenström's Evangelical Movement began in 1856. The Dissenter Law of 1860 gave Nonconformists greater freedom and in 1873 full liberty of worship was granted; henceforth members of the State Church could join these bodies without penalties. The growth of the Free Churches was helped by money and encouragement from Great Britain and particularly from the United States, to which many Swedes emigrated.

The social consequences of the Nonconformist movement were much the same as in England, the Liberal party in its rank

---

[1] Quoted in Lindgren, J., *Per Albin Hansson i svensk demokrati*, p. 35.

and file owing much to Free Church influence. The first big strike, that of 1879, was said to have been instigated by Nonconformists and was accompanied by hymn-singing. The effects of Nonconformity were even greater upon the lower-middle class which grew in numbers towards the end of the century. It was this section of the population which formed the backbone of the Liberal party. In contrast with England, the Social Democrats had anti-religious tendencies, and few of its leaders were religious men.

VIII. *The Free Trade controversy, 1887*

An occurrence of more immediate and direct impact upon Swedish parliamentary development was the Protection dispute of 1887. It has been said with some truth that agrarian parties the world over are more interested in the price of corn than in issues of world or national politics, and the Swedish Farmers'· party was no exception. There was consternation in the 1880's when the import of cheap American and Russian corn reduced the price of rye from 15 to 9 *öre* per kilo and wheat from 18 to 12. The industrial workers gained from this trend but most of the farmers (those who did not consume all the corn they grew) stood to lose heavily. They therefore demanded Protection, and the Committee of Ways and Means which in 1878 had voted unanimously in favour of Free Trade, voted for its repeal in 1885.

The issue cut across party lines, because not all members even of the Farmers' party were equally affected by the import of corn. In Norrland the harvest was too small; in Scania there was more dairy-farming. Officially, the parties in Parliament remained neutral, but throughout the country meetings were held for and against Protection. Finally the Farmers' party in Parliament split into a Protectionist or New Farmers' party and a Free Trade or Old Farmers' party. Many of the latter party associated free trade with the prosperity of the 1870's.

Although the Themptander Ministry (1884–8) was in favour of Free Trade, the chambers were divided on the issue. After the elections of 1886 (the usual annual return of one-ninth of the members) the Protectionists gained ground in the First Chamber and in a division over the rye duty the Free Traders won by only 70–69 with the help of the Ministry's votes. The

Second Chamber voted in favour of Protection by 111–101. Before the Joint Vote could be taken King Oscar II agreed with the Ministry's proposal to dissolve the Second Chamber in the early months of 1887. The Free Traders were returned with a majority, and when the normal triennial elections occurred in September 1887, making two elections in one year, once again there was a Free Trade majority. The town members were overwhelmingly in favour of Free Trade, and nearly half the representatives from country constituencies supported them. However, their triumph was short-lived.

A certain Olaf Larsson, formerly a smelter (not to be confused with the Farmers' party leader Liss Olof Larsson) stood for election as a Free Trader in Stockholm, and was elected on the Free Trade list of twenty-two candidates. The Stockholm members formed the main core of Free Trade strength. It was discovered by the Protectionists that certain taxes, amounting to but a few crowns and dating from some years previously, were unpaid by Larsson. It was pleaded in the Supreme Court that this made Larsson's election invalid according to the 1866 Parliament Act because the franchise and the eligibility of members of the Second Chamber was conditional upon all their debts to the State having been paid. The Court had therefore no option but to declare Larsson disqualified. Moreover, owing to an oversight in the framing of the Act, all twenty-two members for Stockholm were disqualified and forced to give up their seats to their twenty-two Protectionist opponents who were declared to be duly elected. Thus ended the Free Trade era in Sweden after a brief twenty years: Larsson, overcome with remorse, gave up his post as superintendent of a charity soup-kitchen in Stockholm (hence his nickname Ångköks Olle) and emigrated to Canada.

There was no immediate constitutional remedy. The Free Traders in Parliament realized that they could now be outvoted in the Joint Vote, and the King, on whom rested the responsibility for a dissolution, thought that two elections in one year was enough, even though he favoured Free Trade. Dissolution of the Second Chamber was a rare event, this being the first time it had occurred since 1866. Themptander had been accused of sharp practice by the conservatives for dissolving the Second Chamber in 1887 before the Joint Vote could be taken, for not asking the King to dissolve the First Chamber also (which would have weakened the Free Traders' position), and for insisting upon the use of the latest population statistics in apportioning the seats (thereby increasing the number of urban seats, which could be expected to return Free Traders, by six, and the county seats by only one).[1] He was, therefore, in no position to be indignant over the Larsson incident. It has also been pointed out that despite the victory of the Second Chamber Free Traders in the elections of 1887 they were losing ground.[2] There was a gradual movement away from Free Trade, and in the 1890 elections the Protectionists consolidated their position.

The effect of the debate on Protection upon the country was to make many who otherwise had no interest in politics and parliamentary affairs realize how deeply an Act of Parliament could affect their daily lives, even to the regulation of the price of bread. It became useful to have the vote and thus register one's opinion at election time, and it was not long before those who opposed the introduction of Protection but were without the franchise, began to form suffrage associations to press for its extension.

The controversy left its marks on both chambers. In the Second Chamber, the Farmers' party took several years to recover from the split in its ranks. One hundred and fifteen members supported the New Farmers' party led by E. G. Boström, and 50 the Old Farmers, to whom may be added 47 urban Free Traders. The dispute had caused members to act for reasons other than the clear interests of their social class. The effect on the First Chamber was the creation of a Protectionist or Majority party with a programme more definite than the policies of the coteries which were all that had formerly existed. Each chamber became conscious that there were in the country many electors sufficiently interested in its decisions to be both able and willing to change their party allegiance if the policies of the parties was not to their liking. There was here the germ of modern parliamentary government. Boström, who was Prime Minister from 1891 to 1900, was one of the first to realize that the nature of Parliament had changed. His success in obtaining parliamentary approval for his defence *proposition* with ninety days' conscription was possible because he could draw upon the

[1] Petré, T., *Ministären Themptander*, pp. 148–61. [2] Ibid., p. 190.

support of majorities in both chambers—in the same way that the Protectionists had done.

There was also a change in party alignments in both chambers. Instead of the *herrar* of the First opposing the farmers of the Second there was a tendency for each chamber to split into Right and Left groups. The First Chamber Majority party and the New Farmers' party in the Second discovered that their interests coincided in ways other than merely Protection. Both parties viewed with apprehension the increasing radicalism of the towns and it was not long before they took action against it.

According to the Parliament Act of 1866 small towns could combine to form constituencies, and would be represented by a member for every 6,000 inhabitants. As the national population increased more in urban than rural districts, these constituencies became more prolific in members until in 1893 the number of urban constituencies was 82, compared with 55 twenty-five years earlier. Of the total increase of 38 Second Chamber seats, 27 had been awarded to small town constituencies, and the farmers, whose constituencies could number up to 40,000 inhabitants without being given a second member, had reason to feel disgruntled. De Geer had arranged that the number of small town constituencies should be reviewed every decade by Parliament, and in 1894 it was agreed to limit the number of seats in the Second Chamber to 230, of which the towns would have 80. At the same time, the First Chamber seats were limited to 150. Posse had suggested such a 'wing-clipping', as it was termed, in 1867 but without success. It must have intrigued the aged De Geer to notice that the bogey of farmer-domination was now laid. In the voting on the measure there was an omen of a *fronde* in the New Farmers' party: nineteen farmers from the radical and free-trade north opposed the bill.

In 1895, partly as a result of the wingclipping, there was a revival in the fortunes of the farmers. The leaders of the two Farmers' parties agreed to join forces and before the rank and file could discuss the plan the motion was hurried through in meetings of both parties. One hundred and thirty-seven Second Chamber members joined the new party, of whom 131 were country members. Bishop Billing, who had opposed the wing-clipping in the First Chamber in 1892, supported it in 1895, commenting in his diary that the radicals and farmers might join forces, and it was better to support the farmers than the radicals.[1] The First Chamber was not blind to the need to have allies in the Second if radicalism was to be confined to the members from Stockholm and Gothenburg.

The change in the attitude of the farmers was shown in their decreased interest in parliamentary reform. Between 1880 and 1884 they had voted in favour of some extension of the franchise in order to increase their authority in the Second Chamber and Parliament as a whole. But an inquiry by the Constitution Committee showed that the extension of the franchise on any considerable scale might lose the farmers half their seats. In 1888 82 per cent. of country voters were property owners: to offer the vote to all those who, for example, paid local taxes would be to enfranchise a large number of persons who had no similar 'stake in the country'. The farmers were supported in their opposition to parliamentary reform by the Fatherland Association (*Fosterlands förbundet*), a group of town bourgeoisie and craftsmen who wanted increased 'guarantees' if the vote was to be given to groups which might threaten their interests.

ix. *The Universal Suffrage Association*

While the important groups in Parliament were becoming more conservative, the unenfranchised were interested in the movement for parliamentary reform founded in 1890. The Universal Suffrage Association was formed to plead the case for extending the vote to the Second Chamber to all men over twenty-one with certain qualifications. It attracted two small but expanding groups, the liberals and the socialists.

The liberals, who were not yet a political party, were opposed to the Protectionist policy of Parliament, and liberal members of the Second Chamber discovered that their views increasingly diverged from those of the farmers. Too small in numbers to put forward a notion for reform in the Second Chamber, they gladly took the opportunity of convincing the electorate, and those who might one day be enfranchised, of the need for reform. The socialists had formed a party in 1889, but were unrepresented in Parliament.

The platform on which liberals and socialists united was the

[1] Billing, G., *Anteckningar från riksdagar och kyrkomöten 1893–1906*, p. 78.

Folkriksdag or People's Parliament (the idea of which had come from Belgium). At their congress in Norrköping in 1891 the socialists voted in favour of a People's Parliament and a general strike as possible weapons against 'the masters in society'. In 1892 the third conference of the Universal Suffrage Association decided that in view of the 10,000 favourable votes obtained in a plebiscite it organized, a People's Parliament should meet in 1893. It was to consist of representatives from the constituencies and was to show Parliament that a great number of the un-enfranchised were dissatisfied with their present legislature and its lukewarm attitude to parliamentary reform. From the start the socialists were the more active participants, somewhat to the annoyance of the organizers of the assembly, who were liberals. They were given ten of the ninety country seats but were re-fused their claim for eight of the Stockholm places because the Stockholm intellectuals (*kulturliberalerna*) who were the liberals most interested in the People's Parliament, supported by the Temperance enthusiasts and their newspaper *Svenska Morgon-bladet*, also wanted them. One reason for giving the socialists as many as ten country seats was the lack of liberal interest in suffrage reform in some country districts, even where the farmers might be inclined favourably to liberalism. As an urban party the socialists were thought to be ill equipped to deal with country constituencies.

Little resulted from the 1893 People's Parliament. The Prime Minister, Boström, refused to meet a deputation and was not interested in the movement. The King received the leaders but said he could give them no help. When a further meeting of the People's Parliament took place in 1896 the socialists returned no fewer than 30 of the 146 members. On this occasion a dispute arose over future policy. The liberals wanted to do nothing more than to influence public opinion by meetings and cam-paigns, and to influence Parliament by national petitions for reform. The socialists, who in 1891 had agreed to the strike weapon even though they had forsworn 'dynamite agitation', wanted more definite action. The liberals refused either to use force or stage a strike, whereupon the socialists opposed a further meeting in 1899. The liberals went on alone, and in 1898 produced a monster petition of 364,000 signatures, 66,000 of which were by persons possessing the franchise. The movement then faded away, but not before it had helped to arouse interest in the creation of a Liberal parliamentary party. When, a few years later, the time came for the Liberal party to form a government, the period of collaboration with the socialists bore fruit, for relations between the leaders of the two parties were often amicable enough for them to concert their policies.

x. *Conclusion*

In conclusion, it may be said that in the thirty years after 1866 the bicameral system became fully established. At first it depended on a balance of interest between the farmers of the Second Chamber and the upper classes represented in the First, but after 1887, precipitated by the Free Trade controversy, there were many important changes. The social effects of the industrial revolution manifested themselves in the settlement of the farmers' taxation claims and in the growth of a new middle class interested in suffrage and temperance as well as Free Trade. By the end of the period, Liberal and Social Democratic parties were established in the Second Chamber and the Farmers were no longer the main opposition party. Caught between the new alignment of Right and Left, some of them joined the Liberals, while many found an increasing identity of interest with their old opponents, the First Chamber conservatives. These, too, had changed much in forty years, many of them being men who a generation previously could have called themselves liberals. It is not surprising, therefore, that these underlying social and political developments made possible constitutional changes affecting the separation of powers and the position of the King as Executive.

CHAPTER VI

Constitutional Developments, 1866–1905

Although a very important condition of the King's acceptance of the Parliament Act was that there should be no
constitutional change in the separation of powers, it was
impossible in 1866 to foretell the power which the new Parliament might claim. However, so gradual were many of the
changes in the relationship of King, Ministry, and Parliament
that they would appear to have depended on the social and
political events following 1866 rather than on the Act itself.

1. *The Monarchy*

(a) *Its retention of executive power*

In some ways the Crown retained its supremacy. Charles XV
indicated that he intended to uphold his position to the full,
especially in his treatment of the Ministry. This body, weakened
by Gripendstedt's departure and De Geer's unwillingness to
give a lead to Parliament, faced its first important crisis in 1868
when the Second Chamber refused to grant the money necessary
for the Government's defence needs. Four Ministers, led by
Count af Ugglas, the Finance Minister, wanted to resign. The
King returned to Stockholm and declared that the Parliament
Act had not changed the spirit of the Constitution, and that
such a resignation would imply parliamentary control over the
Ministry. Therefore there must be no suggestion of resignation.
De Geer had no alternative but to concur and even liberal newspapers (*Aftonbladet, Göteborgs Handels- och Sjöfartstidningen*) agreed
that resignation was unwise, commenting that the time was not
ripe for *parlamentarism* and that in general there was enough
support in Parliament for the Government to retain office.
Göteborgs Handels- och Sjöfartstidningen wrote a few days later (16
April): 'At least the Ministry ought not itself to take matters in
such a way that every parliamentary majority even in minor
issues can bring about a change of Ministry. The country's
government would thereby lose stability.' Later, at his pleasure,

I

Charles allowed all except the leader, af Ugglas, to resign. In 1870, when Charles was tired of the Ministry, he told af Ugglas that the 'Second Chamber was displeased with him' and requested his resignation on grounds which two years earlier he had averred were inadequate. Later, 'a leading member' of the First Chamber asked De Geer to include the two Speakers, Bishop Sundberg and Count Lagerbjelke, in the Ministry. Since the Speakers were royal nominees, and as, according to Kihlberg, De Geer had cause to suspect that this was a hint from the King, he offered his resignation in June 1870. This was accepted.

Charles replaced De Geer and his colleagues, most of whom were members of Parliament, with a Ministry consisting of several civil servants and only three members of Parliament, two of them from the Second Chamber. It is understandable that Charles wanted to change a Ministry which he had appointed before his accession in 1859 and which had governed contrary to his will. Even so, he had waited four years after the Parliament Act before he dared oppose the author of the reform bill. On receiving De Geer's resignation, he is reported to have exclaimed: 'Now it is I who govern'.[1] Within two years he died, his hope unfulfilled, at the age of forty-six.

His successor and brother Oscar II was more attentive to business and more tactful. He did not attempt to master all aspects of policy and only where the navy was concerned did he make his will felt strongly. However, he still exercised the two powers of appointment and dismissal of Ministers. Like most members of the First Chamber he wanted to increase the country's defences, and formed Ministries with the object of ending the deadlock between the two chambers which prevented this from being accomplished. Failure to pass a defence bill often led to a Ministry's dismissal. Resignation did not occur because of parliamentary disapproval but because the Ministry had failed to meet the King's wishes by bringing the chambers together on a common policy. Boström was the most successful of all the chief Ministers (or Prime Ministers as they were called after 1876), by reason of his solution of the Land Tax controversy in 1892, and he remained in office for nine years.

According to De Geer Oscar II always acted in a constitu-

[1] De Geer, *Minnen*, ii. 108.

tional spirit. His unwillingness to encroach upon the preserves
of Parliament is shown by his attitude to the Protection dispute.
While favouring Free Trade, he wrote to the Prime Minister in
1886: 'It is certainly true that I should consider it neither sen-
sible nor proper to make my opinion prevail against a parliamentary decision, especially as it has been passed with such a
noticeable majority.'[1] Nevertheless, when the chambers disagreed he dissolved the Second Chamber on the advice of his
Ministers in 1887, an act of which Charles had been afraid lest
parlamentarism should result. Oscar II remained aloof from the
Protection debate and accepted the triumph of the Protectionists after the débâcle of the Free Traders in the Stockholm
elections. However, when it was suggested in newspapers like
Vårt Land that Archbishop Sundberg had declined the office of
Prime Minister because of differences over the composition of
the Ministry, the King issued a semi-official communiqué in
Posttidningen stating that Sundberg 'only had to answer yes or no
for his personal participation . . . no so-called request to build a
Ministry has been made to the archbishop, nor have others
received such a commission. This would not be in conformity
with the Constitution.'[2] He added that the formation of a
Ministry 'was a prerogative which belongs to the King alone'.[3]

There was no resignation of office by a whole Ministry until
1905, Oscar II retaining his executive powers largely because of
the support of the conservatives. Rydin, the liberal professor
who became a conservative after 1866, suggested that responsible
ministerial government was suitable for Great Britain, but that
Sweden's division of powers required an Executive independent
of Parliament. Writing in 1904 Pontus Fahlbeck asserted that
the role of the King in this respect was similar to that of the
President of the United States, and maintained that Sweden
was the only European country with a similar type of Constitution. Constitutionally the King retained his powers of economic
legislation accorded in Article 89 as well as his authority over
defence (A. 14) and Civil Service appointments (A. 47). In the
Constitution Committee, Hedin made several attempts to persuade members to alter this section of the Constitution in order to
bring economic legislation jointly under King and Parliament,

---

[1] Hildebrand, K., *Gustav V som människa och regent*, i. 129.
[2] Kihlberg, p. 365.   [3] Ibid., p. 372.

but he failed to get enough support, since the conservatives
were not inclined to request a formal transfer of the powers of
the King. It would seem as though in constitutional matters
even a majority of members of Parliament were conservative: to
want 'ministerial' government was to be a radical like Hedin.

(b) The decline in the royal power

Nevertheless, it is possible to detect a diminution in the royal
power during the period from 1866 to 1905. Charles XV, for
instance, dared not dissolve the Second Chamber lest he should
injure the executive power, which in itself showed how conscious he was of the weakness of his position. His removal of af
Ugglas in 1870 was the last occasion on which a monarch dismissed a Minister without the approval of the Chancellor. Nor
was the return to bureaucratic Ministries in 1870 a regression
to the same type of Council formed by Oscar I, as was indicated
when in the following year Charles called an extraordinary
session of Parliament to approve his defence *proposition*, which
had been defeated in the ordinary session. It was rejected once
again, and the Adlercreutz Ministry, appointed by the King,
asked to resign in a body. In the end only the Minister for War,
Abelin, did so, but he was the Minister whom the Second
Chamber most disliked. Thus four years after pronouncing that
it was *his* confidence which a Ministry required, Charles was
forced to recognize that it was impossible to govern without
parliamentary support. In Norway Charles had to give way
even further. In 1869 he refused the *Storting*'s request for a
change of Ministry on the grounds that it was for the King to
decide—and then changed the Ministry exactly as the Norwegians had requested.

However, since the De Geer Ministry lasted for all but the last
two years of Charles XV's reign, it is difficult to draw conclusions about his attitude towards Ministries in general. Even in
1870, the year in which Charles dismissed De Geer, Gripenstedt
found it necessary to complain of the weakness of the King's
conduct of affairs, though allowance should be made for the
former Finance Minister's desire to divert conservative oppro-
brium from the Parliament Act, which tended to receive the
blame for whatever went wrong.

Oscar II's accession illustrated the changing attitude more

clearly. On the deaths of Charles XIV (1844) and Oscar I (1859) a new Council had been formed on the principle that it was appointed by the King as his personal group of advisers. In 1872 there was no change of Ministers, the Adlercreutz Ministry continuing in office until 1874. In that year Oscar asked De Geer to form a Ministry in conjunction with Posse, thus ensuring support for the Government in both chambers. It was the first of many instances in which the King showed that his main interest was to secure the maximum parliamentary support for the Crown. On this occasion he failed, because De Geer, disliking the thought of party government which a coalition with the Farmers' party would entail, and not on the best terms with Posse, declined the offer. Oscar then took the unusual step of publishing a statement which he added as a royal amendment (*diktamen*) to the Council of State minutes, remarking that he had turned to

'Baron L. De Geer with reference to his special position in the new legislature and his extensive acquaintance with persons and circumstances in Parliament' and he had 'expressed the wish that the baron might take Herr Adlercreutz's place in the King's Council, and had declared himself willing so far as possible to meet the requests which the baron might find himself obliged to make as a consequence of accepting this office. Baron De Geer has intimated that he must decline the proposed office.'

(24/3/74.)

This statement was an implied rebuke to De Geer. Moreover, it seemed to suggest that the King's government should not only be carried on but that leading members of Parliament had the duty to provide the King with a First Minister after a parliamentary defeat of a Council's policy.

A year later De Geer did take office, but his second Ministry was as bureaucratic as its predecessors. A member of the First Chamber defended the relapse of the Ministry into a collection of individual opinions by saying: 'I cannot believe that Parliament should consider it right of the King's advisers to come to an agreement (*sammanrota*) for the empty pleasure of having *one* opinion.'[1]

However, there were soon to be some important constitutional changes. In 1876 the office of the Minister of State for Justice

[1] Bergström in *F.k.*, quoted by Kihlberg, L., op. cit., p. 216.

(Chancellor) became that of Prime Minister on the British model, and the Ministry of Justice was made a separate portfolio. In 1885 the Minister for Foreign Affairs was given direct control of the Foreign Office, which put an end to the curious state of affairs which, for example, in Manderström's time in the early 1860's had caused the Foreign Minister to issue a directive to diplomats insisting that they only obeyed those royal commands which had been countersigned. By giving greater authority to his Foreign Minister the King ultimately weakened the influence of the Crown, and it may have been for this reason that, as has been said, 'it was in the early years of his reign that Oscar II made his most significant contribution in the sphere of foreign affairs'.[1] The departmental reforms were not intended to deprive the King of executive authority but were made necessary by the growing volume and complexity of administration, and the unwillingness of Oscar to take on the heavy burden of concentrating on day-to-day affairs of administration. De Geer was the first Prime Minister, but took no real advantage of his new status. As in the case of the 1840 reforms years passed by before the effects of the change became really apparent. A sign of the future 'democratic monarchy' was perhaps given in 1883 when Parliament changed the title of its addresses to the King from 'Most potent and most gracious Sovereign' to 'To the King' and its signature from 'In deepest humility' to 'With humble respect'.[2]

Oscar's role seems to have become increasingly passive. He did not give his Government much support over Protection and though the transfer from the Free Trade Ministry of Themptander to the Protectionist Boström took three years, the two moderate Ministries of Bildt and Åkerhielm intervening, this was because he preferred to take a middle course rather than because he wanted to delay acknowledging the victory of Protectionism. He preferred to act as 'the honest broker' instead of attempting an active part in political leadership.[3] He never used the royal veto (sanktionsvägran) after 1896, and the only occasion it was again employed was by Gustav V in 1913.[4] Oscar seems increasingly to have allowed Boström, Prime Minister

[1] Lindberg, F., *Kunglig utrikespolitik*, p. 8.
[2] Reuterskiöld, C. A., *Sveriges riksdag*, x. 228. [3] Kihlberg, p. 497.
[4] Malmgren, R., *Sveriges riksdag*, xiv. 144.

for twelve of the last sixteen years of his reign, to direct policy
for him. Yet his firmness in forcing the dismissal of the Staaff
Ministry in 1906, however, makes it unwise to assume that
Oscar was a weak King: it may be that he was passive only so
long as government was in the hands of Ministers who shared
his outlook.

11. *The Ministry*

(a) *Its gradual increase in power*

Neither Charles XV nor Oscar II displayed particularly strong
characters, and yet the Ministries after 1866 relapsed into the
old type of Council which had been so subservient under the
first Bernadottes, and belied De Geer's hope of a 'strong Government with more secure support in the legislature' expressed in
the 1861 memorandum. He himself, however, contributed to
this failure and even Henning Hamilton was driven to complain
that 'the Government spends its time too much on trivialities'
and that 'a party government is proper under the new parliamentary system'.[1] Later he became less convinced of the need
for government based on party support (partly no doubt owing
to the increase in the power of the farmers who had the one
genuine party), and the more common view was perhaps that
of Hugo Hamilton: 'Strongly to discipline the majority, to use
the so-called whippers (*sic*), &c. so that the blind may follow
their leader as is perhaps too often used in England, is not
advisable for us.'[2] Resignations from the Council continued to
be individual and a whole Ministry did not resign at once.
The Ministry was so little in the public eye that the attendance
of De Geer and Gripenstedt at a Gothenburg reform banquet
in 1864 had been exceptional, and apart from a similar public
appearance by Themptander in 1887 ('English fashion')[3] there
were no public appeals by Ministers and few interviews with
the press before the agitation preceding the second reform of
Parliament.

Some Ministers sat in Parliament as members, but were
excluded from committees. Since 1850 it had been customary
for 'the Government' to introduce its own bills in Parliament.

---

[1] Quoted in Kihlberg, p. 130.
[2] *F.k.* 1867, no. 3, p. 327.   [3] Kihlberg, p. 597, n. 1.

After the 1866 Reform Act Parliament sent an increasing number of requests (*skrivelser*) to the Government for legislation to be introduced on a variety of subjects within the King-in-Council's jurisdiction. The Ministry often prepared statements (*utredning*) describing the measures it was introducing and giving the reasons for its legislation, by which process Parliament became dependent for information on the Government, which had the means for acquiring it from the Civil Service. The Government continued to enact economic legislation in the form of executive decrees.

The length of a Ministry varied from four months (Ramstedt) to nine years (Boström's first)[1] but, in view of the frequent changes of individual Ministers, it cannot be assumed that the resignation of the Prime Minister in itself was significant. In the conduct of business the preparatory meetings of the Council increased in importance and the weekly Council of State (*Konselj*) discussed most matters only formally. Attempts were made to give the (private) preparatory meetings (*statsrådsberedning*) constitutional status, but these failed. These meetings were attended sometimes by the whole Council, except for the King, and sometimes by one or two Ministers concerned with a particular policy. Only on more important occasions were all Ministers present, the Prime Minister being in the chair. At other times the Prime Minister might attend if he was interested in the business to be discussed, or if he had a strong personality and wanted to exercise authority. Towards the end of the period the preparatory meetings with the Prime Minister in the chair seem as a rule to have been held weekly.

The Posse Ministry of 1880–3 was an exception to the general run of Councils. Posse seems to have been given a fairly free hand in appointing his colleagues and to have thought that he was in charge of them. His instruction to Forssell, the Finance Minister, that the Prime Minister dictated policy, and that individual Ministers were responsible only for the administration of their departments was most unusual and led to Forssell's resignation. Posse's Ministry did not, however, last long enough to establish precedents, and as a result of the absence of real support by the Farmers' party, by the end of the three years Posse was scarcely in a stronger position than the bureaucrats he had replaced.

[1] See Kihlberg, p. 538 for details.

Oscar, who had begun to distrust him, disliked his arrogance, and was glad to see him go.

The Protectionist crisis had no immediate effect on the constitutional position of the Ministry. Themptander's policy was one of neutrality, the Protectionist system being introduced not by a Government bill but by private motions.[1] He and his Free Trade colleagues took no part in the electioneering of 1887 and remained in office, at Oscar's request, after the defeat of Free Trade. The mixed composition of the next two Ministries was the result of a compromise, and as a whole they were neutral in sympathies.

The greatest change took place during Boström's first Ministry (1891–1900). E. G. Boström was the only chief Minister in the nineteenth century who had never been a servant of the Crown in any capacity whatever.[2] He lacked the legal training formerly regarded as essential in a first Minister, but he had wide political experience and this was henceforth to be a more important qualification. The solution of the problem of the Land Taxes and *Indelningsverk* was one of his earlier achievements and in 1887 when the Farmers' party split he abandoned his opposition to the Land Taxes and became leader of the new Protectionist party. As a Second Chamber politician since 1875, elected by the farmers of South Roslag, he knew the leading members of Parliament, and was able to persuade them to accept his ideas by skilful diplomacy. A thoroughgoing Protectionist, he reorganized the customs duties so that they bore less heavily on agricultural products and more on industrial commodities.

At first, Oscar was somewhat distrustful of a Prime Minister who did not conform to the established pattern, but he soon realized Boström's capabilities and before long allowed authority to pass into his hands. There were many changes in the composition of the Ministry between 1891 and 1900, almost all of which were at Boström's request. As one member put it: 'He whom Boström points to, orders gold trousers; he from whom he turns away ought to order retreat.'[3] He was an admirer of

---

[1] Håstad, E., *Partierna i regering och riksdag*, p. 36.
[2] Posse, like Boström, was a landowner from Scania, but had once served in the Scania Court of Appeal.
[3] Quoted in Kihlberg, p. 419.

Bismarck, from whom he had obtained some of his Protectionist views, and he applied political psychology to parliamentary management. One liberal thought that in his defence reforms he also imported a little blood and iron,[1] and certainly from this time onwards, their own domestic grievances having been redressed, the farmers became less pacific in foreign policy. Realizing that the dispute over Protection had altered the customary division or dualism between the chambers, Boström did not, like his predecessors, rely on the support of one of the chambers, but instead upon whatever majority came to hand in both of them, exploiting the Joint Vote in the pursuance of these aims. He did not treat Parliament condescendingly, but instead allowed its committees greater insight into the processes of government and administration. As an old parliamentarian he knew the value of conducting business with members in the corridors of the Parliament House, in his Stockholm apartment and on his country estate near the capital. He asked for votes of confidence when he was determined to have his way on disputed projects such as the building of the Ofoten railway in northern Sweden in 1898 (opposed by the ironmasters of central Sweden) and the Boden fortress in 1900 (opposed by the Second Chamber). He resigned in 1900 in fact, though not openly, on the Norwegian question, but took office again in 1902, following the bureaucratic interlude of von Otter's Ministry. In his second Ministry he chose his own colleagues, the first time this was specifically permitted by the King, thus setting a precedent for the future.

(b) Changes in its composition

The Ministry changed after 1866 in composition as well as in power. No cleric was appointed to office after 1859 (though Bishop Sundberg was approached). The number of nobles was greatest during the Posse Ministry, but he was succeeded by Thyselius, the first commoner to hold the highest position in the Ministry, and in 1905, at the end of the second Boström Ministry, there were only three nobles in office. (The final breach occurred in 1914 when Knut Wallenberg, a banker and commoner, was made Foreign Minister.) However, most Ministers were members of the First Chamber and, of the three Prime

[1] von Zweigbergk, O., *Svensk politik, 1905–29*, p. 167.

Ministers who were in the Second on taking office, two (Posse and Boström) ended their Ministry in the First.

The Ministry's bureaucratic character diminished by degrees. The De Geer Ministry of 1875 was similar to many of the ministries before 1866, De Geer himself conforming to tradition by becoming a judge (President of Svea Court of Appeal) when he resigned from office. He pointed out in his Memoirs how expensive it was to be the King's First Minister. In the beginning of his career he spent 20,000 crowns a year, but he knew others who found that they needed twice that amount. Adlercreutz, like De Geer, came to office after being President of the Göta Court of Appeal. Many Ministers resigned on reaching the age when they were due to retire on a Civil Service pension, and were gratified by the permission granted in 1888 to use the title 'Former Minister'. Even Boström continued to draw many of his colleagues from the Civil Service. Admittedly he also made full use of Parliament, 'but for the parliamentary system he had no sympathies.'[1] When the conservative election organization was formed in 1904 there was no thought of applying to Boström and his colleagues for support. The Ministry was still considered to consist of servants of the Crown outside or above party.[2] Few civil servants became Finance Minister, the victory of economic-liberalism being signalized by a succession of wealthy financiers and industrialists like Waern (1870–4), Tamm (1886–8), and von Essen (1888–94). Not many of them were connected with, or had much knowledge of, agriculture, still the chief occupation in the country. Waern and Tamm were ironmasters. In 1905 Lundeberg was the first Prime Minister to be an industrialist; he too was an ironmaster, and a conservative. As the proportion of bureaucrats diminished, there was evidence of greater independence in the Ministry. This was particularly noticeable in resignations, which often followed disagreements over policy, whereas the civil servant, putting his loyalty to the Crown first, rarely resigned.

Personal relationships were not always affected by political opposition, as was indicated by the friendship between De Geer and Hamilton. In Sweden, as in Britain, the Ministry could be on good terms with members of Parliament who disagreed with

[1] von Zweigbergk, op. cit., p. 18.
[2] Wåhlstrand, A., *Allmänna valmansförbundets tillkomst*, pp. 29 n. 1, 50–51.

its policy. De Geer remarked once, in an aside, that there was also a tendency not to appoint to office men who seemed very desirous of attaining it. To judge by the formation of Ministries before 1905 there does not always seem to have been any great ambition to become a Minister, least of all Prime Minister, though to appear unambitious may have been a convention in the Civil Service. A member of Parliament did not always aspire to ministerial office, his ambition often being appointment to a committee, preferably the Constitution Committee or Committee of Supply.

The period ended in 1905 when a bureaucratic ministry formed under Ramstedt proved unable to deal with the demand of the Norwegians for a dissolution of the Union. Oscar had no alternative but to let the parties in Parliament provide a Ministry, and a coalition was formed, with the conservative leader, Lundeberg, as Prime Minister, and the leading liberal, Staaff, as a consultative Minister. This Ministry brought about a peaceful settlement of the dispute. Events in Norway had often had repercussions on the more conservative and aristocratic Sweden, and never more so than in 1905.

The composition of the Lundeberg coalition Ministry of 1905 showed how small the changes up to then really were. None of its predecessors had been Ministries of parliamentarians of this type. To some extent the absence of change was the result of the unwillingness of the farmers to take ministerial responsibility. Certainly in the period up to 1887, when they alone formed a disciplined political party, they had not challenged the alliance of conservative bureaucrats and the Monarchy. The economic-liberals for their part were not an independent political force and, moreover, seem to have been satisfied with the 1866 reform and the system of civil service Governments which continued to operate. Apart from De Geer, the two men who most nearly attained the stature of statesmen in the nineteenth century were Gripenstedt and Boström, both of whom were politicians and landowners. It is perhaps significant that although it was during their tenure of office, in the 1860's and 1890's respectively, that the Ministry's independence of the Crown was most marked, neither was an enthusiastic parliamentarian. It required the crisis of 1905 to bring about the replacement of the traditional Council of State by a modern Ministry of leading politicians.

III. *Parliament*

Parliament continued to strengthen its position after 1866 as before, but disagreements between the chambers prevented it from exercising its full authority. The First Chamber was more inclined to support the Crown and its own class against the farmers of the Second Chamber than to defend the rights of Parliament as a whole.

As in the years before 1866, though more effectively, the Constitution Committee was the watchdog of Parliament, but there was no further resort to the futile expedient of impeachment, the committee merely censuring Ministers whose conduct, to judge from the minutes of the Council of State, deserved it (A. 106). Its alternative course of action, to recommend to the chambers that they request the King to dismiss the offending Minister (A. 107), was frequently employed. On eighteen occasions the Second Chamber voted in favour of such action, and on five of these the Minister resigned. This occurred, for example, in 1901 when the Navy Minister, Christensen, was criticized over a disciplinary irregularity. However, to be constitutionally effective the appeal had to come from both chambers, and the First Chamber never joined the Second in its condemnation of Ministers. Thus Article 107, like 106, was never used as the authors of the Constitution had intended.

A feature of Parliament which strengthened its position *vis-à-vis* the Crown was the increased stability of its opinion. Before 1866 the King could hope that parliamentary policies would change between sessions, the intervals sometimes being long enough for memories to become dulled, but the annual Parliaments after 1866 made it impossible to delay action in the belief that Parliament would change its mind: what was the will of members at one session normally remained so at the next. Unwilling to find themselves in opposition to Parliament, Ministries tended to be inactive in matters where Parliament expressed no positive opinion. Towards the end of the century members of Parliament became increasingly interested in social and economic legislation and the Ministry found itself following the lead set by Parliament or one of its committees. On occasion a parliamentary address almost had the force of a directive.[1]

[1] Herlitz, *Grunddragen, &c.*, pp. 255–8.

Nevertheless, by virtue of its control over the administration the Government had access to the necessary documents and was able to exert its influence once the legislative stage was reached.

In Britain, when Parliament was asserting its independence of the Crown, one symbol of parliamentary privilege was the right of members of the House of Commons to nominate their own Speaker. It has already been remarked that the royal appointment of Speakers did not arouse parliamentary opposition in Sweden, presumably because the Crown exercised its prerogative with care. Posse's appointment in 1876 as Speaker of the Second Chamber and Hamilton's elevation to the Chair of the First Chamber in 1877 certainly depended on the initiative of the Prime Minister, De Geer, who preferred to have these opponents in the Chair rather than in opposition. Posse's four years of separation from his party in the Speaker's chair was partly responsible for the lack of co-operation between the farmers and his Ministry when he became Prime Minister in 1880. Speakers could, on occasion, refuse to allow Parliament to discuss certain issues, but the use of this power by the Government was strictly limited by the authority granted to the Constitution Committee to override the Speaker's decisions. On few occasions was the ruling challenged. The Second Chamber disapproved their Speaker's handling of the Boden fortress question in 1900 and voted against his action by 119 votes to 90, but the Constitution Committee supported him. The Constitution Committee of 1906, which had examined the question of royal appointment, reported in its favour and compared it with Parliament's misuse of this power during the Era of Liberty when the Crown did not appoint them. The Second Chamber decided after debate that there was no misuse of power by the Speakers, who it agreed were moderate and non-party, and accepted the Committee's report by 99 to 78. There was no debate in the First Chamber.

A feature of the Swedish political system which might seem to complicate relations between the Executive and the Legislature was the permission granted to civil servants to sit in Parliament. It is difficult to assess the effect of the provision since, despite De Geer's proposal in 1862 to exclude them, the question does not seem to have been the subject of debate.[1] However, on three occasions in De Geer's *Memoirs* mention is made of difficult situations arising out of this arrangement, and in view of the very different principles governing the rights of civil servants in Britain and the United States, the incidents are perhaps worth quoting at some length.

In 1868 the Government and the Committee of Supply approved the creation of an artillery laboratory for the army. When the matter came up for debate in the Second Chamber, a member for Stockholm named Adlersparre who was also Per-·manent Under Secretary (*Expeditionschef*) in the Navy Department and known for his fearless honesty, opposed it as a private member. After the War Minister, Colonel Abelin, had attempted to reply, the chamber voted against the necessary appropriation. It was noted that the Navy Minister, Platen, said nothing in the debate and left the chamber as Abelin spoke. In the Joint Vote, despite the support of the First Chamber, the appropriation was again rejected and so at the next session the matter was raised again. This time the grant was made and was actually larger in amount, Adlersparre remaining silent. In the First Chamber there was sharp criticism of his earlier behaviour by af Ugglas, who said he disapproved of such conduct by a servant of the Crown. Wallenberg, on the other hand, remarked that it was unseemly to comment on the conduct of a member of the other house, and that one had to forget the civil servant when the member of Parliament was speaking. However, his view was not shared by the majority of members. The War Minister, Abelin, felt compromised by the adverse vote on his laboratory and said in the Council that he would resign unless Adlersparre was dismissed. Platen supported his Under Secretary and De Geer,

---

[1] The connotation of 'civil servant' is much wider in Sweden than in England, and may even comprise the clergy, judiciary, and teachers. The number of permanent civil servants in the English sense has been very few, as the following table, based on the Uppsala Studies of 1936, shows:

	Year	Number		Year	Number
First Chamber	1870	3	Second Chamber	1867	6
	1890	7		1876	6
	1910	8		1885	8
	1930	8		1897	4
				1906	8
				1912	3
				1922	2
				1933	4

who was Chancellor, remarked in his memoirs concerning Adlersparre's proposed dismissal 'and I too thought it ought not to take place for an utterance in Parliament, at least not immediately'.[1] This was equivocal enough and it is perhaps not surprising that Platen's 'inability to deal with his subordinates' resulted in his own dismissal shortly afterwards. His successor, Thulstrup, retained the services of Adlersparre for a short while as Permanent Secretary and then prepared an honourable retreat for him as head of the commission for naval affairs. As Under Secretary Adlersparre had held one of the temporary 'positions of trust' (*förtroendeämbeten*), but as a civil servant he could not be dismissed the service entirely for his opinions. The incident, however, perhaps illustrated the inadvisability of opposing the Government if a civil servant wanted to end his career with a seat in the Ministry.

The second instance occurred in 1878 when a Provincial Governor and former Chancellor (Adlercreutz) opposed a Government amendment to the '*skjutsstadga*' or road-transport regulations[2] and was supported by nearly all the other Provincial Governors in Parliament. There was some talk of dismissing him from his Governorship, but the Minister of the Interior and De Geer opposed such action on the grounds partly of his great services and partly the injustice of punishing public servants for their utterances as members of Parliament, the consequences of which might be that no more civil servants would be elected to the Second Chamber.

The third instance involved the former War Minister, Abelin himself, when back in service as a lieutenant-general.[3] Posse, as Prime Minister, issued an ordinary printed request-card asking him to see him at his office. When Abelin arrived he was asked if as a member of Parliament he had made a reservation to the Special Committee's report on army reorganization. He replied in the affirmative, and was then requested to withdraw his reservation. Pointing out that his opinion was unchanged, Abelin refused and was then told by Posse that he must take the consequences. The newspaper *Dagens Nyheter*, which supported Posse, announced later that the Government could not tolerate opposition to its proposals by its servants holding 'positions of trust'. Having advised Abelin to hold to his opinion, De Geer

---

[1] De Geer, *Minnen*, ii. 72.   [2] Ibid., 217.   [3] Ibid., 262.

told Posse that he deplored this policy, whereupon the matter was dropped.

These cases are interesting, but it should be noticed that they affected only senior public servants holding 'posts of confidence', from which, like Ministers, they could be constitutionally dismissed. The question of a permanent civil servant of lower grade does not seem to have arisen in De Geer's experience. The number of such members of Parliament was, moreover, usually only about half a dozen.

Parliament continued to extend its authority in its own sphere of finance. By refusing to increase the Civil List Parliament is even said to have forced Oscar II to pay for his own coronation expenses.[1] The one important field to which it was denied access by the Constitution was that of economic legislation. It was over Article 89, and the rights of Crown and Parliament in this regard, that controversy developed.

Although Adolf Hedin insisted in the Constitution Committee that Parliament should demand that all laws be joint laws of Crown and Parliament, this suggestion was rejected as an attempt to weaken the power of the Crown. In any case it would have required changes in the Constitution, involving the King's assent and that of two successive Parliaments, and would probably have been opposed by the Ministry on the Crown's behalf. There was no formal abandonment of Article 89 and it remains in force today.

Parliament clashed with the Crown over the Article none the less, not because it wished for a formal transfer of power but because it became increasingly difficult to distinguish an economic from a civil law, many bills involving both civil and economic legislation. Parliament would not surrender its jurisdiction on civil matters and the Crown was unwilling to pass hybrid laws, part of which were passed according to Article 89 and part according to 87. Yet where there was deadlock the King had to give way if he or the Ministry were anxious for some solution. Thus rather than pass a hybrid law in the legislation governing private banks, over which there had been disagreement since 1830, the Crown in 1886 finally allowed the law to be enacted as a civil law.

The definition of economic legislation was complicated by

[1] Nisbet Bain, op. cit., p. 434.

the changing social and economic ideas of the later nineteenth century. Where formerly, as in the case of the granting of patents, the criterion tended to be the economic and financial advantage to the country, there came to be concern for the rights of inventors over what was their own private property. Thus legislation which the Crown had long regarded as economic was challenged by Parliament on the grounds that it was in fact civil. The granting of patents was agreed to be a civil law in 1897. Other controversial issues were the factory acts and the law of master and servant. However, in the last few years of the century, when Annerstedt was Minister of Justice in the first Boström Ministry, the Crown agreed to many of Parliament's demands and the dispute died down. The Crown, it is true, had frequently applied to the Supreme Court for a decision whether a given law was civil or economic and had abided by its decision, but the main difficulty was that in most cases both elements were present and the Supreme Court was unable to say which was primary.

The Crown seems to have tried various methods of dealing with the problem of economic legislation. In the first place it has refused the formal transfer of power and the constitutional amendment that this would imply and sometimes merely asks Parliament for its opinion (*yttrande*). Secondly, in certain cases it has agreed to 'delegation' and has thereby allowed Parliament to enact the law jointly. Thus the local government decree of 1862 was passed according to Article 89 but after the parliamentary reform of 1866 the right to enact local government legislation was transferred to the Crown and Parliament jointly (RF. A. 57. ii). Thirdly, the Crown has agreed to the request of Parliament for a share in economic legislation and passed laws 'with Parliament'. Amongst these are the patent, private bank, factory, and master and servant acts already mentioned. However, not all economic legislation has been transferred, and these laws form a fourth category. The decree permitting the detention of alcoholics was not made a law requiring parliamentary consent until 1913, and the law affecting the insane was a prerogative of the Crown until 1929. The Free Trade decrees and certain health decrees remain within its jurisdiction.[1]

[1] For a fuller discussion of economic legislation, see Malmgren, R., *Sveriges riksdag*, vol. xiv, chap. iv.

Yet the dispute over economic legislation was not an attack on the royal prerogative, but was rather an attempt by Parliament to protect its constitutional rights. Parliament was restrained in the exercise of its demands, partly because the Constitution Committee was dominated by First Chamber friends of the Executive and was not, in this particular instance, opposed by an equally strong and homogeneous Second Chamber body of opinion. It therefore refused to follow Hedin's guidance and did not press for a formal transfer of the powers of Article 89.

Yet even in its other dealings with the Crown, Parliament seems to have been restrained. The Second Chamber does not appear to have used to the utmost the few weapons it possessed to check the Monarchy and Council of Ministers. Interpellations played little part and were used mainly to inform Parliament of government policy.[1] There were only ninety interpellations put in the whole period from 1867 to 1905, forty-seven of them in the last ten years. In 1906 something of a sensation was caused by the presentation of sixteen in one session.[2] In general, however, the bicameral system and the absence of an Order of the Day procedure whereby a vote could immediately be taken, prevented full exploitation of the device. From 1885 onwards there came into use a mass assent to an interpellation, which served in its way as a motion of censure. Yet according to Andrén, surprisingly few attacks on the First Chamber were made in the Second.[3]

Indeed there was in some ways a tendency to transfer power back to the Executive. The National Debt office relinquished its control over the money for Supplementary Estimates in favour of the Exchequer (*statskontoret*), which was under Crown control. In 1897 Parliament permitted the Crown to appoint the chairman of the board of the Bank of Sweden and thus exclusive control over another parliamentary bastion in the central financial organization was given up by both chambers. There does not appear to have been sufficient need to alter the Constitution at this time for an issue to be forced.

Parliament's acceptance of the separation of powers is all the more remarkable when contrasted with the demands of the

[1] Herlitz, N., *Grunddragen, &c.*, p. 257.
[2] Öman, K. I., *Karl Staaffs första ministär*, p. 299.
[3] Andrén, op. cit., p. 381.

Norwegian *Storting*. In 1869 Charles XV had to accept the *Storting*'s request for a change of Ministry and annual Parliaments. In 1880 there arose a crisis when the *Storting* for the third time demanded the presence of Ministers in the chamber and their responsibility to it. Although, since 1860, the Swedish Ministry had been able to address Parliament, Oscar II feared that a similar rule in Norway would weaken the executive power, owing to the *parlamentarism* which he rightly believed would follow its introduction. Owing to the feeling in Norway, the King had to give way and in 1884, after a judgement by the court of impeachment, Norway acquired parliamentary government thirty-three years before it arrived in Sweden.

Admittedly, the immediate cause of the 1905 dissolution of the Union was a grievance over diplomatic representation, a political rather than a constitutional issue. Norway's merchant fleet had increased to such an extent that it was felt desirable to have consulates in the larger ports of the world. The diplomatic service was still under Swedish direction and there was not the same anxiety for consular representation abroad. Yet underlying the political dispute was the difference in the tempo of constitutional change in the two countries. Norway had several radical governments after the early 1880's and introduced universal suffrage in 1898; in its eagerness for *parlamentarism* Norway was no easy partner for a conservative Sweden still attached to the royal Executive.

The *Storting* was able to weaken the influence of the Monarchy partly because the Norwegians were conscious of a national awakening (it was the time of Ibsen and Grieg). Another important factor was the unicameral Norwegian parliament in which the upper class was in the minority. The decline of the native Norwegian aristocracy in the sixteenth and seventeenth centuries was in contrast to the continued domination of Sweden by the upper class throughout the nineteenth century, when by creating two chambers, one of which was dominated by the upper class, De Geer delayed the social revolution. The dualism between the chambers, resulting from their social disparity, prevented the Swedish Parliament from challenging the Monarchy.

Moreover, even the Second Chamber, unlike the *Storting*, was not anxious to introduce *parlamentarism*. The Swedish farmers did not want the responsibility of government and made little attempt to strengthen their position. A remark of Liss Olof Larsson, a noted member of the party and Deputy Speaker of the Second Chamber in 1886 expresses this attitude clearly: 'We who do not take part in higher politics take each issue on its own merits. If we consider a Government proposal is good we accept it. But if we cannot support it we work against it. And this we do without any idea of upsetting the Ministry or bringing about political changes.'[1] The senior and most typical leader, Carl Ifvarsson (who is said to have directed the voting of the party by waving different coloured handkerchiefs)[2] went so far as to say: 'It does not really matter to me who sits at the King's advisory table: but on the other hand it is certainly not a matter of indifference for me how things are carried on.'[3] So true was this that in 1877, having defeated De Geer in a vote, the Farmers asked him not to resign. This happened again in 1880 when he made his army reform a vote of confidence in his Ministry and the 1866 Parliament Act: the Farmers defeated him by 121 votes to 75 without demanding or desiring his resignation. Very often Parliament passed resolutions against the Government without precipitating a crisis.[4] The behaviour of the Second Chamber, and of course especially the Farmers, in its attitude to the Government was best portrayed by Ifvarsson when an opportunity came for his party to form or take part in a Ministry. He said simply: 'The Farmers' party will accompany Count Posse to the door of the Council Chamber, and no farther.'

In hoping that the new legislature would work more as a team than the Estates De Geer was mistaken. The old dualism between chambers and between Parliament and Crown remained. The result was the continuation of chronic delays in the enacting of legislation. The First Chamber accepted in principle the abolition of the Land Taxes in 1873; their final abandonment came in 1892. A proposal for Workmen's Compensation made in 1884 was not realized until 1902. The Second Chamber asked for a measure of parliamentary reform in 1880 (though

[1] A.k. 1886, no. 21, p. 29.
[2] Håstad, Partier, &c., p. 50.   [3] A.k. 1875, no. 30, p. 12.
[4] Kihlberg, op. cit., p. 568. In eighteen Joint Votes on various estimates on 10 April 1886, the Government won only two, one by the barest majority (Petré, op. cit., p. 119).

later the Farmers themselves vetoed it). The second reform bill was not passed until 1907 and came into force in 1909.

iv. *Conclusion*

Thus in this period the chambers did not unite in opposition to the Crown. There were many reasons for their inability to do so, the chief of them being the predominance of the conservative majority in the First Chamber, which regarded the Crown as its support against the lower classes. The Farmers were never strong enough in the Second Chamber to control the Joint Vote, and so, as De Geer prophesied, the more homogeneous First Chamber despite its smaller numbers, was often able to hold its own with the help of the 'annexe' in the Second Chamber.

However, far from being hostile to the royal Executive, Parliament, including the Second Chamber, remained on good terms with the King. One explanation for the comparatively good relations between Crown and Parliament was the policy of Oscar II. Although he expected his Ministries to be outside the orbit of Parliament, he required them to work with, and not against, the legislature. He was happiest when acting as mediator and approved of Boström because he was such a successful parliamentary manager. His announcement in 1887 that he would not presume to influence Parliament in its discussion of Protection contrasted sharply with the willingness of his predecessor to indulge in parliamentary machinations. Unlike Charles XV he was able to dissolve the Second Chamber without fear of *parlamentarism*. Moreover, he was careful to point out that the appointment of Prime Minister was his responsibility and did not accept Themptander's resignation immediately Free Trade was defeated. Preferring to follow the Bernadotte custom he appointed two Ministries from the moderates in the First Chamber in the hope of winning support from the Second Chamber as well as the usually reliable First before finally choosing Boström in 1891. On the latter's resignation in 1900 he did not call in a Ministry of the Right lest he should alienate the new Liberal party of the Second Chamber. Oscar II's moderate policy had caused him in 1880 to ask Posse to be Prime Minister and later to appoint him Speaker and other members of the Farmers' party (the real farmers) as Deputy Speakers of the Second Chamber. Because the First Chamber shielded him from direct conflict with the Second, he was able to avoid using the royal veto.[1]

It was, however, doubtful whether the growing Liberal and Social Democratic parties would much longer tolerate an executive power which lay in the hands of the King. Moreover, if Government was to depend on the support of Parliament, did this mean both chambers or the popularly elected Second Chamber? Ostensibly the agitation for the second reform of Parliament was concerned with the franchise, but underlying the dispute were these two important issues. Three years before Lloyd George presented his ultimatum to the House of Lords, the Liberal leader in the Second Chamber was to attempt a similar *démarche* in Sweden. Suddenly, after nearly four decades of constitutional peace, controversy arose over the doctrine of separation of powers and over the 'equal competence and authority' of the chambers.

[1] Andrén, op. cit., p. 245.

CHAPTER VII

The Liberal Party and Parliamentary Reform, 1900–1906

1. *The rise of the Liberal party*

IN May 1899, Sixten von Friesen, a leading member of the Second Chamber of liberal outlook, asked all those members of Parliament interested in forming a Liberal party to meet him at Tattersall's restaurant in Stockholm. For some time the idea of such a party had been mooted in the corridors of Parliament and on 15 April the Liberal newspaper *Dagens Nyheter* had stated that there were several coteries which might be brought together to form a single party, and that people were waiting for a coalition signal. On the 24th the evening Liberal paper *Aftonbladet* remarked that 'it is no secret that in Parliament preparations are being made to bring about unity'. Over seventy members attended the Tattersall meeting on 5 May 1899 and it was decided to form the Liberal Coalition Party (*Liberala samlingspartiet*) when Parliament met in January 1900. The meeting pledged itself to support a Second Chamber franchise extended to all men over the age of twenty-five who paid local taxes.

Von Friesen was responsible for the final act in the formation of the Liberal party, but there does not appear to have been any single cause of the emergence of this large group of Second Chamber members under one banner. Encouragement was derived from the example of David Bergström's radical People's party (*Folkpartiet*) which had been founded in the Second Chamber in 1896 and which comprised three distinct elements: fifteen farmers from the radical north; ten Stockholm members; and seven small-town representatives.[1] After the Tattersall meeting and the formation of the Liberal party, Bergström and his friends agreed to join forces with Friesen. It was especially necessary for the various liberal forces to unite in view of the

[1] Thermaenius, E., *Sveriges riksdag*, xvii .141–2.

reunion in 1895 of the Farmers' party whose tendency now was to ally with the First Chamber conservatives, in sharp contrast to its traditional policy. In its fear of liberalism and particularly socialism, the Farmers' party had ceased to attract radicals. Nor were all the farmers conservative, and those who regretted the change in the party's programme were another important group who joined the new Liberal party.

It has been estimated that at least five different elements coalesced in the new party.[1] In addition to the liberal farmers there were the social reformers, older radicals like Hedin, and nonconformist teetotallers. Finally there were the intellectuals (*kulturradikaler*) who had been influenced by Hedin when studying at Uppsala in the 1880's and who had founded the Verdandi radical student organization for the dissemination of liberal ideas. These intellectuals, each of whom is said to have possessed a copy of Mill's *On Liberty*, were to be the most important group. Among them in their student days were David Bergström, founder of the People's party and a vice-chairman of the Universal Suffrage Association, Hjalmar Branting, later leader of the Social Democrats, and Karl Staaff, a member of the People's party and later leader of the Liberals.

However, none of the intellectuals had a place in the leadership of the Liberal Coalition party. As its name implied, the party was a compromise, and it was agreed that to stress the radical element would only alarm the farmers, since if the party was to become a force in the Second Chamber it must at all costs attract agricultural representatives. This was borne in mind in 1900 when Parliament met and a meeting of the coalition at the Hotel Continental selected the council or steering committee of the party (*förtroenderåd*). Von Friesen was appointed chairman not only because he was the leading liberal but also because he was an urban member of Parliament who possessed the confidence of the farmers. Although the People's party had increased the number of its seats in the Second Chamber to 43, it was offered only 2 of the 6 seats on the *förtroenderåd*, whereas no fewer than 4 farmers were appointed. It was hoped that by giving the farmers such a large share in the governing body, membership of the party would increase from 82 to over 100 when the Second Chamber met. (It was, moreover, a tradition

[1] Rönblom, H. K., *Frisinnade landsföreningen 1902–1927*, chap. 1.

in the Second Chamber to favour the farmers; when the People's party itself had been created in 1896, 5 of the 9 seats on its *förtroenderåd* had been allotted to them, although less than half the party were farmers.) Five deputy-members were appointed, bringing the total number of members and deputies up to 12. Of the 5 deputies, 3 were representatives of the People's party, and only 1 was a farmer.

The Liberal Coalition party pledged itself to social reform in a programme thought by Rönblom to have been written by von Friesen. Among its demands were factory inspection, State insurance for accidents, legalized collective agreements, arbitration, home ownership, and sick pay. It was clearly not a party of economic-liberals. The Norwegian policy of the party was the same as that favoured by a majority of Second Chamber members, namely, an equal voice for the Norwegians in foreign affairs. It reiterated the Tattersall programme of parliamentary reform—the franchise for men over twenty-five who paid local taxes—but without a sense of urgency.

II. *Proposals for parliamentary reform*

When Parliament met in 1900, the Prime Minister, Boström, presented a bill for the introduction of conscription. The Second Chamber agreed to support it on condition that the Government introduced a reform bill, and in 1902, after the Conscription Law had come into force, Boström complied. The Government's proposal met the Liberal demand for manhood suffrage at twenty-five for taxpayers, but with certain restrictions. Thus, for example, in order to be entitled to vote, a man was required to be liable for military service. Moreover, married and older men were to receive an extra vote. These additional 'guarantees' as the conservatives euphemistically called them, were unacceptable to the Liberal party. The bill did not receive enough support from either chamber and was rejected.

However, the conservatives in both houses, anxious to meet the rising demand for reform, began to show an interest in a new type of 'guarantee', that of proportional representation. The Second Chamber majority, with some Liberal support, accepted a motion by Månsson of Trää in favour of general manhood suffrage and PR. More surprising, even the First Chamber (the reform of which was not considered) suggested the holding of an inquiry into the possibility of basing the Second Chamber franchise on PR. This idea had first been put forward by Bishop Billing ten years previously because, so he later asserted, the condition of working men in his diocese led him to consider a suitable method by which they could have some voice in Parliament.

The Liberals were thus compelled to reconsider their policy. They could hardly demand that the franchise should be restricted to taxpayers now that the conservatives seemed to be abandoning property qualifications, the traditional 'guarantee'. The moderate Liberals agreed with von Friesen when he gave PR his support on 31 July 1902, by stating 'no party and no class ought to have anything against it'. The radicals, however, were less enthusiastic. Some regarded Bishop Billing as the 'father confessor' of the conservatives, and thought that his PR proposal was providing them with a subtle means of evading a real reform. Consequently in his election speech at Gnesta in August 1902 Staaff argued that although PR was unquestionably just, it ought to apply to First Chamber elections as well.

These differences did not prevent the victory of the Liberal party in the Second Chamber elections in September 1902, when they won ten seats and achieved their first aim—control of a majority of the Second Chamber seats on the joint standing committees of Parliament. The Liberals obtained 27 of the 48 places, the Farmers 18 and Independents 3. Only in the Committee of Supply did the Farmers' party remain in control.

At the same time the radicals improved their position within the Liberal party. They had been leaders of the Universal Suffrage Association which was wound up in 1900. Before finally breaking up, the Association had hopefully asked the 365,000 petitioners for parliamentary reform to subscribe one day's pay in each of the next five years to a fighting fund. By October, 1901, 2,000 people had subscribed 40,000 crowns. Experience in Britain, the United States and Norway had shown the need for a national organization which could finance candidates for Parliament, and in 1902 the National Liberal Federation (*Frisinnade landsföreningen*) was formed under the leadership of Karl Staaff and David Bergström in order to support candidates who were sympathetic to reform. As the use of the word *frisinnade* instead of *liberal* in its title indicated, the new organization was not officially tied to any parliamentary party. However, eleven members of Parliament, mostly Liberals, sat on its *förtroenderåd*, and its first meeting was opened by von Friesen, a moderate Liberal, and the more radical northern farmer, Persson of Tällberg.[1] Yet although the National Liberal Federation was led by radicals, its first programme for reform had favoured, after a close vote, the old programme of a Second Chamber franchise restricted to taxpayers, rather than one based on general manhood suffrage.

. On 3 November 1903, the inquiry into PR proposed by the First Chamber in 1902 having been held, Boström presented a new reform bill in which the Government recommended PR. On 14 November the National Liberal Federation met to discuss its attitude towards the PR principle. Persson of Tällberg favoured the adoption of PR for the Second Chamber, but the meeting adopted Staaff's proposal that it should only be supported if it was applied to both chambers. Failing such a policy, the Federation should advocate the limitation of the powers of the First Chamber.

This decision implied a change of front on the part of the Federation, and meant that there were now three different proposals for reform. There was the First Chamber's proposal of PR applied to the Second Chamber alone, or, as it was called in Sweden, single proportional representation (SPR). Secondly there was Staaff's proposal for PR applied to both chambers, or double proportional representation (DPR). Lastly, there was his new suggestion of retaining single-member constituencies with a wider franchise (SMC), and of ultimately so limiting the power of the First Chamber that the Second would effectively govern. The adoption of PR, in contrast, implied that the First Chamber would continue to be equal in status, either unreformed (SPR) or reformed (DPR). Staaff's opponents were later to suggest that in adopting SMC as his aim he abandoned the position he had held at Gnesta, when he had called PR 'unquestionably just'. However, he had then maintained that he would accept only DPR, whereas the 1903 Government bill was offering only SPR. It is true that Staaff changed his mind. Once he realized that the Liberals might be able to control the

---

[1] Farmers with common names like Persson or Petersson added the name of their locality to make identification easier.

Second Chamber he preferred to leave the First alone in order that, like the British House of Lords, it would seem unrepresentative of the people and indefensible. His final plan, for SMC, was designed to reform the Second Chamber alone, and in such a way as to favour the Liberal party. The mistake he made was to overlook the possibility that his conservative opponents, faced by the prospect of lower-house *parlamentarism* under Staaff's leadership, might seriously propose DPR as the lesser of two evils.

The decision of the National Liberal Federation to support Staaff's proposal of limiting the powers of the First Chamber had its repercussions upon the parliamentary party, still led by von Friesen, the supporter of SPR. Realizing that he no longer expressed the feeling of the party, he recanted in *Dagens Nyheter*, saying: 'The proportional method is dear to me, but far dearer is the reform of the franchise itself.' He admitted to von Zweigbergk, the editor of the newspaper, that while the principle of PR was being discussed in committee he had been working out the fascinating mathematics of the various methods of applying it, having been a mathematics teacher himself, instead of studying its wider implications for parliamentary reform. Zweigbergk comments that von Friesen had been brought up, parliamentarily speaking, in the Committee of Supply, where the elucidation of arguments for a proposal was the responsibility of the secretary appointed from the Civil Service.[1] If this was so, and if such a narrow approach was common, it helps to explain that attention to details rather than principles which appears to characterize the discussion of the second reform bill.

Leadership of the Liberal parliamentary party passed to Staaff, the most prominent member of the National Liberal Federation. Yet as a radical he was not even a member of the parliamentary party's *förtroenderåd*. Indeed, although he had been a member of Parliament since 1896, he had played little part until the formation of the National Liberal Federation. He was a new type of Liberal, a man whose concern was not so much for the middle class who had prospered from the industrial revolution as for the 'little man', the *småfolk* whose numbers had been increasing and who now formed a not inconsiderable part of the electorate. Staaff was given the loyalty and affection of

[1] von Zweigbergk, op. cit., p. 72.

these people, who felt that he understood their ways and had their needs in mind. He was neither a Nonconformist nor a teetotaller, but Freechurchmen and temperance enthusiasts regarded him as their champion. Unlike Posse he has not been accused of using his followers for his own political ends.

Under Staaff the Liberals drew upon themselves the hostility of the upper classes and the conservatives. Partly this was the result of the party's policy towards the First Chamber; partly it was because the stigma of radicalism, which in Britain was distributed between the Liberals, Independent Labour party, and Fabians, was concentrated in Sweden upon the Liberals; and partly it was the outcome of Staaff's personality. To his opponents he seemed lacking in humour and somewhat self-righteous, and he committed several psychological blunders in his dealings with them. Moreover, the upper classes distrusted a man who was a private lawyer, and even suggested that his clients were not always respectable.

To this day he has so many ardent admirers and fierce detractors, even amongst scholars, that it is still difficult to discern his true nature. His motion for reform in 1904 gave grounds for the accusation that he was an opportunist. Knowing that his support lay in the small provincial towns, he suggested that these towns should increase their representation, even if it meant reducing the number of representatives from the cities (where the Social Democrats were expected to increase their strength). He attacked the First Chamber in his speech, and pleased many of his friends, but there were many who were not impressed by the partisan nature of his proposal. Staaff spoke of 'the people' but in practice he meant neither the workers nor the farmers but the *småfolk*, and his motion was defeated.

A year later he was appointed Consultative Minister in the Lundeberg coalition Government. His moderation and competence on this occasion, however, won him the confidence of the Court before he became Prime Minister himself.

III. *The first Liberal Government, 1906*

The Second Chamber elections in September 1905 increased the Liberal party's seats to 106, and the Social Democrats' to 13, giving the Left a majority in the Second Chamber. The farmers were now split into two groups by the formation of the National Progressive party under the leadership of Peterssen of Påboda and Anderson of Nöbbelöv. Between them the farmers' parties could muster about 100 members, but it remained to be seen whether the farmers would present a united front against Staaff, who was now appointed Prime Minister. At this time only the Social Democrats formed a homogeneous party in the sense that they could be relied on to vote together on any issue.

The Liberal Government took office in the autumn of 1905, and met Parliament when the new session opened in January 1906. During the next five months, no fewer than 163 Government bills were presented, making the session the busiest since 1866. Despite a large conservative opposition, Staaff controlled the Second Chamber, but there was no Liberal party in the First. Of his ten Ministers, several were non-party men and only four were members of Parliament, all from the radical wing in the Second Chamber. No members of the Liberal party's *förtroenderåd* were given office. Conservatives were shocked by the appointment of a journalist (Bergström) as Consultative Minister, but there was an even greater surprise for a country where intellectual accomplishments are a reason for social esteem in the appointment of a primary schoolteacher (Berg) as Minister of Church and Education. He symbolized the rise of this important group in the previous decade; there were now a dozen primary schoolteachers in the Second Chamber. Staaff himself was the first private lawyer to be a Minister of the Crown, and held office as Minister of Justice in addition to being Prime Minister.

In one appointment Staaff stored up future trouble for himself. Owing to his distrust of Persson of Tällberg, the leader of the Norrland farmers, he appointed as Minister of Agriculture Gösta Tamm, a landowner who had been defeated in the 1905 election when standing as a Liberal. Tactically, Staaff's plan to have with him a small group of reliable friends and a few more or less non-political Ministers of the traditional type was sound, since the reform of Parliament needed the driving force of only a few Ministers, as Louis De Geer's Ministry had shown. On the other hand, in the difficult task of securing at all costs a majority of the Second Chamber in favour of his proposal, it was strategically unwise to risk the alienation at a critical point of an important *fronde* which might one day hold the balance of political power.

Though the Liberal parliamentary party in 1906 claimed to represent the interests of the nation, and of the *småfolk* in particular, few members could themselves claim to belong to this section of the population, as the following table indicates:[1]

Agriculture		Civil Service and Armed Forces	
Landowners	4	Permanent civil servants . .	6
Farmers	30	Minor judges	11
		Officers	1
Commerce and Industry		University and secondary school	
Ironmasters and factory owners	5	teachers	8
Business men	8	Primary school teachers . .	12
Small business . . .	7	Other minor civil servants .	1
Craftsmen	2		
		Professions	
Workmen and Trade Union Officials.	1	Lawyers	2
		Doctors	2
		Journalists	5
		Ministers of religion . .	2

The Liberal party felt that the time for reform was at hand despite being in a majority only in the Second Chamber, and there only with Social-Democratic support. The elections had shown that it stood high in the favour of the electorate, and its members believed that their mandate was more important than the views of the First Chamber. It was with a light heart that Staaff introduced his reform bill designed to bring that chamber to heel.

IV. *A House of Commons for Sweden?*

Events since 1866 had shown how misplaced was the optimism of De Geer in expecting two chambers of equal standing but unequal composition and interests to work together harmoniously. When Staaff took office in 1906 it was clear that there would be a struggle for power between the two chambers, and the omens of the time favoured victory for the Liberals in their demand for a powerful Second Chamber, or Swedish 'House of Commons'. Parliamentary government had become part of the natural order of things in Norway, now a Kingdom in her own right, the Liberals had won a great victory in the British elections, and in Russia's Grand Duchy of Finland a new

[1] *Studier, &c.*, p. 176.

Parliament based on universal suffrage was conceded by the Tsar. In Sweden a large student demonstration promised the new Government the support of the rising generation. 1906 was a year propitious for a radical change in the representation.

Staaff was especially influenced by the political controversy in Britain, where the Liberal Government of Campbell-Bannerman took office in the same year that he himself did. He believed himself to be a Prime Minister on the British model and out of office he was to act the part of Leader of the Opposition. Indeed, he was even interested in Home Rule, and when questioned about Liberal policy towards Ireland is reported to have said: 'I believe in Gladstone more than I believe in God.'

It was a sign of the times that there was no question of any royal interference with Staaff's presentation of his bill to Parliament in the manner of the earlier Bernadottes. As expected, the bill was devised to increase the authority of the Second Chamber, and incidentally to be of advantage to the Liberal party. Each constituency was to return one member, thus giving the Liberals the opportunity of using their local advantage in many districts, especially in the small towns. Where a candidate failed to secure an absolute majority there was to be a fresh election, Staaff hoping that since the Liberals were the centre party they would gain from any transfer of votes. It was an ingenious proposal. Moreover, instead of the towns being awarded 80 seats and the country constituencies 150 (as laid down by the Wing-clipping of 1894) the proportion was to be 65 to 165. In favouring the country districts Staaff hoped to attract some of the farmers to his proposal, and also to satisfy the rural members in his own party. It was a far-sighted move, because the basis of the Liberal party's strength was gradually shifting towards the country. The Social Democrats were already capturing the large cities, and later were to obtain control of some of the towns.

There was no dispute over the extent of the Second Chamber franchise. Apart from lowering the minimum age from twenty-five to twenty-four Staaff preserved the conditions of the bills of 1903 and 1904 by the Boström government. The chambers had to choose between Staaff's single-member constituencies and Boström's proportional representation. With Socialist support the Liberals could expect victory for their bill in the Second

L

Chamber: it was equally certain that the First Chamber would not approve of Staaff's measure without considerable persuasion.

The bill went through three stages. It was presented in February 1906, and debated in general terms in a *remiss* debate. Afterwards it went to the Constitution Committee, where the First Chamber members supported proportional representation, and the Second Chamber, it is thought, single-member constituencies.[1] The third stage was the final debate and vote in the chambers. The most important was the second, the committee discussion, because clearly the bill as it stood would not pass both houses. However, if the committee could reach an agreement which it could recommend to the chambers it was possible that in a modified form the bill might succeed. Needless to say, Staaff was quite prepared to take the necessary steps once the First Chamber had rejected his bill, and to ask for a dissolution.

In the *remiss* debate[2] on 27 February, following the presentation of the bill to Parliament on 24 February 1906, there were one or two interesting speeches. One was by Professor Kjellén, the only conservative member among thirty-nine urban representatives, and one of the first propagators of the study of geopolitics. He spoke mainly for the benefit of his conservative colleagues, and offered them advice which, unfortunately for their party's future, they were unable to take. He advised his party not to rely on the Farmers' party, which was decimated at every election, but like Disraeli urged the need of obtaining the votes of the workers in the towns. If the conservatives were to do so they would find that proportional representation would help them. Turning to the subject of reform, he remarked that in previous reforms the class giving way to the demand for change had always been able to act as a brake, but on this occasion it was doubtful whether the farmers, as the losing group, would have the power to be a brake at all on the new class rising to power. It was an astute speech, calculated to make the farmers think that it was their political power which was threatened rather than that of the upper class in the First Chamber. Of this

[1] There is no record of any actual voting on the principle as such.
[2] A *remiss* debate is usually held on the Address or the Budget, but it can also be used whenever, on the submission (*remiss*) of a bill to a committee, there is general debate.

chamber he declared that he could not accept the Liberal view that it was 'a sort of national park where national curiosities enjoy an artificial protection for their otherwise hopeless exist-ence'.[1] Daniel Persson of Tällberg countered Kjellén by saying that the farmers (of whom he was one, though some said he was more an auctioneer and middleman than a true farmer) need not be intimidated by talk of the workers. Quoting the words of one of his predecessors, Nilsson of Österlof in 1871, he exclaimed: 'They are flesh of our flesh and bone of our bone.'[2]

Ministers had the right of addressing both chambers. Staaff took the opportunity of addressing the First Chamber and sug-gested that DPR was becoming attractive to the members of their chamber now that they knew that the Liberals in the Second Chamber were opposed to SPR. If DPR was to be acceptable to his party he said, it must

go to the root of the matter and permit the electors of the Provincial Councils and Town Councils, as well as their members who voted for the First Chamber, to vote according to the proportional method. But I wonder if I should be very wide of the mark when I say that such a far-reaching reform is most definitely less attractive for the overwhelming majority of this house than the principle of single-member constituencies on which the Government bill is based.[3]

Thus Staaff extended the principle of DPR to include not only the election of the First Chamber by the proportional method, but its electoral colleges as well.

Certain private motions were put forward for consideration by the Constitution Committee when the bill was being dis-cussed. One compromise suggestion, known as the Mossebo programme, was that the present system of constituencies should be retained but that small towns with a population of over 1,000 should elect their own members. This attempt to give Staaff part of what he asked for did not, however, receive much Liberal support. Another proposal, by Lundeberg, the conservative leader in the First Chamber, was for the extension of DPR as proposed by Staaff but with the proviso that any proposal to introduce a progressive income tax should be excluded from the Joint Vote. Lundeberg, the ironmaster and man of property,

[1] *A.k.* 1906, no. 19, p. 9.
[2] Ibid., p. 11.   [3] *F.k.* 1906, no. 17, p. 2.

would probably have been a liberal in 1866 but in 1906 was the
most respected member of the conservative group in the First
Chamber. The importance of his motion lay in the fact that he
had discussed double proportionalism as a possibility.

This being so, there was considerable interest in the motion of
Petersson of Påboda. He supported DPR but opposed its extension to the franchise of the Provincial and Town Councils. He
also suggested that the maximum number of votes in the countryside should be reduced from 5,000 to 1,000 per person or business
company, thus making his proposal attractive to the farmers of
the Second Chamber, if not to the First Chamber conservatives.
'Påboda', as he was sometimes called, was an important figure
in Swedish politics. One of the new type of farmers with a folk
high-school background, he was intelligent and capable enough
to be made Minister of Agriculture in the coalition Ministry and
to make history by being the first farmer to hold office. He was one
of the leaders of the Progressive party, and there could be little
doubt that if the battle between the Liberals and First Chamber
developed, each side would need him and his party as ally.

The Påboda motion was presented later than the others, 23
March, at a time when the Constitution Committee was reaching a deadlock. It soon proved attractive to the conservative
members, and with the support of Påboda and Elowson they
were able to reject the Government's bill and pass the Påboda
motion instead. A deciding factor was the conversion of Lundeberg to the proposal. Påboda himself defended his position skil-
fully and described the effect of single-member constituencies in
London where the Liberals had polled 248,000 votes and won
40 seats in the 1906 election compared with the Conservatives'
230,000 votes and 19 seats. Proportional representation, on the
other hand, did not waste anyone's vote and prevented the sort
of anomalies which occurred under the old system. In supporting his motion the committee recommended the chambers to
raise the minimum age to twenty-five and to require that
electors were State taxpayers. (The findings of the committee,
which were issued on 7 May, filled 384 pages.)

v. *The defeat of the Liberal reform bill*

A week later the Government *proposition* and the committee's
proposal were debated in the chambers simultaneously. Staaff

was faced with the situation he had regarded as most unlikely, a First Chamber which now supported DPR. Admittedly the conservatives on the committee had refrained from 'going to the root of the matter' in their proposal, but there was no guarantee that they might not go further. He could do little except tell the First Chamber that this was 'a complete volte-face' and that it was a sham reform (*skenreform*). Instead of realizing that the time called for delicate diplomacy if he was to succeed he bluntly remarked in the First Chamber debate:

'I believe that the Second Chamber ought to have greater significance than the First', and went on to say 'It is the duty of the Second Chamber to see that the clock goes: it is the First Chamber's duty to note what time it is.'[1]

Professor Blomberg replied that it was the duty of the chamber to make sure the clock kept correct time, and reproved Staaff for using language more appropriate in addresses to his admirers than in Parliament. Staaff's speech antagonized his hearers and the Government bill was defeated by 126 votes to 18 (of which 14 were thought to be registered by members who favoured another proposal on which they were unable to vote owing to the rules of Parliament requiring a bill and counter-bill). The Påboda motion was accepted by 118 to 26.

᾽ In the Second Chamber Påboda argued that in the long run his proposal was more far-reaching than Staaff's. However, the immediate issue was Second or dual chamber control, and Påboda's motion definitely postponed the time when the Left would be able to dominate Parliament. For this reason Branting, whose small party stood to gain from proportional representation, supported Staaff. He feared that the conditions laid down by the First Chamber in recompense for the application of DPR would be severe, and might even include greater restrictions to the Second Chamber franchise. The Social Democrats were pledged to universal suffrage at twenty-one. Sweden's two neighbours, largely owing to Socialist influence, were already far advanced towards universal suffrage. Norway obtained general manhood suffrage in 1892 and Finland (as Lindhagen remarked, 'this outpost of our national culture against the East'), though a Grand Duchy of the Tsar, became in 1906 the

[1] *F.k.* 1906, no. 48, pp. 42–43.

first country in the world to have universal suffrage for men and women. The agreement of the Liberals and Socialists ensured the victory of Staaff's *proposition* in the Second Chamber by 134 to 94: Påboda was defeated by 132 to 96. The chambers had reached opposite decisions and there was no hope of the Staaff proposal becoming law, at least during the present session.

Everything now depended upon the reactions of the Government. Branting had made the suggestion that violence might result when on 13 May he said he thought political development lay in a 'sort of class war', but he softened the impact of his words by adding that 'he hoped it would not take a wild and brutal form'. The important pronouncement came from Staaff who followed up his tactlessness to the First Chamber in the *remiss* debate with a volley in the Second Chamber in the final debate on the bill before the vote was taken: 'Should I be mistaken, should the struggle in its coming stages present a more stubborn character than I consider probable, then it will go on to some extent to another field than that of suffrage. Shall the power of the King and his people rule over Sweden—or the power of the King and the gentry?'[1] They were words very similar to those Lloyd George used to denounce the House of Lords. On hearing them Staaff's Minister for War, General Tingsten, rose and left the chamber. Billing commented in his diary that Staaff 'had an unfortunate habit of ending a speech with some churlish or foolish remark'. Two days later Tingsten and the Foreign Minister Trolle resigned. The speech had been made without consulting either them or two of the Consultative Ministers, for Staaff had given strict instructions to Biesèrt, the Finance Minister, not to divulge the contents to his colleagues.[2]

There were two alternatives for Staaff. He could either resign, having been defeated in his aims, or he could bring in a new measure the following year, hoping for greater support. As he had not made his bill a vote of confidence he was in a position to wait and see. Instead, as apparently he had intended from the beginning, he asked the King to dissolve the Second Chamber. However, he had not warned Oscar II of this intention when he took office because, he said, he did not want to upset a sick man.[3] (The King died the following year.) When

---

[1] *A.k.* 1906, no. 57, p. 11.
[2] Öman, op. cit., p. 259.   [3] von Zweigbergk, op. cit., p. 28.

the vote was taken, Oscar was away from the capital and so, on 18 May, Staaff told the Crown Prince Regent (later Gustav V) that he wanted to have the views of the electorate on the two proposals. What he really intended to do was to start agitation amongst the public in order to obtain the moral defeat of the First Chamber by a new election,[1] after which the mandate of the people would prevail. (This was what the Liberal Government in Britain succeeded in doing four years later in its attack on the House of Lords.) Gustav, however, was not in favour of a dissolution of the Second Chamber and suggested to Staaff that he should wait a year and then make a further attempt.

Oscar returned to Stockholm the following day and consulted the Speakers and Vice-Speakers, whereupon he reiterated the suggestion of the Crown Prince. Staaff still preferred a dissolution. There was an interval of about a week, after which the King issued a communiqué on 25 May explaining that 'he did not consider it logical or correct parliamentary procedure to dissolve a chamber which had assented to a Government bill'. Thereupon the Ministry felt they had no alternative but to resign. Whereas in Britain the King was compelled to recognize the superiority of the House of Commons, no such convention governed the relations of the Swedish chambers. Oscar was therefore acting with constitutional propriety when he announced at the end of the meeting of the Council of State on 25 May: 'the equal standing of both chambers must be recognized by the King and preserved by him'. This proved to be the end of the Liberal party's reform bill.

VI. *Reasons for the Liberals' failure*

The Liberals had no right to be surprised at the King's action. However, Hellner, a Consultative Minister, afterwards remarked: 'We did not believe he would be against it; that he should refuse never entered our heads.'[2] He and his colleagues had underestimated the opposition and had not paid sufficient attention to its strong constitutional position. Caught unawares, the Liberals and Social Democrats did not call any special congresses to discuss the situation, nor did the Social Democrats seize the weapon they had attempted to use in 1902 when

[1] Timelin, R. E., *Ministären Lindman och representationsreformen 1907–9*, p. 77.
[2] Hildebrand, op. cit., i. 476.

balked of the reform of Parliament they wanted—the general strike.

Had Staaff argued simply that the will of the people was more important than outdated constitutional forms, he would have been on stronger ground, but in doing so there would have been two difficulties. He could hardly have claimed that he represented the will of the wholenation when as many as ninety-four members of his own chamber voted against him. Secondly, if he believed that, given the opportunity, the electorate would express its wholehearted support for his bill, he could have waited a little longer. The Liberal newspapers supported him, and if the leaders of the party had stumped the country they might have increased the party's majority at the 1908 election to such an extent that the First Chamber dare not oppose it. Instead of taking this long-term view, Staaff persisted with his proposal and justly deserved the criticism of Baron Nils Palmstierna in the *remiss* debate in the First Chamber that though he had opposed a possible solution to the reform problem in 1904 and 1905 because it had contained proportional representation, Staaff would consider no alternative to his own measure. Indeed, he was insisting that a quick solution was essential. But, asked Palmstierna,

> Why has this solution not already been reached? The Crown has twice put forward proposals on the basis of universal suffrage. The First Chamber has twice passed the Crown's bill, and in the Second Chamber it was rejected by a hair. Had it been passed here, a speedy solution would already have been found. Whose responsibility is it that this did not happen? Everybody knows.[1]

This was certainly true. Staaff had said in 1905: 'We are willing to take responsibility for postponement [of the Government's bill], and we have fully realized what this responsibility implies.'[2]

Staaff could not complain, like the Liberals in Britain, that the other house was pursuing a general policy of obstruction. A record number of bills had been introduced. Apart from the reform bill, only five had been rejected, and on only two of these occasions was the First Chamber responsible. There was thus

[1] *F.k.* 1906, no. 17, p. 4.
[2] For Staaff's attitude in opposition, see for example *A.k.* 1904, no. 66, pp. 65–66, *A.k.* 1905, no. 51, pp. 29–31.

'no sort of obstructionist policy from a First Chamber opposed to a pro-Government Second Chamber.'[1]

Given wiser leadership, it is possible that the Liberals might have succeeded in their aim for a 'House of Commons'. Boström had prepared the way for them in May 1904, when in the debate on the franchise he said that the balance of political power lay in the Second Chamber.[2] When rebuked by Blomberg he agreed that 'the Swedish people are represented by the First Chamber as well as the Second' but continued:

I stand for this interpretation. It depends partly on the greater number of members in the Second Chamber, partly on the circumstance that its members are elected more frequently and chosen more directly by the electorate than the members of the First Chamber . . . Besides, this is not a unique characteristic of our system but holds good of England's upper and lower houses, of France's Chamber of Deputies and Senate, and so on.[3]

He did not point out that in other countries the chambers were not equal in all their powers. However, if even Boström could be so persuaded, the outlook for lower-house supremacy was certainly promising.

The issue in 1906 was complicated by bad relations between the Prime Minister and the Court. Oscar had approved of Staaff's handling of the Norwegian crisis, and expected the Liberal leader to show a restraint towards the Monarchy similar to that which he had displayed towards the Left Government in Norway. Unfortunately Staaff did little to smooth his path with the King, even though he needed his support if he was to introduce Second Chamber control of the Government. In trivial instances he showed lack of understanding of the monarchical system. For instance, after the dissolution of the Union, when it became necessary to alter the Swedish flag, the King wanted to keep his own three-tongued standard. The Ministry thought that one flag was sufficient for all purposes. In the end Staaff told the King that he could keep his royal standard—and could have a green or a red one if he wanted. Not unnaturally the King was annoyed at his effrontery.[4]

A more important source of bitterness was Staaff's handling of the Civil List. The dissolution of the Union reduced the

---

[1] Öman, op. cit., p. 288.   [2] F.k. 1904, no. 57, p. 16.
[3] F.k. 1904, no. 58, p. 15.   [4] Billing, G., op. cit., p. 313.

income of the Court, and in particular of the Crown Prince, and Staaff agreed to discuss with his colleagues an increase in the sum provided by Parliament. They suggested that the proposal should be made from the floor of the House on the grounds that the Government (i.e. the Crown) should not itself take the initiative.[1] Because of its vacillating policy towards Norway in 1905, the Court was unpopular with both radicals and conservatives, though for opposite reasons. Parliamentary opinion in 1906 was therefore generally unfavourable to the King, and no motion was raised in either chamber for an increase in the Civil List. Defenders of Staaff have pointed out that as a good parliamentarian he was powerless to act if his colleagues and party disapproved, but there is no indication that Staaff used any pressure on them. When, in 1907, Lindman raised the amount of money voted by Parliament for the royal household from 192,000 to 260,000 crowns annually, Staaff opposed the proposal and suggested a single payment of 550,000 crowns instead.[2] Moreover, since Staaff's was not a bureaucratic Ministry, the refusal of the Liberal Government to take the initiative suggested not so much modesty on the part of the Crown as stubborn disinclination by radical members of Parliament, newly raised to the executive power, to assist the Court in a very delicate task.

Oscar was glad when Staaff resigned. Staaff on his part had made little effort to keep the King informed of policy, and could not object to a similar attitude by Oscar, who refused to see him in the week following the request for a dissolution on the grounds that he was 'tired'. None the less, the King spent the week approaching various conservative leaders, and when he had assured himself of a new Ministry he published his communiqué and immediately accepted the resignation handed to him. It is possible that the week's delay in issuing the communiqué was necessary to give the King time to form a new Ministry behind the backs of the Liberals;[3] it might, on the other hand, have been caused by the King's desire to wait until the parliamentary session was completed.[4]

---

[1] Öman, op. cit., p. 202 (cf. *supra*, p. 62, n. 1).
[2] Hildebrand, op. cit., i. 487.
[3] Brusewitz, A., *Kungamakt, Herremakt, Folkmakt*, p. 19.
[4] Hamilton, Hugo, *Hågkomster*, p. 348.

One great hindrance to Staaff during his first Ministry was the tradition that Ministry and Parliament were separate. He was unable to exercise influence over the Constitution Committee to which his bill was submitted. Early in the session he tried to overcome the gap between himself and the parliamentary committees by writing a letter to the Law Committee on 28 January, but this was described by the influential *Stockholms Dagblad* on 15 February as an indication of the way in which the Government intended to influence the work of the committee. No further communications were addressed to any committee and no consultations took place over the reform bill between the Ministry and the Constitution Committee.[1] It was, moreover, considered by some Liberals to be contrary to the spirit of the Constitution for Staaff to be present at the party meeting which chose Liberal members of the Constitution Committee. Staaff made sure that those chosen were anti-proportionalists.

There was co-operation between the Ministry and the Liberal party council, but there was little liaison between Ministers and the party as a whole. The party refused to allow its meetings to be dominated by the Ministers, and Staaff for his part did not take the whole party into his confidence. As many as one-third of the party opposed the Government on important issues, the radicals and farmers, especially, showing considerable independence as committee members. A large proportion of members were against the proposal for immediate dissolution in 1906, even though Staaff was given his greatest support over the reform bill. The loyalty of the party in general must not be overestimated. One of Staaff's weaknesses lay in the fact that he represented not the centre but the left of his own party.

He did not altogether resent the separation of the executive and legislative powers once he had obtained office. Despite having opposed the Crown's exclusive control over the power of economic legislation, he found it a very useful constitutional device as Prime Minister.[2] In opposition, he had also pleaded for a freer interpretation of Article 90, which restricted the right of members of Parliament to inquire into the day-to-day activities of the Administration. On 3 March 1906, however, he replied

[1] Öman, op. cit., pp. 304–5.   [2] Ibid., pp. 289 ff.

to a Socialist interpellation concerning the Government's prosecution of a Socialist journal for *lesé-majesté* with a refusal to
recognize 'the propriety of extending the right of interpellation
to the sphere of the Minister of Justice's power of prosecution'.
Constitutionally he was correct, but in 1897 he had wanted to
extend this article to cover such individual decisions as these.[1]

VII. *Conclusion*

The events leading to the failure of the Liberal attempt at
reform in 1906 were in marked contrast to the circumstances of
1865. In the first place, public opinion had not had time to be
aligned on the side of the Government, nor could the moral
pressure put on Charles XV and the *Riddarhus* have been applied
to the First Chamber and Oscar II. Indeed, they could regard
themselves as the champions of the 1866 Parliament Act and all
that De Geer had stood for in his insistence on two chambers and
a division of power between King and Parliament.

Secondly, Staaff made it plain that he *did* intend to 'land the
country head over heels in *parlamentarism*'. De Geer had found
it advisable to mitigate the anxiety of Charles XV by an increase
in the Civil List. Staaff, who was in a very real sense threatening
the power of the Monarchy, and who had good grounds for
assisting the King in his financial difficulties, made no compensation whatsoever. Unlike De Geer, he was not prepared to work
with his Monarch, and in his over-confidence worked against
him, believing that power was on his side.

Thirdly, the homogeneity of the Staaff Ministry was not as
great as in De Geer's Council of Ministers. After the resignation of Hamilton in 1860 De Geer had been able to shape his
Council into a team, each one of whom was at least reconciled
to their Chancellor's policy. But Staaff had appointed several
colleagues who had no particular interest in his reform, and at
the time when his reform bill was still in the balance, had
actually encouraged the departure of the Foreign Minister
Trolle and the War Minister Tingsten. Their resignation at a
crucial moment seriously weakened the standing of the Ministry.

The parliamentary support for Staaff provides a fourth point
of comparison. De Geer could rely on the full support of the
two lower Estates and a considerable number of the Nobles.

[1] *A.k.* 1897, no. 42, p. 2.

Staaff had almost no following in the First Chamber, and not much more than half of the Second.

Finally, the policy of the Right was very different in 1906 and 1907 from the conservatives of 1865. In 1906 the conservative leaders were able to present an alternative proposal which was in some ways better than the Liberal *proposition*; they were able to advise the King on his constitutional duty; and they were prepared to take over government as soon as the Liberals admitted defeat. Viewed as manœuvres, the honours in the battle between the Right and the Left went to the Right. It was they who appeared to make concessions, to be reasonable men who treated the King with respect, and to be acting in the spirit of the Parliament Act. The central issue, whether or not the upper classes should continue to have a large share in Parliament through the control of the First Chamber, they glossed over.

As far as many of the farmers were concerned, the choice lay between the First Chamber they knew and a Parliament controlled by Liberals and Socialists whose real intentions were still somewhat obscure. They were not at all sure that they preferred the Left to the Right. The farmers were fighting a battle for existence as a class exercising political power. In 1866, when three-quarters of the population were engaged in agriculture, they obtained control of the Second Chamber. By 1910 their numbers had dropped from 3,000,000 to 2,700,000 while the number engaged in industry, commerce and the public service had risen from 1,200,000 to 2,800,000. In 1906, therefore, the farmers were about to become a minority of the population. If the Liberal bill was passed, they would be doomed to minority status, which would worsen as industrialization increased; if proportional representation was introduced and a friendly First Chamber prepared to side with them on occasion, they might still be a power in the land. The choice, however, did not present itself to them as clearly as this because of their deep-seated doubts about the identity of their interests with those of the First Chamber. It remained an open question in 1906 whether the Liberals or Conservatives would offer them most security. The divisions amongst the farmers illustrated their demoralization. Some, like Påboda, formed the Progressive party, while others joined the Liberals. Among the latter were

Tällberg and his friends who hovered uneasily between the point of view of Staaff and that of Påboda.

Upon Staaff's resignation Oscar offered the premiership to Påboda, the author of the motion which had received greatest support, and the first farmer to be asked to become Prime Minister. He declined, and once more the opportunity for political power was missed by the farmers. They would now have to see what the conservatives of the First Chamber had to offer.

CHAPTER VIII

The Passing of the 1907 Reform Bill

1. *The Conservative Ministry takes office, 1906*

IT was a sign of the speed with which the times were changing that Påboda should have been asked to be Prime Minister. However, he preferred to become Minister of Agriculture once more.[1] In this capacity he played an important if subordinate role in the next two years. He is said to have been responsible for the exclusion of certain more conservative elements when Lindman formed his Ministry, and Brusewitz's study has even suggested that the policy of Påboda overshadows that of Lindman.

In calling upon Lindman to form a Ministry, Oscar recognized that a new generation had come to power. Just as Staaff replaced Von Friesen, so Lindman took over leadership from Lundeberg. At first sight it would appear that the King was returning to the old type of Ministry, since Lindman was both a First Chamber conservative and an ex-civil servant who had been Director-General of the Royal Telegraph Board. But he was chosen because of his political, not his administrative, position, and was very different from the usual civil servant. He had resigned from the navy as a Commander in 1892, at the age of thirty and then, like Lundeberg, had become interested in the iron industry, making his mark first as Managing Director of the ironworks at Iggesund and later in the new iron-ore mines in the north, at Kiruna. Possessing remarkable powers of organization, and an ability to make friends with all sorts of people, this short and rather impish figure attracted the attention of Boström, who recognized his ability and offered him the post of Finance Minister in his second Ministry. Lindman declined and was then appointed Director-General of the Telegraph Board. After some persuasion he was encouraged to enter the First Chamber in 1905, and in the same year took office as Naval Minister in the Lundeberg–Staaff coalition. Only two members of the First Chamber were younger than Lindman.

[1] The department was created in 1900.

Oscar was a sailor himself, but though this may have inclined him towards Lindman as a possible premier, the appointment was justified on personal grounds; there was no other Conservative who could pilot the Conservative party through parliamentary reform. Lindman was an important figure throughout the period of twentieth-century parliamentary change, being Prime Minister at the time of the second reform bill and a leader of the opposition party during the 1918 debates on the third. His moderate conservatism and restrained counsel enabled him to play a difficult part very well.

The Ministry of 1907 was, in many ways, conservative, but it could more accurately be described as a Ministry of friends of proportionalism.[1] Trolle and Tingsten, the two non-party men who had resigned from the Staaff Ministry, agreed to serve in their former capacities. Among the others were Roos, a Second Chamber Liberal who had supported in turn single proportionalism, single-member constituencies, and later double proportionalism; Påboda and Hammarskjöld, who were National Progressives in the Second Chamber; and Swartz, a colleague of Lindman in the First Chamber who supported double proportionalism. The Ministry was completed with the addition of three Ministers who were not politicians and one Right wing conservative, Juhlin, who was not a member of Parliament.

11. *Lindman's policy*

The new Government took office on 29 May, immediately after Staaff's resignation, and on 6 July Lindman outlined his policy. Speaking to his supporters he said bluntly that to persuade the Liberals to overcome their opposition to the conservative point of view the conservatives would have to accept a reform in the composition of the First Chamber which would give opposition members some representation. If Lindman could bring about an adequate reform of the First Chamber, the main ground of Liberal opposition would be removed. However, it was going to require considerable diplomacy to convince members of the Second Chamber that the First would be reformed and at the same time assure the First Chamber that it could approve the proposal because it would not harm the position of the Conser-

---

[1] Timelin, op. cit., p. 103. Brusewitz (op. cit.) argues that it was Right-wing and in fact the first Right Ministry (p. 21).

vatives. Lindman therefore directed the attention of the First Chamber to the short-term advantages of his proposal (that the Conservatives would retain control of the First Chamber), and that of the Second Chamber to the long-term effects (that, beginning with the Joint Vote, the hegemony of the First Chamber would ultimately be ended).

Lindman could count on the support of his Conservative colleagues in the First Chamber, and upon the large minority of proportionalists in the Second, led by Påboda and his National Progressive party. The task before him could be summarized as the conversion of twenty-one Second Chamber members from support of Staaff to support of PR. He himself put the case:

> Could I not perhaps obtain the necessary twenty-one votes if, for example, I were to suggest that the election of members to the First Chamber (i.e. of Provincial Councils) should also be subject to the proportional principles? This thought has not the character of anything definite and I risk offending certain First Chamber members who perhaps found our proposal this spring concerning the First Chamber radical enough: but parliamentary life is composed of just such dangers.[1]

Svenska Dagbladet (moderate-Liberal) commented that the aim of securing twenty-one converts was not high enough for a Government dealing with the reform of Parliament. The newspaper was wrong. Lindman knew that Staaff's strength lay in his appeal to principle and in contrasting the power of the people with that of the plutocracy, a level on which the conservative groups could not compete. By preventing the debate turning on the principle underlying parliamentary reform, by concentrating on details and by being 'practical' he was able to stop the Liberals from using their main armament.

Staaff was not in a strong position. He was unnerved by his defeat in Parliament, and exposed his willingness to compromise a few days before Lindman made his speech. On 24 June at Nackarpsdal he repeated that he did not oppose DPR in principle, and would accept it in the event of a thorough reform. But what did he mean by a 'thorough' reform? Supposing the conservatives made an offer which they considered thorough and Staaff did not: what would happen then? The differences

[1] *Svenska Dagbladet*, 6 July 1906.

M

might be narrowed down to details and the whole principle of a proper reform of the upper house reduced to a series of minor points in which the 'conservatives could score. Moreover, if Staaff wanted a really thorough change, his opponents could argue that he was not acting in the spirit of the 1866 Parliament Act, and there would have to be discussion over precisely what was the 'spirit' of De Geer's measure. Again, Staaff would not want to be pressed too far, lest the floodgates of universal suffrage be opened to socialism. *Arbetarbladet* (Social Democrat) put the Socialist point of view of the Nackarpsdal speech: 'with such unreliable and irregular pace-setters, Liberalism certainly will not win decisive battles. From the Liberals one can clearly expect nothing but compromises.'

Too late Staaff realised that Lindman might accept his challenge. At Östersund on 26 August he said that the Liberals would only accept DPR if the Second Chamber was to dominate Parliament. Lindman contented himself with the reply at Delsbo that DPR had originated in the Second Chamber where it had received two-fifths of the votes cast.

Seven months elapsed between these speeches and the meeting of Parliament in January 1907 to discuss reform. In this period Lindman wasted no time, and followed the Liberal example of building up a nation-wide organization intimately linked with the parliamentary party. The conservative organization (*Allmänna valmansförbundet*) which had been formed in 1904 in preparation for the 1905 elections had not so far found its feet. Under G. F. Östberg it was made into a vehicle for propaganda, the conservative parties in both chambers being linked with it. Many of the farmers of the Second Chamber, for example the National Progressive party, were persuaded to side with the Right, and from this time it is possible to use the generic term Right (or Conservative) to describe opponents of Staaff in both chambers. Lindman's Delsbo speech was only the fourth time a Prime Minister had taken the opportunity of expressing his political views on a public platform. On 23 September the Liberal *Dagens Nyheter* was able to say that 'undeniably there has come an offensive spirit into the Right's policy altogether different from the spring'. Lindman was planning a bold stroke, and needed to pacify his own supporters almost as much as to convert some of his opponents. One of his most significant acts was to call a meeting of forty Conservative newspaper editors shortly before presenting his bill to Parliament.

As a preliminary move, he set up a committee of inquiry consisting of six members of Parliament who were advocates of PR to examine every aspect of the franchise question. The findings of the committee were embodied in the Government bill presented to Parliament on 2 February 1907. As expected, it applied PR to the Second Chamber. Fifty-six constituencies were to be formed, in which, except for the six large town constituencies, town and country were mixed. In the introduction to the bill, which was drafted by his Department, the Minister of Justice said that PR was inserted to preserve the balance of power between the farmers and the rising industrial class.[1] He pointed to the constituencies of Great Britain which varied very much in size, and added that the Swedish electoral districts would be roughly equal. Division of the seats according to votes was to be made in conformity with D'Hondt's rule, that is to say the party with the largest number of votes was given one seat; its votes were then halved, the party which now had the largest number being also awarded one seat; the votes of this second party were then divided by three. Thus, supposing there were three parties, receiving 40,000, 36,000 and 24,000 votes respectively, and five seats to be allotted,

	1st Count	2nd Count	3rd Count	4th Count	5th Count
A party	40,000 (1)	20,000	20,000	20,000 (1)	8,000
B party	36,000	36,000 (1)	12,000	12,000	12,000 (1)
C party	24,000	24,000	24,000 (1)	6,000	6,000

A would receive two seats, *B* two seats, and *C* one.

The minimum age for voters was to be twenty-four. It was a bill which, to judge from the Minister's statement, was intended to attract the farmers.

Nevertheless it was the First Chamber reforms which aroused greatest interest and caused most surprise. Not only did Lindman accept DPR, but he applied it down to elections to the Provincial Councils, thus meeting Staaff's most serious objection. In addition he drastically reduced the number of votes permitted to the First Chamber electorate. The graded scale,

[1] *Kungl. Maj:ts Nåd. Proposition*, no. 28, p. 13, 1906.

whereby the rich had more votes than the poor, was so modified that the maximum number of votes which any one person could exercise was forty. For this, an income of 12,000 crowns was necessary in the towns and 15,000 in the country. Previously, the maximum number of votes had been 100 in the towns and 5,000 in the country. The term of First Chamber members was reduced in length from nine to six years. In its scope, the bill went far beyond what the Left expected and Branting was reduced to writing in *Social Demokraten* on 4 February that the Conservative intention was that 'it would *seem* but not *be* an effective reform'.

III. *The Debate in Parliament*

The Liberals and Social Democrats presented motions before the debate began. The Socialists, as previously, were in favour of universal suffrage at twenty-one to the Second Chamber and a First Chamber with only a suspensive veto. As they themselves pointed out, they were at least consistent in their demands. Seven Liberals, led by Lindhagen, abandoned the Staaff point of view and joined Branting's small band of thirteen. Staaff and seventy-two other Liberals placed a motion in favour of Second Chamber government and criticised the bill for not seriously touching upon the question of the composition of the First Chamber. The electorate, so they maintained, was to be altered, but the members were to be the same group of rich men. For this reason Olsson of Viken put forward a suggestion, which was to be important at a later stage, for a reduction in the qualifications for admittance to the Second Chamber from property assessed at 80,000 crowns or income at 4,000 to 40,000 and 2,000 crowns respectively. He also proposed that members of the First Chamber be given a salary. Without such an amendment to the bill he maintained the Government would be:

rather like a landlord who, as a gesture for the numerous inhabitants of a cellar flat, constructs a spiral staircase up to a reading room in the flat above, but has the staircase blocked by a door well barred and bolted.[1]

There were few speeches in the *remiss* debate. In the First Chamber the Minister of Justice, Albert Petersson, introduced

---

[1] *Motioner i Andra kammaren*, no. 197, p. 2.

the measure by saying that there was need for a First Chamber elected on a broad popular basis: although this might cause concern, members could be assured that this was no leap in the dark.[1] Only three other members spoke, two of them die-hard Conservatives. One, Benedicks, deplored the Minister's 'funeral oration' and said that many members would dislike the bill even if they did not get up and say so. He admitted that the Government had done its best to get a good press (presumably the meeting of the editors had not been without success), but doubted whether such a radical measure was necessary instead of the step-by-step reform of Great Britain. The experience of democratic countries was not reassuring: the anti-trust legislation had exposed corruption in the United States; in France deputies pandered to their constituents instead of furthering the national interest; and in Australia the number of immigrants only just exceeded the number of emigrants, so great was the distress caused by Socialism. Members ought to remind themselves of the Era of Liberty and how it was necessary for Gustav III to save Sweden from the fate of Poland.[2]

There was more debate in the divided Second Chamber. The Prime Minister himself introduced the bill and described it as a radical offer. Proportional representation was not being adopted in order to restrict manhood suffrage but to protect minorities so that all might be represented.[3] Staaff's speech was not one of his best. It was marred by a forlorn attempt at jocularity and showed an inclination to trivial criticisms. Once again he said that the Liberals would consider a far-reaching application of DPR, and after admitting that the bill went surprisingly far he congratulated the Prime Minister on his concessions.[4] It was left to Branting to argue categorically that the bill was unacceptable and that it was a device for keeping power in the hands of the rich. The new forty-grade scale merely meant that in commune elections one-seventh of the people possessed 90 per cent. of the votes instead of one-tenth. The power of business firms was unaffected. Even England attempted to give each person one vote in local elections, the maximum number in exceptional cases being only six. As the qualifications for admittance to the First Chamber now stood, in two whole

[1] *F.k.* 1907, no. 6, p. 5.
[2] *F.k.* 1907, no. 6, pp. 6–14.
[3] *A.k.* 1907, no. 8, p. 6.
[4] *A.k.* 1907, no. 8, p. 13.

provinces only one Social Democrat was eligible for election. He ended an inspiring oration with words to be as famous as Staaff's the previous year. The bill did 'not make the Swedish people master in their own house'.[1]

Professor Kjellén put forward a theory fashionable amongst some Conservatives. He accepted the party system but did not think it followed that these parties should oppose each other in the same chamber as in England (and there only in recent decades). Sweden's tradition was bicameral, the two chambers performing the function of the two parties in the House of Commons. As illustration he referred to industry, where management and workers nominated equal numbers of representatives in a dispute. The chambers similarly represented the two main classes, and to allow the workers to have access to the First Chamber would flout this principle.[2] Like many other Conservatives who supported the two-chamber system, Kjellén did so on grounds of class interest. The more subtle arguments used to defend the House of Lords in England would have seemed hypocritical if employed to defend the First Chamber.

The bill was then referred to committee. Instead of following the usual procedure of sending it to the Constitution Committee, Parliament agreed to set up a Special Committee, in order to allow the Liberal ex-Ministers (but not the present Ministry) to take part in its deliberations. Another reason for this procedure lay in the provision to make alterations in the commune franchise, which was outside the purview of the Constitution Committee. The Special Committee could deal with the whole bill. Several newspapers agreed with the decision, though the Social Democrats argued that the 1905 elections had given no mandate for it.[3] The Liberals were pleased when Lindman promised that of the committee's 24 members half should be supporters of single-member constituencies and half of proportional representation. Of the twenty-four, nine of the supporters of proportionalism were members of the First Chamber and three were from the Second. Three members of the First Chamber and nine of the Second were in favour of single-member constituencies. Of these nine, one was a Social Democrat (Branting) and one a Farmer. The three proportionalists

[1] A.k. 1907, no. 8, p. 21.   [2] A.k. 1907, no. 8, p. 31.
[3] Timelin, op. cit., p. 282.

included two Farmers and one National Progressive. Five of Lindman's committee of inquiry were included on the Special Committee, of which Lundeberg became chairman and Staaff vice-chairman. Discussions began on 18 February and continued until 30 April. No fewer than 38 motions were submitted and examined.

Owing to divisions within the Liberal ranks, it soon became clear that PR would be accepted by the Committee. Staaff agreed that the reduction of the grades in the First Chamber franchise to forty was a thorough reform and did not support Branting's proposal to abolish plural voting altogether. At the end of February a vote resulted in a victory for PR by 14 votes to 10. When the National Liberal Federation met in Stockholm on 7 March, northern representatives insisted on the need for a reform of the commune franchise so that business firms in the north did not swamp the vote of the local inhabitants. Lindman's proposal, which was the first to suggest the ending of this anomaly, sowed dissension in the Liberal ranks. Whereas the Conservatives were unanimously in favour of PR, and the urban Socialists of single-member constituencies, the Liberals were now divided into town and country members, whose sympathies varied. In a by-election in Stockholm two Liberal candidates fought each other on the proportionalist issue, the supporter of single-member constituencies being successful.

In April the Conservative editors were called to Stockholm once again and were warned that the Government was about to make an offer which some Conservatives might consider too high a price for reform. There was, however, little sign of such an offer in the report of the Special Committee, which supported most of the proposals of the committee of inquiry and also adopted a motion of Persson of Tällberg that taxpayers should receive an extra vote for the grade in which they stood and not, as heretofore, only for every completed grade. For instance, supposing a man received the vote on payment of 100 crowns in taxes; under the old method he would receive a second vote when he paid 200 and a third at 300; by the new stipulation he would receive a second vote at 101 crowns, and a third at 201.

The Government made its offer between the publication of the report and its debate in Parliament, proposing the adoption of the suggestion of Olov Jonsson of Hov (rejected by the Special

Committee) that members of the First Chamber should receive a salary. Jonsson had pointed out that although salaries had increased by 55 per cent. since 1866 and a professor who then received 4,500 crowns now earned 7,000, the cost of being a member of the chamber had risen to 6,000 crowns, and thus the bar on entry was in reality also 50 per cent. higher than in 1866. The main obstacle to admission to the First Chamber was no longer the property qualification, but the absence of a salary. Certain Conservatives, notably Lundeberg and Trygger, asserted that the Government had no right to change its mind before the chambers had debated its original bill.[1] Lindman, who had remained passive while the committee discussion was taking place, replied that the Government was not prepared to be a dumb spectator of affairs.[2] This statement won much support in the country, and when the amended bill was put to the vote in the First Chamber it was accepted by 93 votes to 52.

The position at the beginning of the Second Chamber debates, which now took place, was that the Conservatives were ready to accept PR and had made a series of concessions purporting to show that they were seriously reforming the First Chamber. They had reduced the scale, widened the franchise, and had offered to pay members. The Second Chamber was presented with a difficult choice. It could either oppose the bill entirely because it was not a thorough reform (a difficult position to assume) or it could try to gain as many changes in the First Chamber as possible and then accept the Government's bill. Staaff took the former line, but one or two of his followers showed signs of weakening. Tällberg, as a representative from the north where the business vote had greatly increased, was concerned with commune reform, and was influenced by the Conservative promise of legislation. He therefore proposed that the qualifications for membership of the First Chamber should be halved. This had been made before without much success, but now it formed a step in the bargaining process. Andersson of Nöbbelöv proposed a compromise solution—reduction of the property qualification to 50,000 crowns taxable value and of the income to 3,000. This was supported by Branting, who would have liked greater concessions, declaring that no Social Demo-

[1] Timelin, op. cit., p. 410.   [2] Ibid., p. 413.

crat official received more than 2,700 crowns, except for certain newspaper men who earned up to 3,300. The Social Democrats having temporarily deserted Staaff, the motion was carried by 122 to 105. It remained to be seen whether any more of the Liberals could be weaned away, and the necessary twenty-one votes transferred.

For the moment the chambers had reached different decisions, but the situation was not like that of 1906 when the reform bill was rejected by the First Chamber; the differences now were slight. The bill, the Special Committee report, and the decisions of the chambers were referred back to the Special Committee once more for arbitration (*sammanjämkning*). It was now the duty of the committee to present a new proposal which embodied the views of both chambers and was acceptable to both. On Sunday, 12 May, Lundeberg was persuaded to accept the Andersson proposal, whereupon the committee voted in its favour by 14 to 9. When the proposal was put to the chambers as it stood (i.e. with the committee recommending the First Chamber to accept the decision of the Second) the vote in its favour was 110 to 29, compared with the earlier 93 to 52 when payment of members had been hurriedly put forward by the Government. The majority was now almost as great as for the Påboda motion a year earlier, despite the concessions Lindman had forced the members to make. He had led the Conservatives step by step nearly to victory.

There remained the Second Chamber vote. Now, at the final hour, the Socialists remembered their pledge to support Staaff and voted against the bill. But of the 106 Liberals only 83 were loyal to their leader, exactly twenty-one voting in favour of the reform. Thus Lindman achieved his ambition. He more than achieved it, for some Independents and National Progressives accompanied them, making the total number of converts 31. The voting in favour of the Government bill was 128 to 98.

This time there was no rejoicing in the streets as in 1865. The bill lay *vilande* until after the Second Chamber elections and was passed without a division in 1909. Recognizing the defeat of his lower-house *parlamentarism*, Staaff voted for the bill and both chambers agreed that proportional representation should henceforth be applied to the distribution of committee seats.

iv. *The aftermath*

Lindman's victory was recognized even by his opponents. The Liberal *Stockholmstidningen* said of him on 15 May: 'No one can but admire him for the strength and cool determination with which he has fought his battle.' The Socialist *Arbetarbladet* remarked that the strength of the Right over the past two years had increased considerably. The turning-points were Lindman's acceptance of the proposal of the committee of inquiry to reduce the graded scale, and his decision to concede further points when the report of the Special Committee was published. Unlike Staaff he did not treat the newspapers as politicians' servants. By taking the Conservative editors into his confidence he won their support. Before the issue was settled he had converted several moderate-Liberal papers which had previously supported Staaff to his own point of view. Chief amongst them were *Aftonbladet* and *Svenska Morgonbladet*.[1]

From a Conservative standpoint, the bill left the First Chamber intact. The number of Liberal and Socialist members increased to about sixty, but they were still a minority. The Left could console itself with the knowledge that the Conservatives had consented to a reform of the chamber, and the time could not be far off when the remaining anomalies would be removed. Still, it was a setback to have to wait a few more years, when in 1906 immediate victory had appeared in sight.

The Liberals had been in a difficult position after their defeat of 1906. They could hardly abandon their demand for single-member constituencies after having raised this to the level of principle. They had, it is true, agreed to consider any thoroughgoing proposal of DPR, but to abandon their own plan in favour of extracting maximum concessions over PR seemed to many members of the party to be abandoning principle in favour of opportunism. They found themselves in the embarrassing position of having to say that only single-member constituencies were fair and democratic, and at the same time that thoroughgoing PR was satisfactory. In assuming that timidity and bad faith were characteristics of the Conservatives, they certainly maligned their opponents. Moreover, to base their policy of parliamentary reform on this assumption was un-

[1] Timelin, op. cit., p. 201.

realistic. Branting summed the situation up in the closing debate in the Second Chamber: it was a 'fatal mistake for the Liberals not to conform to the general advance in the summer of 1906 and widen their base over the franchise issue so that it embodied a reform of the Constitution which affected the First Chamber as well'.[1] Staaff, however, was too stubborn and too determined to have his own proposal accepted to change his policy even after defeat. Nor was he, unlike Branting, able to support PR provided it was accompanied by the maximum concessions possible. For Staaff, as his support of the forty-grade scale and opposition to Branting's proposal for its abolition indicated, was afraid of the masses. It was the misfortune of the Liberal party that it came into existence too late, when already the Social Democrats were increasing their hold on the workers by means of a highly organized party under competent leadership. Unable to trust Right or Left, the Liberals were in no position to satisfy either. Hence Branting's remark in a speech at Gävle on 28 June 1906: 'In the long run, Liberalism is an unreliable ally.'[2]

Yet the Social Democrats were loyal to Staaff and preferred to present a united reformist front and keep their promises rather than to be attracted by the offers of concessions made by the Conservatives. At an extraordinary Congress in April 1907 a motion in favour of a general strike was defeated by 36,000 to 17,000 card votes. It has been suggested that they were foolish not to support Lindman's proposal of PR, but its acceptance would have meant compromise, and the party wanted to retain its ideal—complete democratization of Parliament. Staaff's lower-house *parlamentarism* promised this but Lindman's concessions did not.

The bill was accepted by the chambers partly because both sides became tired of the discussion, and this enabled Lindman to take advantage of the general malaise and push through his measure of reform. The First Chamber had opposed Staaff, but was chary of rejecting Lindman's reform out of hand. The Prime Minister had used his influence to insist that some reform was necessary and that proportional representation applied to both chambers would be enough to satisfy public opinion. The Norwegian crisis of 1905 had warned the chamber of the consequences of a stiff and uncompromising attitude, and this may

[1] *A.k.* 1907, no. 52, p. 119.   [2] Quoted in Timelin, op. cit., p. 537.

well have affected their acquiescence in Lindman's suggestions.

As for the Liberals, the miracle worked by Staaff of applying discipline to a large party built of diverse elements could not be repeated. By endeavouring to interest the farmers in the party, the Liberals achieved their aim of being the largest party in the Second Chamber, but at the cost of unity. It was the farmers, who proved the weakest link and who revealed its heterogeneous character. The first blow against the Liberals had been struck by a member of the National Progressive party, Petersson of Påboda, when he produced his motion of double proportionalism in 1906. Within the party Tällberg proved an advocate of making concessions to the Conservatives. He had not only been passed over in favour of Gösta Tamm when Staaff formed his Ministry, but he was somewhat jealous of Påboda's success. Nevertheless he had shown a consistent attitude, having presented a motion for the reduction in the First Chamber property qualification as far back as 1893–4. It was because Tällberg had his own ideas of parliamentary reform that Staaff thought it best not to include him in the Ministry. It might have been wisest to have done so. Tällberg led the important Liberal *fronde* from the north, farmers who felt the impact of the new iron mines and saw mills, and the political power which accompanied them, more keenly than anyone else. Of the twenty-one Liberals who deserted Staaff, sixteen were from the north.

The farmers played a vital part in the second reform bill. After many years in opposition they had now become conciliators. They were as difficult for outsiders to discipline as ever, and Lindman had as much difficulty with Påboda as Staaff had with Tällberg. They continued their old policy of supporting measures rather than men, and still preferred to modify the programme of others rather than to provide their own policy. It was all that they wanted, but it was not a very great political ambition.

From a constitutional standpoint, the negotiations of 1906 and 1907 proved that respect for the 1809 Constitution and the 1866 Parliament Act was too strong for Staaff. The separation of powers might in practice be gradually undermined and parliamentary government introduced, but the formal transfer of the powers of King or First Chamber was unlikely. The King had acted with constitutional correctness and had very little responsibility for the bill itself. Lindman did not have to follow De Geer's example and tell the King what he intended to do. Had Staaff been successful, the traditional system of division of powers between Crown and Parliament, the equality of the two chambers, the elaborate committee system, and its check upon the Ministry would all have been greatly modified. It was scarcely possible that he could have carried the First Chamber, let alone the Crown, with him. Even the Liberals were critical of Staaff's decision in 1912 to be chairman of both the parliamentary party and the National Liberal Federation, the concentration of power in one man, as in one assembly of men, being considered unwise.

Nevertheless, though the form of the Constitution and the Parliament Act remained, the position of the First Chamber was not finally settled. Meanwhile, moreover, there was to arise the question of the executive power itself, and in this matter once more the King and Staaff did not agree.

CHAPTER IX

The Threat of War, 1908–1917

THE controversy between the Liberals and the King over control of the executive power did not come to a head until early in 1914, after four more years of Lindman's premiership and just over two years of Staaff's second administration. Meanwhile the international situation had steadily worsened and there was considerable bitterness between the Left, anxious for social reform, and the Right, who were concerned over Sweden's unpreparedness in the event of war. It was these differences, expressing themselves in the Government's rearmament policy, which led to the break between the King and Staaff, and the formation in 1914 of a conservative Ministry which, owing to the outbreak of war in Europe, was supported by all parties until 1917.

1. The Lindman Ministry, 1908–1911

In 1908 the triennial Second Chamber elections took place. By gaining 6 seats the Right increased its representation to 98 seats, making it equal to the Liberals, who lost 6. The Social Democrats added no fewer than 21 seats to their small band of 13, and no independent members remained in the Chamber. The new Parliament met in 1909, and once again, as required by the Constitution, passed the reform bill, which then became law. Staaff hoped that there might be a new election in 1909, and believed that under the new Act his party would be more successful than in 1908. Lindman, however, refused to ask the King for a dissolution, and waited until the three sessions of the Parliament elected in 1908 were duly completed. Branting, the Social Democrats' leader, was unperturbed by the delay, since he thought that the Left was too weak to govern in face of a hostile First Chamber. Staaff, however, whose temper was increasingly affected by the stomach complaint from which he suffered, was embittered.

At the outset of the new Parliament there was an interesting constitutional controversy. The Government summarily refused to allow certain information to be given by civil servants to a parliamentary committee, thus creating a situation which could arise at any time under a political system where the executive and legislative branches were separated. In this instance the Fourth Temporary Committee of the Second Chamber was discussing a proposal to increase the opportunities for promotion from non-commissioned to commissioned rank in the Army. On his suggestion, the committee agreed that its secretary, a Social Democrat named Baron Palmstierna, should approach the secretary of the Swedish Non-Commissioned Officers' Association for its views. The secretary of the Association was a sergeant-major in the Household Cavalry, whose colonel, Count Oxenstierna, then appealed to the general officer commanding the Fourth Division to find out if this meeting was in order. The general asked the Minister for War, General Malm, who replied on behalf of the Government that it was improper.

The matter appeared to come under Article 46 of the Parliament Act, which stated:

If a committee requires verbal or written information from any Government official or Agency, the committee has a right, through its chairman, to request the King to order, through the member of the Council of State whom the King shall designate for this purpose at each Parliament, the proper person or Agency to submit the information requested. . . .

Assuming that the Association came under the category of 'Government official or Agency' the proper procedure had not been followed by the committee, since no request had been made to the Minister. In the course of time, however, committees had not always adhered to the letter of Article 46, and it seemed to the Left that the Government was making use of this constitutional provision because it disliked the idea of parliamentary interference in one of the last conservative strongholds, the armed forces. Lindman ascertained the views of the French Government on the authority of Ministers and committees in France, and was assured that in France the Minister had to give permission before information could be transmitted, and, indeed, that such a procedure was in accordance with the separation of powers.[1] The Government did not, however, base

[1] *Lindmans samling*, vol. xxiii.

its case on this argument. It declared that the Non-Commissioned Officers' Association was not a Government agency within the meaning of Article 46, but was an organization formed purely for matters affecting welfare. Therefore, the Government argued, it had no authority to discuss the question of promotion.

At the time it seemed that this might be the signal for a long constitutional struggle between the Government and Parliament,[1] with Lindman afraid lest Parliament should claim its eighteenth-century privileges, and the Liberal and Socialist members defending what they considered to be the rights of the people's representatives. However, for two reasons the crisis did not develop. First, the case itself was really outside the scope of Article 46, over which a battle could have been waged, and thus did not provide a test case for the responsibility of Ministers as intermediaries between Parliament and the Executive. Secondly, the advent to power of Staaff in 1911 reduced the tension between Government and Parliament. Henceforth Ministries did not differ so markedly from the majority in the Second Chamber in policy. Moreover, even in Staaff's conception of parliamentary government there was no room for interference by private members and committees in affairs constitutionally the province of the Executive, an attitude which was upheld in later years by Branting and other Social-Democratic Ministers.

The case was the climax to a period of constant bickering within the Government, which was divided into two factions, the one led by Lindman and the other by Påboda. However, it was not so much the legal merits of the case as the Government's attitude to the committee which offended Påboda, who was a farmer in the old tradition as well as being a parliamentarian. He thereupon offered his resignation. It has been suggested that Lindman used the occasion for a final break with his antagonist, a step which could safely be taken now that the reform bill was passed.[2] The departure of his Minister of Agriculture was a real test of Lindman's ability to establish a common policy, particularly in rearmament, between the Conservatives of the First Chamber and the farmers in the Second. By choosing his time and issue well, Lindman was able to secure the continued allegiance of the farmers, especially of their leader, Carl Persson

[1] Varenius, O., in *Statsvetenskaplig tidskrift*, 1909, p. 178.
[2] Brusewitz, op. cit., pp. 38–44.

of Stallerhut, because of their distrust of the Liberals' defence policy and their dislike of socialism. Lindman had the advantage of being, like Boström, successful in winning the support of · the farmers for a patriotic defence programme in contrast to the Farmers' party's traditional policy of economy. Påboda had dreams of reviving the Farmers' party, but none followed him when he broke with Lindman, and he went into the wilderness alone. After a year or two's sojourn there, he found his way back into the Government—as a colleague of Staaff in his second Ministry.

The difference of opinion between the Liberals and Conservatives over defence was made clear when an all-party committee was set up to examine the proposal of the Government to increase the Defence Estimates from 78 to 97 million crowns and the period of conscription from 245 days to 365. The committee decided that the construction of a Dreadnought (F-boat) came within its terms of reference, whereupon Staaff and the Liberal members of the committee resigned, since it was Liberal policy to oppose heavy naval construction. A year later the committee report (without Liberal signatures) recommended the expenditure of 93 million crowns on defence, 4 millions being for the construction of a Dreadnought. The Second Chamber rejected the Government bill, but it was passed in the Joint Vote. This victory illustrated the weakness of the Left so long as the Conservatives dominated the First Chamber and enjoyed a certain amount of support in the Second. The 1911 elections, when the provision of the second reform of Parliament would come into operation, were awaited with interest.

11. *The elections of 1911 and 1912*

The Liberal Coalition party fought the Second Chamber election of 1911 with the full support of the National Liberal Federation, and Liberal candidates were obliged to accept the manifesto which the Federation issued. There were three main proposals in the programme:

(i) The realization of a parliamentary constitutional system (*statsskick*) with the main source of power (*tyngdpunkten*) in the Second Chamber.

(ii) Overhaul of the national defences. An immediate inquiry in accordance with the resolution of the Second Chamber, to examine the direct reductions, economies, and planned regulation of expenditure which in the future will make the burdens of defence proportionate to the country's financial strength, and give the necessary room for other needs of State. The inquiry is to make clear whether, through prudent arrangements, the present training period for conscripts can be reduced. (During the election campaign, Staaff actually promised to reduce the period of conscription.)

(iii) Local veto. Inquiry into Prohibition according to the resolution of the Second Chamber.

The net was flung wide. By still insisting on lower-house parliamentary government Staaff reiterated his old demand and gave expression to his chief ambition; by allowing local veto he heartened his temperance supporters; and by promising to reduce defence expenditure in order to spend money on social welfare he appealed to the instincts of many members of the party. Staaff argued in the Second Chamber that 'through large and far-reaching social measures, the most oppressed and distressed class can be helped'. He might fear the emergence of a Socialist electorate based on universal suffrage, but this did not prevent him from having regard for the social and economic needs of the working class. Pursuing a common social policy, the Liberals and Social Democrats shared a common electoral organization in fifteen of the fifty-six constituencies. At times the two parties quarrelled, but, on the whole, the spirit of co-operation inherited from the days of the Universal Suffrage Association continued, and, indeed, survived until the end of the Liberal–Social Democrat coalition in 1920.

The Social Democrats, whose trade union supporters had recovered from the disastrous General Strike of 1909, had a more radical policy, and included in their programme the disestablishment of the Church, disarmament, the inauguration of a republic, an eight-hour working day, compulsory social insurance, and taxation reform. Many Social Democrats, particularly the Young Socialists, not only preferred to spend money on welfare rather than armaments, but were anti-militarist in a sense in which the Liberals were not.

On the Right there was a certain amount of defeatism. The Conservatives also had their manifesto, but they relied for their votes upon the support of those who feared the victory of the

Liberals and Social Democrats. Amongst the aims of the Conservatives were the introduction of social insurance, reform of the poor law, the establishment of collective bargaining and, of course, a programme of increased defence expenditure. The desire of the Conservatives to attract the marginal vote was reflected in the minutes of the Conservative Party Organization, which since 1904 had conducted the elections on behalf of the parliamentary parties. In a note it was stated that it was not 'considered suitable that the Right-wing element of the First Chamber should be thought to stand behind this programme'. As a result, Lindman conducted the campaign with the Second Chamber Conservatives in the foreground, giving the Party Organization, which had become identified with the First Chamber, a subordinate role.

The Second Chamber elections resulted in an overwhelming defeat for the two Right-wing parties, who mustered between them a mere 64 seats. The Liberals increased their seats from 98 to 102, but the outstanding gains were those of the Social Democrats, who increased their numbers from 34 to 64 and now equalled the combined Right total. The electorate, which had been doubled by the reform, now numbered about 600,000, half of whom went to the polls.

In theory Lindman could have stayed in office. He still controlled the First Chamber and had enough members in both chambers to dominate the Joint Vote. However, he bowed to the moral defeat which the Right had suffered in the elections and resigned.

Bishop Billing advised the King to approach two 'moderate-Liberals', Hellner and De Geer,[1] men who were known to be unsympathetic to some of Staaff's radical plans, particularly his reduction of conscription and defence expenditure, but Billing on this occasion showed less than his usual grasp of affairs. When approached, the moderate-Liberals said that only Staaff could form a government based on the necessary parliamentary support, a view shared by the two Speakers, whom the King also consulted. The King returned to Stockholm on 29 September 1911, when he was able to sum up the situation for himself and to agree with Lindman and Swartling that Staaff (like Posse thirty years earlier) should be allowed 'to run out the course'.

[1] Son of Louis De Geer.

The Conservatives thought that nothing would do the Liberal party more harm than a term of office.

The King, for his part, looked forward to a Staaff Ministry with almost as little relish as he would have welcomed a Government of republican Socialists. He tried his best to be friendly at the first audience, and assured Staaff that 'all would be forgotten', an unfortunate phrase which caused Staaff to note in his diary 'What! We have never had any quarrel.' This would seem to indicate that Staaff did not realize the effect of his handling of the Civil List in 1906 and other less important issues. He informed the King that 'he naturally considered that he ought to stand outside parties completely'.[1] Whether he and the King meant the same thing by this statement is doubtful, but it does at least suggest that Staaff accepted the tradition that the Ministry was primarily the servant of the Crown and formed the executive power.

In 1906 Staaff had not been clear regarding his power as Prime Minister to request a dissolution of Parliament. This time he wanted to make sure there would be no misunderstanding, especially as he thought that a new First Chamber should soon be elected in accordance with the terms of the 1909 Reform Act. He demanded the King's acquiescence in the dissolution of the chamber as the condition of his acceptance of office. The Conservative Trygger was opposed to the idea of any promise, but his opposition to a dissolution 'aroused even His Majesty's surprise and embarrassment'.[2] The other Conservative leaders advised the King to agree to a dissolution provided Staaff proposed a definite date. After some discussion the Liberals and Social Democrats decided upon an immediate dissolution although some members thought they ought to wait until after the 1912 Provincial Council elections, which were expected to be in their favour. Lindman regarded the decision as a tactical mistake. On the other hand, it might have been unwise for Staaff to put off the dissolution after complaining so much of similar dilatoriness by Lindman.

The Liberal leader felt it was correct parliamentary procedure, in view of the large Socialist gains in the Second Chamber, to ask them to form a coalition, but he was very relieved

---

[1] Brusewitz, op. cit., p. 48.
[2] *Lindmans samling*, ii, p. 8, 30 September 1911.

when a vote in their parliamentary party in both chambers resulted in only six of the seventy Social Democrats being in
favour of the project. If they had accepted, 'I really would have
been in the soup', Staaff is said to have remarked afterwards.[1]
Instead, they offered a 'well-disposed policy of wait-and-see'
(*välvillig avvaktande hållning*). King Gustav remained suspicious
of the Social Democratic party, and Staaff could not persuade
him that much of their anti-militarist and republican propaganda was not to be taken too seriously and would be laid aside
the day they took office. The King persisted in his distrust of
Staaff partly because of his apparent co-operation with Branting.

In the first week of October 1911, Staaff formed his second
Ministry. His friends from 1906, who now appeared to have
formed a 'shadow Ministry' in the meantime, were once more
appointed to office. (The conservative leaders now had their
'shadow' Ministry.) The King gave Staaff a free hand. On this
occasion the composition of the Ministry showed that he had
been more daring in his appointments, no fewer than nine of his
Liberal colleagues being appointed to office. Påboda, who had
reconciled himself to Staaff's liberalism, returned to the Ministry
of Agriculture, and for the first time civilians were appointed to
the Ministries of Land and Sea Defence (i.e. War and Navy).
The two Liberal politicians who received these portfolios, Bergström and Larsson, knew little about either Service, and there
was some resentment in Conservative circles. Lindman commented that it was possible to have a civilian First Lord like
McKenna in England, or a Minister like Delcassé in France,
because the admirals themselves decided how the lump sum
allotted to the Navy should be spent. If there were a change in
the departmental administration of the Swedish Services, there
would be no objection, on principle, to civilian Ministers. As it
was, it appeared as though the armed forces were to be in the
hands of men who not only were ignorant of many of their
needs, but were generally regarded as unfavourably disposed
towards them.[2]

The First Chamber elections took place as promised in 1912

[1] von Zweigbergk, op. cit., p. 97.

[2] *Lindmans samling*, ii. 13, 7 October 1911. Lindman makes some adverse
comments on the two Ministers, neither of whom could address foreign visitors in
any language but Swedish. Some Conservative newspapers made fun of them in
cartoons. (See those collected in *Sveriges Nya Historia*.)

and reduced the representation of the Conservatives from about 130 out of a total of 150 to 85. The number of Liberal members increased from 15 to 51, and the number of Social Democrats from 2 to 12. The Conservatives still had a majority in the First Chamber, among their 86 members being 32 servants of the Crown, 20 landowners, 7 farmers, 17 business men, and 9 professional men.[1] By now the Conservatives were thoroughly alarmed at their future prospects, and a reorganization of the various Conservative groups took place. They had long lacked the discipline and cohesion of the Liberals and Social Democrats, and were weakened by being divided into several 'conservative' parties. These were now reduced to one for each chamber, the attempt to have one Conservative party for the whole of Parliament breaking down in the face of the strong tradition that the Farmers' party and its successors in the Second Chamber had different interests from the upper class in the First. However, the Conservatives of all types in the Second Chamber, sixty-four in number, were able to unite under Lindman's leadership, and the last remnants of a separate farmers' party disappeared.

III. *The policy of the second Liberal Government, 1911-1914*

The Liberals took office supported by Social Democrat allies who were now a large and well-disciplined party. They were opposed by Conservative parties in each chamber, the First Chamber Conservatives dominating that house. It was no longer possible for the Liberals, as it was in 1906, to regard themselves as the only large organized party.

Staaff had learnt the lesson of the consequences of the division between Government and party and made sure of his position by becoming chairman of the parliamentary party in 1912 in addition to being Prime Minister. Henceforth, his ministerial colleagues became ex-officio members of the party council.

Difficulties soon presented themselves to the Liberals once they were in power. Their three-point programme seemed clear enough in the election manifesto, but its simplicity was deceptive. Moreover, the moral courage required of the parliamentary party for its execution was considerable. Once the election was over there was less enthusiasm for putting the controversial

---

[1] Thermaenius, E., *Sveriges riksdag*, xvii. 213.

Prohibition programme into practice, and Staaff's cherished *parlamentarism* seemed premature.

Staaff had claimed that there would be no compromise over Liberal policy, but he was soon challenged when he announced his intention of lowering the sugar duty. The committee set up to investigate the question was not whole-heartedly in favour of his proposal and suggested a compromise solution. Members of Parliament who represented Scania constituencies (where sugar-beet was grown) objected to the lowering of the duty on imported sugar and finally Staaff accepted the committee's proposal, even though it ran counter to official Liberal policy. To pass the compromise *proposition* by 139 votes to 78, Staaff had to depend upon the support of the Conservatives to overcome the opposition of the Social Democrats and some Liberals. After listening to his speech in the Second Chamber, Branting coldly observed: 'It is more the lawyer than the statesman who speaks.'[1] Similarly, in order to pass his proposal to introduce old-age pensions in 1913, a bill which was described as 'mean' by some Left critics, Staaff once again had to take his majority where he could find it. In the style of a Boström he had become a 'zealous vote-catcher'.[2] Moreover, he who had so scorned the Conservatives' use of the Joint Vote now had recourse to it himself. Undoubtedly much play could be made over these developments, but it was the primary object of the Prime Minister to make sure of his majority in order that his Government might stay in office. Despite the Left's dominance of the Second Chamber and its control of the Joint Vote, 228 of the 380 seats in Parliament being held by the Left, the First Chamber was still overwhelmingly Conservative. To add to Staaff's difficulties, the ideas of the Social Democrats did not always coincide with his own.

The fate of the Ministry ultimately hinged on its rearmament policy. In fulfilment of his pledge to reduce arms expenditure, Staaff stopped construction of the Dreadnought on 15 December 1911, at a time when the Conservatives on their part were convinced that the international situation demanded an increase in naval armament. During the following year there were renewed rumours of Russian spies in disguise wandering through the country as saw-sharpeners, and the explorer Sven Hedin

[1] *A.k.* 1913, no. 18, p. 75.   [2] von Zweigbergk, op. cit., p. 60.

wrote *A Warning Word* to emphasize the Russian threat. No fewer than a million copies of the booklet were printed. To appease the incensed Russian Court the King and Queen paid a visit to the Tsar, warmly supported by the British Minister, Sir Cecil Spring-Rice, whom Lindman termed 'an extremely clever man'. The rank-and-file Conservatives followed the lead of a young schoolmaster, Manfred Björkuist, and subscribed money for the building of a Dreadnought. Seventeen million crowns were donated, whereupon the Government had no option but to accept the money and start construction. In 1913, as the danger of war increased, Staaff himself began to have doubts about his defence policy, and finally he became convinced that rearmament was necessary and that the period of conscription should be lengthened. However, he did not carry all his party with him, about 70 of the 152 Liberals in both chambers opposing his new policy. Moreover, thinking that he had received a mandate for a reduction in armaments at the 1911 election, Staaff was reluctant to betray the electorate by lengthening the period of conscription after promising to shorten it.

In December 1913 Staaff made a long-awaited public pronouncement upon the defence question in a speech at Karl-skrona. In it he virtually abandoned previous Liberal policy by promising his hearers that he would ensure an adequate rearmament programme to meet the present danger. He did not, however, say he would extend the period of conscription. This important step would have to wait until the election of September 1914 gave the electorate the opportunity to make its decision.

The King asked Staaff if he would advance the date of the Second Chamber election from September to the spring of 1914, but on 28 December 1913 Staaff replied that he could give no answer to this question, Thereupon, the King, angry at the prospect of a year's delay in the settlement of the conscription issue, asked several moderate-Liberals who were favourable to rearmament to be ready to form an alternative Ministry. They advised him to wait until Staaff had received the report of the Defence Preparatory Committee and had presented his bill to Parliament.

The country seems to have been sharply divided on defence policy. Many of the Liberals and Socialists who had supported disarmament in 1911 retained their beliefs, and disapproved of Staaff's Karlskrona speech. The moderate-Liberals who had supported rearmament as a group in 1911 had increased slightly in numbers. A large number of Conservatives, who were by no means confined to upper-class circles, definitely wanted re-armament. No longer, like the previous generation, radical in their political views and opposed to any form of defence ex-penditure, the more conservative farmers who supported Lind-man were eager to see a strong Sweden even if this meant a longer period of conscription. Those who remained of the old persuasion tended to be recalcitrant liberals, as difficult for Staaff to manage as the Farmers' party had been for Posse between 1880 and 1883. However, the greatest anti-militarist feeling was now to be found in the towns.

iv. *The Palace Yard Address, 1914*

On 6 February 1914, after long preparation, over 30,000 people, most of them farmers (hence the description *bondetåg*), marched through Stockholm to present an Address to the King and Ministry, and to hear the King speak to them in the Palace Yard. Naturally, many Conservative leaders were interested in this procession, but to regard its organization as a Conservative manœuvre is not entirely fair. Lindman himself later admitted that the procession consisted of at least 80 per cent Right-wing persons, and that its leaders were in many cases officers of Con-servative party organizations,[1] but the numerous farmers who marched were genuinely convinced that the Liberal Govern-ment was not being patriotic in its defence policy and needed a spur to action. They did not realize how much the King, and even more the Queen, welcomed the opportunity of showing sympathy for their cause.

King Gustav modified some of the remarks he intended to make on this occasion, but his speech was significant enough none the less. Particularly striking was the part:

There are certainly not lacking in our country those who are of the opinion that the period of conscription for our infantry may not be fixed now, but I by no means share that opinion; on the contrary, I am of the opinion which you have just expressed, namely that the

[1] *Lindmans samling*, ii. 144, 1 March 1914.

·defence issue ought to be discussed as a whole and decided now without delay and in one piece.

The procession moved on to the Government offices where
Staaff, unaware of the King's words, welcomed the farmers and
made a short speech in reply to their Address.

When Parliament met a day or two later there were angry
questions from members of the parties of the Left. Branting
described the King's action as unwarrantable; Professor Edén,
leader of the Second Chamber Liberals, expressed himself with
more restraint. Social Democrats in both chambers who referred·
directly to the King's speech were ruled out of order by the
Speakers.

The more moderate Conservative leaders professed disapproval of the Palace Yard speech. Lindman expressed in his diary
the opinion of a moderate-Conservative concerning the relations
between the Liberal Ministry and the King:

> But to understand the situation properly it must be remembered
> that these were men who openly told him that it was they who ruled
> and that he had only to sign their decisions. They had shown this
> many times—witness Staaff's Karlskrona speech, which was not
> given to him before its delivery. In other words, they wanted to re-
> introduce the Era of Liberty 'rubber stamp' [monarchy]. It is not
> surprising that the King should react to this.[1]

The first·reaction in the Ministry was that the Government
should resign, but calmer counsels prevailed and it was decided
to approach the King and obtain assurance from him that he
had not meant to act contrary to his Ministers' constitutional
advice. The Ministry therefore put two questions to him in
order to make sure that there would be no repetition of·such
incidents. They asked the King

1. Whether he considered he had committed himself to a
   particular standpoint with regard to the still unpublished
   proposition on defence, and

2. Whether in the future he would hear his Ministers' advice
   before making a public pronouncement.[2]

These appear to be fairly moderate demands. They were made

---

[1] *Lindmans samling*, p. 136, 10 February 1914.
[2] The correspondence is quoted in Hildebrand, op. cit. ii. 120–4.

privately and there seems to have been no question of taking advantage of the King, should he agree to meet them.

In reply to the first question Gustav said: 'As I have not yet seen the Government's proposal regarding defence, and still less the views of the military experts in the matter, it is impossible for me to answer this question before it comes up for decision.' Later, on the telephone, he added: 'This therefore means that I did not come to any decision in advance.' The answer of the King to the second question was as follows: 'It is clear that according to the Constitution I could not reach any definite decision in a question without first hearing my constitutional advisers' opinions or suggestions in the Council Chamber.'

This evasive statement did not satisfy the Ministry, which suggested the following text:

It should be made clear that my speech in the Palace Yard on February 6th was not intended to have any sort of official character, and in answer to the first and second questions I hereby declare that it was not my intention in any way to anticipate the examination I have to give to the forthcoming proposal of the Ministry for improving the national defences. This examination will be in all respects constitutional and consequently cannot be bound by any previous attitude on my part.

To this the King replied: 'This request I cannot grant, for I will not deprive myself of the right to speak freely with the Swedish people.' It was obvious that the King did not want to retract his statement in the Palace Yard. He even sent the whole correspondence to the Press. The Ministry therefore resigned on 10 February 1914, four days after the speech.

v. *The controversy over the King's Palace Yard Address*

The significance of the King's decision 'to speak freely with the Swedish people' so publicly demonstrated in the Palace Yard, has long been a subject of controversy between conservative and liberal historians in Sweden. In defence of the King it can be argued that he was primarily concerned with the dangerous international situation, and as head of the armed forces regarded himself as responsible for the safety of his people. It could hardly be said that he had not first reasoned with his Ministers; indeed, from 1911 onwards he had brought all his influence to bear to make them realize the seriousness of events on the Continent, but apparently in vain. Nor could it be suggested that the Liberal party itself had an agreed re-armament policy. At a meeting held four days before the Palace Yard address, when half the parliamentary Liberal party was present, a majority appeared to be opposed to an increase in the period of conscription. Hence occurred the King's remark to Staaff: 'You haven't even got your own party with you.'[1] Moreover, the Prime Minister had hardly taken Gustav into his confidence. In 1912 the King complained to Lindman that Staaff was impolite, that he did not visit him, and that he made no reports.[2] Staaff certainly did not consult him in advance of the Karlskrona speech in the manner which the King could expect of a Prime Minister about to initiate a major change in policy.

Nevertheless the King went farther than was necessary to emphasize his belief that a more adequate defence programme was required. Having read the proposed speech on 29 January, Lindman told the King that it would cause the Government's resignation, and that he should let Hellner and De Geer II also read it in order to be sure that an alternative moderate-Liberal Ministry was feasible. Like the moderate-Liberals when they were approached, Lindman suggested that the King could not properly take action until the Defence Preparation Committee had issued its report. The Crown Prince and the King's bro-thers also attempted to dissuade the King. He must have realized that he was about to act contrary at least to the spirit of the Constitution.

Staaff's attitude, like the King's, is defensible, but only in part. He was not alone, either in Sweden or abroad, in being slow to realize the danger of world war in 1914. It is to his credit that he was prepared to make a change in policy, going as far as he dared without risking a split in his party and the accusation of breaking his election promises. He believed that a Government had a duty to fulfil its mandate, and could have replied to the King's sugges-tion of an early election (though he refrained from doing so) that the same argument applied in 1914 as in 1906, when it was Staaff who wanted a dissolution of the Second Chamber: namely,

[1] von Zweigbergk, op. cit., p. 110.
[2] *Lindmans samling*, ii. 31, 28 February 1912.

that it was neither logically nor parliamentarily correct to dissolve a chamber which supported the Government. It is true that Staaff did not treat the King as a friend he could trust, but this was because he believed that the King had other advisers such as Sven Hedin, Trygger, and the ultra-Conservatives of the Court. Lindman himself noted: 'The King, however, seems determined not to alter the speech. It is clear that there are advisers behind the King, and I think I know who they are.'[1] Among them may be included the German-born Queen Viktoria, who disliked Staaff's aim of parliamentary government on the English model. Faced by these people, many of whom were *Junkers* whose influence was unknown to the general public, and yet who might betray his confidences to the King, Staaff defended what he regarded as the constitutional rights of the Prime Minister and his colleagues in a parliamentary system. It is difficult to pronounce judgement on the personal relations of Gustav and Staaff. It is true that the King never had such problems with any other Prime Minister throughout his long life, and it seems probable that Staaff's temperament made it difficult for them to work together. But it could be argued that something more than personalities was involved, and that it was Staaff's fight for constitutional propriety which made the King careful in future not to encroach upon the sphere of his Ministers.

In one respect at least, however, it is difficult to defend Staaff's actions. Having himself decided that rearmament was necessary, and yet believing that a mandate from the people was required to endorse this change of policy, he should have accepted the King's proposal of an early election. The very state of affairs which made this desirable—division within the Liberal party on the subject of rearmament—restrained Staaff. Under the circumstances, the Liberals could hardly fail to lose seats. Staaff may therefore be accused of putting his party before his country.

Not everybody was so conscious of the constitutional significance of the King's speech. Eighty-five Conservatives in the First Chamber and sixty-three in the Second issued a communiqué stating: 'Our people have no time to waste on fruitless and heart-rending constitutional struggles in view of the serious world situation.'[2] There was much to be said for this point of view. Yet in retrospect, because as it happened Sweden escaped the holocaust

---

[1] *Lindmans samling*, ii. 126, 29 January 1914.   [2] Hildebrand, op. cit., ii. 127.

of war, it is possible to assert that the constitutional aspect of the controversy was of greater ultimate importance. The King's action can perhaps be explained according to the traditional theory of the King as the Executive under a Constitution which established the separation of powers and gave Ministers only an advisory capacity. According to present-day notions of ministerial responsibility, however, such an explanation would be quite indefensible. In fact it is impossible to apply either standard of judgement since, more perhaps than any other event in modern Swedish history, this episode marks the watershed between the century of the separation-of-powers doctrine and the era of parliamentary government.

It was not immediately apparent that there had been a test of the Constitution and that the King would no longer act as the repository of executive power. Indeed the King seemed to have made a successful defence of his constitutional prerogative. In the special Second Chamber elections which followed the resignation of the Liberal Ministry, the Conservatives increased the number of their seats to 86 and the Social Democrats to 74, the Liberals being heavily defeated and obtaining only 70. The ordinary elections of September 1914 gave the Right 86 seats, the Social Democrats 87, and the Liberals a mere 57. In opposing Staaff in 1906 the King had enabled the Conservatives to pass their own reform bill. Now in 1914 he had again ousted a Liberal Government, giving heart to those forces who wanted greater armaments. By dissolving Parliament he demonstrated Staaff's weakness in the country, since the elections reduced the Liberal party to the smallest in the Second Chamber. Staaff never recovered from his second defeat and died the following year.

The King's victory was, however, more apparent than real. He never again tried to speak to his people, or intrigued behind the backs of his Ministers. Nor did he argue with his Ministers that as chief Executive he had the right to pursue a different policy from theirs. The age of the Monarch as Executive in Europe was almost over, and it was perhaps fortunate for Gustav that the issue was settled before war broke out and not later, in 1918, when monarchies were being overthrown throughout the Continent.[1]

[1] There were some Conservatives in 1914 who thought that if the elections went

The events following Staaff's resignation in February 1914 illustrated once again the importance of the centre in Sweden. It was the moderate-Liberals and moderate-Conservatives who dominated the political scene on his departure. Although there were *Junkers* in Sweden, as in Germany, these men were only important at Court, for real political power rested with members of Parliament where plutocratic business men like Lindman and Hellner were men of consequence. The government which Gustav wanted to succeed Staaff would have been led by Trygger, but the Conservative leaders politely told this aspirant for office that he was unacceptable. The final choice, Hammarskjöld, was not a parliamentarian but a civil servant, former Minister, international jurist and banker. Several of his colleagues were from the board of the Stockholm Private Bank. Business men and bureaucrats, not *Junkers*, formed Conservative Ministries in Sweden.

VI. *War, 1914–1917*

For the next three years, Government was carried on by a predominantly Conservative Ministry. Hammarskjöld showed the gift for conciliation he had already demonstrated at the Hague Court, and his war policy of strict neutrality was supported by the people. He set up a Defence Committee and made Staaff its chairman, and after the outbreak of war many of the old differences were buried. Much of the spark seemed to have gone out of the Left parties, Staaff's death in 1915 deepening the gloom in Liberal circles. At this time the King's policy seemed to have succeeded.

The year 1917 brought inflation, scarcity of food, and unrest to Sweden. Hammarskjöld's neutral policy prevented him from signing a commercial treaty with Britain in which the British proposed that in return for 90,000 tons of timber and a restriction on supplies of materials to Germany, thirty-three food ships would be allowed through to Sweden. It was generally believed that Britain wanted the resignation of Hammarskjöld before signing the commercial agreement. On the other hand, the Foreign Minister, K. A. Wallenberg the banker, was pro-Entente, as were the Liberals and Social Democrats. A monster petition signed by 600,000 people was presented in support of

against their party the King might have to abdicate or face revolution. See Clason's letters in *Historisk tidskrift 1951*, ii, p. 194.

Hammarskjöld, but after growing disharmony in the Ministry, the Government resigned, being defeated by the Left in the Second Chamber in the spring of 1917. Elections were due in September and meanwhile an interim Government under the moderate Swartz took office. Lindman became Foreign Minister, and the British treaty was signed. A few months later the Luxburg affair exposed the Diplomatic Service to the charge of having aided the Germans. Coming as it did in a year of shortages and misfortunes this news helped to turn opinion in favour of the parties of the Left at the September election, though there was less change than might have been expected in the circumstances. The Right admittedly lost 29 seats, but 14 of these were to a new party of farmers, who could still be called Right-wing. The Liberals obtained only 62 seats, and the Social Democrats actually lost a seat for the first time, but only because their party had also split, the Left Socialists, who later sympathized with Bolshevism, obtaining 11 seats, mainly in the north. Swartz resigned and the King had to form a new Ministry. On 5 October the Liberal parliamentary party met to discuss future policy, the first time it had done so in the long parliamentary vacation which often lasted from May to January. It was an important meeting because it seemed probable that the Liberals would be asked to form a Government.

If the fiascos of 1906 and 1914 were to be avoided it seemed advisable to the Liberals that a government of the Left should be as broadly based as possible. Moreover, now that the Social Democrats were the largest party in the Second Chamber it seemed important that they should be asked to take part in a coalition Ministry. Although much had happened to the Social Democratic party in the past quarter-century, it remained to be seen whether the party would support a policy of *minister-socialism*, and whether Gustav V would accept Social Democrat Ministers as suitable persons to be members of the King's Council of State. It is worth turning at this point to an examination of the rise of the party and the way in which its early revolutionary philosophy was abandoned in favour of the acceptance of the parliamentary system. It was this change which made possible the coalition Government of 1917, and the reconciliation of the King and Branting.

CHAPTER X

The Rise of the Social Democratic Party

1. *Its origins*

THE origin of Swedish Socialism has been traced back to 1831 when a bookseller named Per Götrek translated Saint-Simon and introduced French Socialist thought to Sweden. In 1845 the Stockholm Educational Circle was formed by men of liberal persuasion who dreaded the prospect of the evil effects of industrialism in England spreading to Sweden, and tried to bring culture and enlightenment into the lives of working men. But a much more significant event was the strike at Sundsvall on the north-east coast in 1879. Here for the first time there was evidence of collective action by the workers against their employers, and it was no accident that it should occur in an expanding new industry without traditions, the timber industry of northern Sweden.[1]

During the next ten years the Socialist movement established itself. The first piece of propaganda was *Folkviljan* (The Will of the People), published in 1882 by August Palm. In 1885 he founded the newspaper *Social Demokraten*, the editorship of which passed the following year to Hjalmar Branting, then still in his early twenties but already showing great promise as a gifted and intelligent writer and a wise counsellor. Branting was not by nature a revolutionary. Born in the same year as Karl Staaff, 1860, he attached himself to Staaff's Verdandi group at Uppsala University and decided to give up his career as a scientist. He is thought to have been converted to Marxism because it seemed complementary to Darwinism.[2] A visit to Germany, where he met several Socialists, confirmed him in his new beliefs, and on returning to Sweden he became a journalist. With a small legacy he helped the Socialist propagandists. He was twice fined for articles he published in *Social Demokraten* and in 1889 was sent to prison for three months.

---

[1] For a short account of the early development of Socialism, see Lindgren, J., *Från Per Götrek till Per Albin*, chap. 1.

[2] Boëthius, B., *Svenskt biografiskt lexikon*, vi. 18.

O

It was in this year that the constituent Congress of the Social Democratic party was held, Branting acting as secretary. It had the added distinction of being the only political party to have originated outside Parliament. Congresses were held in 1891, 1894, 1897, and 1900. But there were never more than a few dozen delegates, and few members were present at more than one meeting. Emigration was still considerable and many promising young men departed for the United States. By 1900 only Branting and Thorsson had attended all the congresses. The number of members was 10,000 in 1895, 67,000 in 1905, and 86,000 in 1915.

11. *The Social Democrats and Marxism*

The Swedish Social Democrats were not original political theorists. In their early years they brought ideas back with them from Germany and particularly from international conferences. The 1886 programme of inheritance taxes, eight-hour day, regulation of womens' work, and protective laws for workers was based on the German Socialists' 1875 Gotha Programme. At this time the policy of Branting and the party was orthodox Marxism. At Gävle in the same year Branting made a speech in which he attacked the bakery monopolies and prophesied that economic development might wipe out the middle classes. In that event 'the millionaires will stand alone against the hungry masses'.[1]

In 1891 the party had to decide whether or not to support the Liberals in the new suffrage movement. Its decision to co-operate was the first indication that it was prepared to compromise. For its vote did not favour infiltration, of which Marx would have approved and which had been successfully applied in 1885–6 to overcome the 'bourgeois' leaders of the trade union movement. It implied a definite partnership with liberal-minded people and though the Suffrage Association broke up when the liberals would not assent to direct action the friendships formed during the 1890's remained. In theory Freechurchmen and Social Democrats were opposed to one another, but their numerous common interests—opposition to the Established Church, humanitarianism, franchise reform, and temperance—brought about many useful personal contacts.[2] The co-operation

[1] Tingsten, op. cit., i. 151.
[2] Thörnberg, E. H., *Politiska partier och samhällsklasser*, p. 98.

of Branting with the Liberals in Parliament followed as a matter of course. Curiously enough, the opponents of the 1891 decision were anarchists rather than Marxists, and in so far as there was an opposition to Branting's middle-of-the-road policy, which was supported by the Fourth Scandinavian Workers' Conference in 1892,[1] it came from them. However, they were not excluded from the party.

The change from Marxism became more evident in 1897, six years after the publication of the German Socialists' Erfurt programme. The theme of the new Swedish programme, unlike that of its German counterpart, was evolution rather than revolution, the Social Democrats having discovered that it was not practicable to apply the Marxist theory to the Swedish situation. There was no large proletariat and even if the Socialists waited until the growing industrialism created one, Sweden would probably remain mainly an agricultural country with an urban proletariat which was but a minority of the population. Further, it was difficult to plead that the workers were being exploited at a time when the country, workers included, was experiencing a period of great prosperity. Nor did the simple Marxist formula of two main classes, bourgeoisie and proletariat, apply to Sweden, where the groups which Marx called petit-bourgeois were increasing in numbers and power, as the Liberal Party with its influx of elementary school teachers and countless *smâ-folk* was demonstrating. According to Marx's argument, this group should have been losing and not gaining in importance. In 1897 the doctrine of the Iron Law of Wages was dropped from the programme and in its place a project of State help for producer-associations was included. The nationalisation of the means of production was referred to, but not with the expectation that it would create a new society. Most important of all, it was agreed to support parliamentary and social reforms during the period before full socialization could be introduced.

Thus the party largely abandoned Marxism in practice. Partly this was due to the need to attract supporters, and partly because Marxist theory had never deeply affected the pragmatic Swedish Socialist movement. In endeavouring to win the trade unions and workers to their cause, the Social Democrats were competing with other organizations such as the Nonconformist

[1] Tingsten, i. 184–5.

churches and the temperance societies. These bodies influenced the main source of recruits, the trade unions. A trade union newspaper in the 1880's bore the slogan 'Help Yourself and God Will Help You'.[1] During the general strike of 1909 Prohibition was willingly accepted. Freechurchmen tended to support the Liberals owing to the hostility of many Socialist leaders to religion. However, the party did not become anti-clerical, and by abandoning its more doctrinaire policy it retained the support of trade unionists. Indeed, during a short interlude from 1898–1900 it was able to enforce the ruling that membership of the Trades Union Congress should be confined to Social Democrats. Attempts were increasingly made to extend the Social Democratic vote, and as the nature of the party changed, so its Marxism faded more and more into the background. The theory to which lip-service was paid and which at moments of crisis frightened the conservatives, was never put into practice.

III. *The importance of Branting*

Branting entered Parliament in 1897, with Liberal support, and was the solitary Social Democrat until 1903, when he was then joined by three others. During this period he established his unquestioned leadership of the party, and at the same time proved himself a good parliamentarian and popular member of the Second Chamber, sitting on committees and taking part in debates. There was a noticeable difference between the vociferous Branting who was the editor of *Social Demokraten*, and the restrained member of Parliament, representing a Stockholm constituency. The change in his attitude was not wholly due to the mellowing effect of Parliament: his opposition to violence had appeared as long ago as 1891.

Perhaps the most significant events in the development of Swedish Socialism were the times when Branting's point of view was challenged by rival and more revolutionary ideas. In 1886 there was the choice between him and more fiery Socialists for the editorship of *Social Demokraten;* in 1891 the Congress was presented with the alternative of anarchism; and in 1897 Branting asked the Congress to use the parliamentary method of securing power. Each time Branting carried the party with him. In 1899 the more extreme Axel Danielsson and Sterky both

[1] Tingsten, *Den svenska, &c.,* i. 71.

died before reaching middle age, and no one was left of Branting's stature. When a younger generation in the twentieth century fought for the succession, so great was his influence on the party that it was upon the shoulders of the more moderate Hansson and Möller that his mantle fell rather than upon Left-wing Socialists like Höglund. The party's choice perhaps typified the Swedish preference for moderate men to lead political parties.

As a leader, Branting proved himself more Swedish than Socialist. He favoured the nationalization of the northern iron-mines, but based his argument not on Socialist grounds but on the Swedish tradition of co-operation as in, for example, the old Bergslag mining region in central Sweden. Like other members of Parliament he treated each issue on its merits. Nor was there occasion for a parliamentary discussion of socialization or state ownership, since the only subjects for debate in Parliament were concrete proposals which could be referred to a committee.

The Swedish parliamentary system made it difficult for Branting, and later for his party, to persist in irresponsible opposition, because they had to take their place on committees, Branting serving on the Special Committee which discussed the reform bill in 1907. He somewhat distrusted the Liberals because he felt that the partisan attitude they sometimes adopted was to the detriment of Left co-operation, and Staaff for his part did not forgive the lapse of the Socialists in their support of DPR during the latter part of the 1907 debates. Branting himself, however, was personally popular. His honesty and good nature won him friends in Parliament even amongst those to whom intellectualism and atheism were anathema. Surprisingly perhaps, for a man of the Left, he had an aristocratic personality, and, like Staaff, was somewhat reserved in his private life.

The Socialist party was pledged not to take part in government with other parties, though as early as 1899 Branting commented sympathetically on Millerand's decision to enter the Waldeck–Rousseau Ministry in France.[1] By refusing to take part in a coalition government in 1911, Branting perhaps showed wisdom, since the party thereby escaped the fate of the Liberals in the 1914 elections. In late 1914 the party became the largest

[1] Höglund, i. 336. At the Amsterdam Conference of Socialists in 1904, Branting did not support the general opposition to *ministersocialism*.

in the Second Chamber and the question of eventual participation in government came to the fore. At the outbreak of war the Socialist parties in Europe had supported their respective governments, and in France they had broken the rule made some years previously that the party should not co-operate in government. Branting was wise enough to settle the issue of *ministersocialism* in Sweden before the matter became urgent. The 1914 Congress approved by 90 votes to 68 a motion to co-operate with the Liberal opposition, to support the neutrality policy of Hammarskjöld, and, when the time came, to take part in a government of the Left. Branting's 'Swedish' line defeated the policy of the internationalists.

The Young Socialists who by 1914 were not so much the younger members of the party as those who were to the left of Branting and the majority point of view, did not approve of this policy, but were unable to obtain control over the party newspaper or the parliamentary party, both of which were dominated by Branting and his friends.[1] They were particularly opposed to the independence of the parliamentary party and put forward a motion that its minutes should be examined by the Party Congress. They also proposed that the number of members of Parliament on the party council should be reduced. Branting strongly opposed this 'primitive democracy which originates in the belief that from the beginning the masses understood everything better than those who have insight and knowledge'. The opposition believed something different: they objected to Branting's 'Right-Socialism' and wanted perhaps not the anarchism proposed in the 1890's but at any rate a more independent and militant policy. Matters first came to a head in 1912 when the Party Council presented Sandler, Ström, and Vennerström with the alternative of resigning from the Young Socialists or from the party council on the grounds that no split should be allowed within the leading counsels of the group. For the time being the three elected to stay in the Party Council. However, the division within the party became so serious that in 1915 the party introduced a rule that a majority of the parliamentary party could make its decision binding on all members, who were forbidden to speak against it in the chambers. In the event of a division, they could absent them-

[1] See Edenman, R., *Socialdemokratiska riksdagsgruppen 1903–20*, passim.

selves but were not to vote against the party. This was the most serious attempt at party discipline in Sweden and was abandoned in 1919. Nor was it obeyed unconditionally, partly because, as Branting admitted, it was contrary to the Constitution. Nevertheless, the party council kept a watchful eye over the activities of the parliamentary party. Early in 1917 the Young Socialists at last decided to break away and to form the Left Socialist party. Its members sympathized with the Bolshevik revolution. However, they were not as successful at the polls in September 1917 as they had expected, and obtained only eleven seats. Six years later they applied for readmittance to the Social Democratic party.

Branting's success in retaining the support of the trade unions and Socialists for a policy which was rather a Right-wing Socialism may be attributed largely to his political flair. In smaller issues he tended to wait for the opinion of the party to crystallize and in 1911, when he had no definite opinion about entering the Government, he took a vote of the Social Democratic members of Parliament. On the two occasions when the fundamental policy of the party was at stake, however, he showed himself determined that it should follow him or choose another leader. The first was in 1891 when he presented the Socialist congress with the alternative of proceeding on parliamentary lines under his leadership or of choosing anarchism and receiving his resignation. In 1914 the party had to choose between accepting what Branting regarded to be the consequences of its position as the largest Second Chamber party and losing his services. He knew he was indispensable and the threat hardly needed to be uttered. Yet the result of his action was that the party which Branting in his youth had encouraged not to compromise with the bourgeoisie now committed itself to a series of alliances with bourgeois parties, the 'pure' Socialism of the early years being increasingly diluted as the years went by. The Swedish Democratic party confirmed Marxian prognostications in one respect: that a Socialist party which enters into partnership with the bourgeoisie loses its soul. This does not of course prove that the soul of the 1880's was worth saving.

The Congress supported Branting partly because there was no qualified alternative leader. Much of his support came from

the workers in the Stockholm *arbetarkommuner*, many of whom
were older men who had known Branting in his early days and
did not approve of the sniping tactics of the new generation.
The Left Socialists did not endear themselves to the rank and
file as a whole. Versatile, superficial, and inconsistent men
without staying power, they lacked the power of leadership and
were poor psychologists.[1] They looked upon Socialist policy as
one of immediate day-to-day tactics in the war against the
bourgeoisie and were not perturbed at a sudden change of front
if they thought the situation demanded it. A Lenin could have
succeeded in this manner, but not Hinke Bergegren or Zeth
Höglund, who were no match for Branting. His reasonable and
loyal demeanour when he differed from the party impressed his
followers in contrast to the abuse in which the Young Socialists
indulged when they found themselves in a minority.[2] The more
responsible of the younger generation felt a certain kinship with
Branting and became his loyal adherents. Thus when at the
time of the second reform bill in 1907 younger men like Möller,
Hansson, and Ström were dissatisfied with official policy and
thought that the party ought to rouse the workers against the
measure, Branting appointed them to the party committee
which discussed the bill. They soon ceased to talk of a general
strike and listened instead to lessons on parliamentary tactics.[3]
On the whole, opposition stemmed from young intellectuals
and not from the trade unionists, whose loyal support was
always forthcoming.

Branting's policy worked admirably. He was fair and tolerant
and set an example in co-operation with other parties and in
the acceptance of parliamentary institutions. The Young Socialist
who attacked him was treated so gently that he felt like Aneurin
Bevan in the House of Commons in 1929: 'the stone he thought
he had thrown turned out to be a sponge'. When at last the
split came in 1917, it was not unwelcome to the party, which
did not want to be burdened by extremists when it was accepting
responsibility for government. By this time the Social Democratic party considered that it represented the majority of the
people and not just a section of the population. It had even
made advances to the country dwellers, though without much

[1] Lindgren, J., *Per Albin Hansson i svensk demokrati*, p. 269.
[2] Edenman, R., p. 145.   [3] Lindgren, J., op. cit., p. 123.

success; like the Liberals, the Socialists discovered that vote catching was an important necessity. Although this was a long step from the anarchism that had been seriously discussed in 1891, it was the logical implication of the acceptance of parliamentary institutions in that year.[1]

[1] It is interesting to compare the rise of the Swedish Social Democratic party with the generalizations made by Roberto Michels in his *Political Parties*, pp. 161 ff.

CHAPTER XI

The Third Reform of Parliament

1. *Formation of the Coalition, 1917*

THE traditional disinclination of the Social Democrats to accept the responsibility of Government was only one of the obstacles in the way of a Left coalition. The other was the attitude of Gustav V towards leaders of a party which was pledged to republicanism at home and to a pro-Entente policy abroad. He feared for his crown and for the neutrality of Sweden. Yet it was clear to him that it was impossible to form a government from which the largest party in the Second Chamber was excluded. His first endeavour to minimize the influence of the Social Democrats consisted of an appeal to the Conservatives, Liberals, and Social Democrats to form a national coalition. However, the Liberals and Social Democrats were pledged to a programme of parliamentary reform, and to such action the Conservatives were unwilling to commit themselves.

The King then turned to Widén, a moderate-Liberal and Speaker of the Second Chamber, and asked him to form a Ministry primarily of the Centre, but containing elements of the Right (controversial figures like Trygger and Lindman to be omitted) and the Social Democrats. It proved impossible to attract any leading Conservatives, most of whom were members of the First Chamber, to this project. Swartz maintained that co-operation in such a Ministry would prejudice his position in the First Chamber. Edén and Branting told Widén that if authoritative Conservatives did not take part a 'clearly' Left Government must be appointed. Realizing that the former was impossible and that the latter would require a different Prime Minister, Widén gave up his attempt.[1] When informing the King of his failure, he pointed out that Gustav would have to reconcile himself to Socialist participation, and assured him that he need have no fear of republicanism, despite Lindhagen's attempt before the war to introduce a motion urging the creation

---

[1] See Gerdner, G., *Det svenska regeringsproblemet 1917–20*, p. 15.

of a republic. In October 1917 the King accepted the idea of a Liberal–Social Democrat coalition and contented himself with insisting that Edén, whom he called upon to form the Ministry, should appoint a reliable Foreign Minister pledged to the policy of neutrality. The moderate-Liberal, Hellner, was appointed to the general satisfaction of all parties. However, he was not altogether in favour of parliamentary reform, in which the Left had become increasingly interested since their victory at the polls, and took office on the understanding that he was not associated with the Government's domestic policy.

The Social Democrats accepted Edén's invitation to take part in the Ministry and were awarded four of the ten portfolios. However, there was some delay in the announcement of the names of the new Ministers owing to doubts about Branting's participation. At first the King thought he could exclude the Socialist leader on the grounds that he was really an atheist, having, in the days when a man had to profess some religion, registered as a Methodist because this was the only alternative to remaining in the State Church. Moreover, Ministers of the Crown were required to subscribe to the 'true evangelical faith', and Branting, even registered as a Methodist, failed to qualify in this respect. When it became clear, however, that Branting could not be excluded from the Ministry, it was discovered that he had forgotten to contract out of the Lutheran Church, and that his name was still on the register. Thus, after all, he was a Lutheran of the 'true evangelical faith'. He was appointed to the Finance Ministry, much against his will, and because he had no aptitude for figures he resigned three months later from the post. It then seemed curious that so much concern had been expressed about the appointment such a short while previously.

The new Prime Minister, Nils Edén, was very different from Staaff. He was forty-six years old, a professor of history at Uppsala, and one of the council of five who took over the leadership of the Liberal party on Staaff's death. Because he had been one of the Liberals who opposed Staaff's treatment of the King in 1914 he was able to placate Gustav, who told Lindman that he would be loyal to the new Ministers if they were honest with him.[1] Under Edén the coalition became a strong united Ministry.

The 1917 coalition Ministry was the first Government in

[1] *Lindmans samling*, ii. 229, 15 October 1917.

which politicians who were party leaders in the Second Chamber governed with the pledged support of a majority of members in the lower house. In the nineteenth century Ministers were rarely politicians or party leaders, and never received a pledge of support from a reliable majority of the Second Chamber. The support usually given was that of the First Chamber and was not guaranteed by party discipline. After the dissolution of the union with Norway in 1905, Ministries came to depend more on the support of the Second Chamber than on the First. Nevertheless both Staaff and Lindman led minority governments, and during Staaff's second Ministry the Social Democrats, though well-disposed, remained outside the Government and gave no pledge of support. Hammarskjöld governed by virtue of the passive acquiescence of the Left between 1914 and 1917. Now, for the first time a Ministry could rely on a majority of the Second Chamber, comprising 62 Liberals and 86 Social Democrats in a house of 230. Moreover, there were 45 Liberals and 16 Social Democrats in the First Chamber. Although the Government was in a minority in this chamber, these 61 members, added to the 148 in the Second Chamber, were sufficient for the Government to control the Joint Vote. Out of 380 members of the Swedish Parliament 209 were pledged to support a Government composed of leaders of their own parties.

This event, therefore, is considered an important milestone in Swedish constitutional development. It signified the victory in Sweden, not of the lower-house version of *parlamentarism* so dear to Staaff, but of a system of government in which the support of Parliament was clearly the over-riding fact. It indicated that the separation of powers as laid down in 1809 was no longer fully appropriate.

Before accepting office Edén obtained two pledges from the King. The first was a promise not to allow anyone to come between him and his constitutional advisers; the second was to dissolve the Second Chamber if the First Chamber proved obstinate in its attitude towards parliamentary reform. The battle of the Liberals with the Crown was over, the King having been forced to support the Government whatever might be his personal inclinations. Constitutional development had been swift, and it had taken all the energies of the Liberal party to achieve it. Enough strength remained for the passing of the

third parliamentary reform of 1918 before the Liberal party
began to break up.

11. *The first reform bill of 1918*

In Sweden, as in many other countries, the First World War
completed the emancipation of women, politically as well as
socially. The introduction of women's suffrage was almost a
foregone conclusion by 1918. Immediately after the passage of
the 1907 reform bill, Staaff had adopted women's suffrage as
part of his programme, despite his rejection of the principle of
universal suffrage in 1906. At that time his energies were concentrated upon lower-house *parlamentarism* and not upon the
small Swedish suffragette movement. However, petitions were
submitted by women's organizations for the extension of the
franchise, and, since the local government decree of 1862
awarded women the commune vote, there could hardly be a
rejection of the petitions on the grounds that women were
unsuited by nature to political responsibility. The Liberals
therefore put universal suffrage in their programme in 1907,
one year after its adoption in Finland. The second Liberal
Government introduced a reform bill in 1912 for women's
suffrage, and at the same time proposed the abolition of the
legal persons' (business premises') vote. Both bills were defeated
by the First Chamber.

Staaff's lower-house *parlamentarism* was less attractive to the
Liberals once the one man who really believed it was feasible
died in 1915. Edén realized that in supporting further parliamentary reform the Liberals must make sure that it should not be
to their disadvantage. The extension of the franchise to women
seemed harmless enough, since it could be assumed that their
vote would be distributed roughly in the same proportions as
men's. On the other hand, there remained the serious problem
of the composition of the First Chamber. The Liberals wanted
to deprive the Conservatives of their power but did not want
to transfer it to the Social Democrats. In 1915 Gunnar Rexius
published his book on the operation of the bicameral system
in Sweden. He compared it with the American system and
pointed out that the difference between the two houses of Congress was the result not of financial qualifications of membership

but of the different method of election.[1] The book offered Edén the solution he sought. Even if the financial franchise qualifications of the First Chamber were removed, its more conservative (i.e. non-Socialist) character could be preserved by means of indirect election, longer period of office, re-election by stages, and so on. Thereupon the Liberal party quietly dropped its programme of lower-house *parliamentarism*.

Early in 1918 the Liberal–Social Democrat Government introduced its first reform bill. The main provision was an extension of the First Chamber franchise to all taxpayers equally, thus abolishing the forty-grade scale and the business premises' vote. Some of the younger Social Democrats pressed for universal suffrage irrespective of taxes paid, and even asked for the abolition of the First Chamber, but the majority of the party approved of the Government's proposal, which was passed by the Second Chamber. The Liberals had more than won their point. Not only did the First Chamber retain the characteristics which Rexius had said marked the more conservative house from the popularly elected chamber, but it still retained certain financial qualifications. Voters were required to be taxpayers, and members had still to be in possession of property valued for taxation at 50,000 crowns or income of 3,000 crowns annually.

Nevertheless the bill was defeated in the First Chamber because it was considered to be too radical a measure by the defenders of plural voting. The Right argued that De Geer had intended the composition of the First Chamber to be different from the Second, and that the Parliament Act of 1866 provided for the representation of various interests. They added that those who had a greater stake in local affairs (i.e. those who owned more property) should have a correspondingly greater number of votes when electing the Provincial and Town Councils which appointed members of the First Chamber. The bill was defeated by 70 votes to 48, and thus at the end of the 1918 session Parliament broke up for the long vacation still no nearer to the settlement of the reform question.

III. *November, 1918: fear of revolution*

Some months later, Parliament convened in special session on 30 October 1918 to deal with the rise in prices and, in particular,

---

[1] Rexius, p. 305.

its effect on civil service salaries. Edén had discussed the matter of reform with Swartz on 17 September, and had then met Lindman and Trygger. The Conservatives rejected his proposal for an all-party reform and would not even promise to co-operate in a committee of inquiry to prepare a measure for the 1919 session which met in January. The outlook for Edén was not hopeful since he required the votes of about a dozen First Chamber Conservatives if any future reform bill was to become law.

No progress had been made when Parliament assembled. Early in November Edén approached the Conservatives again, but without success although this time the King and Crown Prince put pressure on the Conservative leaders. They insisted on waiting until their party met on 15 November and refused to advance the date of its meeting. Moreover, they held that an extraordinary session was incompetent to deal with questions affecting the fundamental laws. As Lindman was to put it in the final debate on the third reform bill in the Second Chamber on 17 December 1918, he could 'scarcely believe that it was the opinion of the framers of the Constitution that such an important question should be dealt with among the special issues the settlement of which the King could constitutionally put in the hands of an extraordinary session of Parliament'.[1] In this the Conservatives were constitutionally correct, but events in Europe were not waiting upon constitutional rectitude. When at last the Conservatives did bring forward the date of their meeting to the 13th and on the 14th agreed to a measure of reform, it was too late.

On the same day, the 14th November, Edén put forward a second and more radical proposal which no longer required that voters should pay direct taxes. The Government had decided to go forward without conservative support, to the chagrin of Lindman and Trygger.

There was reason for Edén's haste. No one quite knew what effect the armistice was having upon the workers, and certainly the tone of the Left Socialists was not reassuring. On 11 November they had issued a communiqué calling for workers' and soldiers' soviets, the end of the monarchy and the First Chamber, a constituent National Assembly, land division, control of

[1] *A.k.* no. 17, p. 10, *Urtima*, 1918.

industry by the workers and preparations for a general strike. The Social Democrats and trade unions arranged a great meeting for 14 November in the People's House (*Folkets Hus*) in Stockholm to decide what was to be done at this crucial period. Fearful that there would be resentment at the delay in reforming Parliament and that the meeting might even resolve to abolish the First Chamber or even set up a republic, the Liberals hastened to make their second offer prior to the meeting. The King saw Branting and impressed upon him the need for strong leadership at this time of crisis.

The People's House was filled, and overflow meetings were held in other halls. Between speeches the crowd sang the Marseillaise and Internationale, but appeared willing to follow its leader provided he could give them adequate guidance. This is said to have been Branting's greatest hour. He rose to the occasion in masterly fashion. He was able to tell his audience that he had seen the King, whose attitude towards the international and national situation was encouraging, and that the workers had nothing to fear from the Monarch, who understood the need for reform better than the Conservatives. Branting had, moreover, been invited to Petrograd and, seeing for himself what Communism meant, had not liked what he saw. Speaking with direct knowledge of the Russian revolution, he rejected the arguments in favour of Bolshevism in Sweden. Finally and most important of all, he was able to announce the new proposals by the Government promising universal suffrage to the First Chamber. The meeting accepted his advice to support them and agreed to postpone the discussion of the abolition of the monarchy until 'the majority of the people express themselves in favour of this course through a referendum'. Nothing was said about the First Chamber, the general view being that the proposals of reform would solve this problem automatically.

The next day Socialist and Trade Union headquarters speedily dispatched a million copies of the resolutions to all branches throughout the country to check the revolutionary ferment. Two days later the danger of revolution was over. The Conservatives, still apparently unaffected by what was going on, at first issued a guarded communiqué on the subject of reform, . but a few days later accepted universal male and female suffrage for the First Chamber as well as the Second. On the 22nd of

November the Government bill was presented and a Special Committee set up, its chairman being Hjalmar Branting.

The Government had introduced a measure of parliamentary reform at an extraordinary session of Parliament. The speed of events and the danger of revolution were held responsible for this unusual step, many people undoubtedly being influenced by developments on the Continent. The King was particularly anxious for the safety of the Queen, who was in Germany. He was alarmed by the spectacle of monarchies throughout Europe being swept away by revolution, and his old fears of the Socialists and their threat of a republic in Sweden were revived. The Police Chief of Stockholm reported that even the Horse Guards were unreliable and that only the police and volunteer *Landstorm* were not affected. Bolts were taken out of army rifles.[1] On 11 November the War Department received the report of the IVth Army Division in which the grave effect of anti-militarist propaganda on the troops was described.[2] On 12 November the two Defence Ministers reported that the attitude of the Army and Navy was revolutionary. For four years the armed forces of Sweden had been mobilised but inactive, and it was not surprising that now that the danger was over the effect of the relaxation of tension should be in some ways similar to that of the defeated armies on the Continent. There appears to have been good reason for the decision of Edén to prepare new reform proposals and not wait for the Conservatives to approve them.

Nevertheless the suggestion has been made by a Social Democrat historian that the threat of revolution of 11 and 14 November was nothing but a bluff on the part of the Social Democrats, and that in fact at no time were they prepared to use unparliamentary means of obtaining power.[3] The evidence suggests that there was at least some bluffing by the Left. It seems hardly probable, in view of Lindman's appreciation of people and events, that the Right could be so unaware of the danger of revolution that they could continue prevaricating before, during, and after the meeting of 14 November. Lindman later described the presentation of the reform bill to the extraordinary session

[1] Hildebrand, ii. 290.
[2] Lindgren, *Per Albin Hansson*, p. 412.
[3] See Lindgren's chapter *Den stora bluffen* (The Great Bluff).

as being in the nature of a *coup*.[1] Indeed, the Conservatives' chief reaction was that the Liberals had stolen a march on them. At first they opposed it, but a few days later recognized their diplomatic defeat and accepted Edén's new measure. In the debate of 17 December 1918 Trygger and other Conservatives were still complaining that the Liberals and Social Democrats had forced their measure on to Parliament by constantly harping on the revolutionary times in which they were living, as though Sweden were in the same state as the defeated Powers on the Continent.[2]

A revolution in Sweden would have required leadership, presumably from the one revolutionary party, the Left Socialists. They numbered only 20,000 compared with Branting's 120,000 Social Democrats and, in addition, the party was completely unprepared for action. Not one of its leaders was a practical man with the gift of organization and the military grounding required. One of the few victories of the Left Socialists (or Young Socialists as they then were) over Branting had been a resolution passed by the Social Democratic Party Congress in 1908, when, in opposition to the Government's defence policy, it encouraged anti-militarist propaganda and dissuaded members from entering sharpshooter organizations. The result of this was apparent ten years later: neither Socialist party was capable of using force. The Young Socialists had defeated themselves. In April 1917, at the time of the potato famine, there was considerable unrest and a procession of workers went to the Parliament Building. On this occasion the Young Socialists missed their opportunity of leading a revolutionary movement by letting the orthodox Per Albin Hansson come out of the chamber and address the crowd. Consequently, it did not surprise Hansson, at any rate, when the Left Socialists, having issued their manifesto on 11 November, waited for someone else to give a lead. Three days after the meeting in the People's House they meekly agreed to co-operate with Branting, whom they had called a lackey of Entente capital and a dictator blindly followed by the workers.

---

[1] *A.k.* no. 17, p. 12, *Urtima*, 1918.

[2] *F.k.* no. 10, p. 12, 1918. Both the Government bill and the committee's report laid great stress on the events on the Continent, the committee quoting with approval Wilson's remark: 'The world must be made safe for democracy.'

The more moderate views of the Social Democrats were summed up by Hansson in *Social Demokraten* (to which he had succeeded Branting as editor) on 14 November 1918: 'We do not allow ourselves to be either frightened or seduced into going the adventurous and, for the working class, fateful way of Bolshevism. Democracy and dictatorship are enemies. We fight *for* the former, *against* the latter.' Hansson had used all his authority in February 1918 to prevent the party from supporting the Finnish Social Democrats on the grounds that they had resorted to arms instead of using their parliamentary majority.[1] In this attitude he differed sharply from Left Socialists like Vennerström who gave the Finnish Reds whole-hearted support.

Yet the Social Democrats, Branting excepted, cannot be excused all blame for the excited state of public opinion. Hansson himself made a speech at Linköping on 1 December 1918, when the Special Committee was beginning its deliberations, in which he threatened strike action if the Conservatives did not accept the Government's proposals. He reminded his hearers that threats had not been absent in 1865: 'When the decision was reached there stood great crowds outside the *Riddarhus*, among them several of Blanche's sharpshooters. It is illustrative of the feeling of the time that afterwards August Blanche expressed his gratification that "Stockholm's streets did not need to be dyed red with the Nobles' blood".'[2] It was the oratory of the moment, and did not mean so much as opponents of the Socialists like to read into it. The party ultimately depended on the sober words of Branting, who admittedly in the final debate on the reform bill still maintained that the Social Democrats were not satisfied with the bill and looked forward to the time 'when the democratic republic will be general in civilised countries', but nevertheless agreed that this question, like that of a unicameral system and the executive power was 'not so thoroughly discussed and so clearly formulated that one can say there is a definite public opinion in favour of one or the other'.[3] When challenged, the party could look back upon this period with some pride in its restraint.

The Liberals and Socialists had good reason to be thankful for the turn of events in November 1918. There had been very

[1] Lindgren, pp. 368-70.   [2] Lindgren, p. 402.
[3] *A.k.* no. 17, p. 29, *Urtima*, 1918.

little disturbance, but sufficient threat of it to alarm some of their opponents. They could not have been unaware of the effect of the crowd upon the *Riddarhus* in 1865, and of how the lack of popular support in 1906 had contributed to the victory of the First Chamber. Had outside pressure not been applied in the autumn of 1918, the Conservatives might have repeated their tactics of the spring and summer, waiting until the Government fell, when they could introduce a milder reform of their own. They had not anticipated the sudden end of the war, nor the quick action by which the Liberals and Socialists, as Edén admitted, took advantage of the psychological moment.[1] The Liberals seem to have been able to make a nice calculation of the extent to which they needed to modify their proposals. If there had really been danger of revolution, the concession over the franchise was hardly sufficient to arrest it, considering that the property qualifications of the First Chamber members were left untouched. As for the Social Democrats, they were undoubtedly excited by the revolutions in Europe, and naturally believed that this would hasten the Socialist millenium, but there was little enough indication that violence might result. In November 1918 there were disturbances in Denmark, Switzerland, and Holland but there were none in Sweden.[2]

IV. *The passing of the third reform of Parliament, 1918–1919*

The Special Committee set up under Branting as chairman began its work early in December and took only a week to make its recommendations. Among its twenty-four members was a strong body of Conservatives, including Trygger, Lindman, and Swartz. They were relieved that they were not being forced to accept a Socialist reform, while the Social Democrats for their part realized that their chances of success in the First Chamber were greater if the bill was sponsored by the Liberals.

The report of the committee was issued on 14 December. It bore the marks of compromise and much hard bargaining. All were agreed that women should vote on equal terms with men, and the Liberals succeeded in their aim of abolishing plural voting and the business premises' vote, privileges which had assisted the Conservatives in controlling the First Chamber. Owing to the pressure of events, however, they had been com-

[1] *K.p.* no. 34, p. 44, *Urtima*, 1918.   [2] Lindgren, p. 396.

pelled to acquiesce in a further extension in November 1918, and agreed to allow everybody, whether taxpayers or not, to vote in the commune elections which indirectly elected the First Chamber, thus satisfying the Social Democrats. The age at which a man might vote for members of the Second Chamber was lowered from 24 to 23, but the commune franchise was at the same time raised from 21 to 23. Members of the Provincial and City Councils were to be at least twenty-seven. No change was made in the financial qualifications of members of the First Chamber. Several other changes in the electoral system, however, deserve noting. Second Chamber constituencies were to be large enough to appoint at least five members. The First Chamber was to be elected for eight years instead of nine, and the Second for four instead of three. In the cities, special electoral colleges replaced the city councils in the election of First Chamber members.

The third reform, which extended the franchise to 3,200,000 people, was the last important reform of Parliament. Some parts were passed by the special session, but those which involved a change in the Parliament Act had to wait until the regular session of 1919. These received their second assent in 1921 after the Second Chamber elections of September 1920.

The swift passage of these bills is in strong contrast to the long-drawn-out negotiations of 1906-7. The vital stages were those preceding the setting up of the committee, and consisted of the Conservatives' refusal to co-operate with Edén, the Liberals' adoption of universal suffrage to the First Chamber as well as the Second, and the acceptance of the Liberal proposals by the Social Democrats. Thus one member, Ericsson of Aaby, openly admitted at the beginning of the reform debate in the First Chamber on 17 December 1918, that the issue had already been settled before the debate began. All parties agreed with the Special Committee's recommendations, even the reluctant Trygger.

Thus ended the great period of parliamentary reform in Sweden. The 1866 Act had replaced the Estates with a popularly elected Second Chamber and a senatorial upper house. In 1907 the franchise to the Second Chamber had been widened and the various property qualifications abolished. The franchise for the indirectly elected First Chamber was extended in 1907,

but the restrictions upon it were only ended in 1919. Nevertheless, after all the reforms the First Chamber remained different
from the Second. The property qualifications of members, its
indirect electoral system, the longer tenure of members, and the
higher mimimum age for council electors (27) and members
(35) ensured that it would have a more conservative flavour.
In introducing the bill Edén had answered the Conservative
criticisms by saying, 'far from conflicting with the basis of the
Swedish bicameral system, it must be considered a return to the
principles on which it was originally based'.[1] Nevertheless, by
passing this measure, in contrast to the effect of their assent in
1865 and 1907, the Conservatives allowed the Liberals to put an
end to the control over the Swedish Parliament by the 'gentry'
of the First Chamber. In 1921 the number of Conservative
members of the upper house was reduced to thirty-seven. The
Social Democrats, in contrast, numbered fifty.

[1] *K.p.* no. 34, p. 55, *Urtima*, 1918.

CHAPTER XII

Parliament since 1919

I. *Further reforms*

IT was clearly only a matter of time before the remaining
disqualifications in the electoral system would be amended
or removed. In 1922 the franchise bar against men who were
not liable for military service was abolished. After 1936 convic-
tion for a criminal offence ceased to entail permanent dis-
franchisement and after 1945 bankrupts and persons on poor
relief were enabled to vote. The minimum age for exercising the
franchise was gradually lowered, the first change taking place in
1937 when the age of special electors of the First Chamber was
lowered from 27 to 23, becoming the same age-limit as for other
electors. In 1945 the minimum age for all electors became 21.
The minimum age of members of the First Chamber was reduced from 35 to 23 in 1953. Possibly the most important
financial barrier, the property qualification of First Chamber
members, was removed in 1933. In recent years, sessions of
Parliament have lengthened considerably, so much so that in
1949 the distinction between ordinary (*lagtima*) and extraordinary or special (*urtima*) was abolished. Since 1921, the
Chambers have appointed their own Speakers.

II. *Proposed changes*

Many proposals were made, but not all were successful. For
example, the Liberals frequently proposed the reallocation of
seats to make the proportional system work more fairly; the
Conservatives, until the onset of the Depression, wanted to
restore the tax qualification, and the Farmers' Association, in
1933, wanted to exclude civil servants from Parliament. Two
questions, the ending of proportional representation and the
abolition of the First Chamber, were discussed at some length.
  In the 1920's some Social Democrats thought that the multi-
plicity of parties which prevented a strong, stable (and probably
Social Democratic) government from obtaining power was the

result of proportional representation. The party leaders replied that the system reflected the divergent views of the nation, but was not their cause. In answer to suggestions that the British system of single-member constituencies was perhaps preferable to large electoral districts returning several members, they argued that the British experience of single-member constituencies was different from the Swedish, and that it was an oversimplification to attribute the strength of British government to the two-party system. Moreover, there were many disadvantages in the British type of parliamentary government. The majority party in England, they said, was composed of heterogeneous elements and was not so strong as was popularly supposed. There was often no party with an absolute majority of seats, and when there was a majority it often bore little relation to the votes cast in the election. In Sweden, on the other hand, where personality and leadership counted for less, and general agreement within Parliament for more, there was less need for an absolute majority. P. A. Hansson replied to suggestions for changing the electoral system by saying that the Swedish tradition was to put policy and programmes before men. Parliamentary committees treated measures on their merits, and members did not support or reject them because of loyalty to the proposers or oppose them because they did not approve of the Government in power. This interesting discussion of the electoral system died down in the 1930's after the Social Democrats obtained power. It then became evident that no changes in the system would radically alter the balance of power.

The future of the First Chamber was discussed during debates on constitutional reform in the 1953 session. A Liberal proposal to abolish the chamber was not, however, supported by the other three main parties, although the unicameral system had long existed in Norway and Finland and was introduced into Denmark in 1953. The Swedish Social Democrats in particular did not favour the abolition of the chamber in which their majority now resided. Parliament agreed to press the Social Democratic Government to present proposals within the next three years for the extension of the advisory referendum and for a definite regulation of the Second Chamber's electoral system, and at the same time the Government was asked to report on the position and functions of the First Chamber, i.e. the bicameral system. Among other proposals the Government was asked to consider were successive instead of simultaneous debate by the Chambers and proportional instead of equal representation of the two chambers on committees. 'The truth seems to be that the inclination is towards the creation of a First Chamber which can not only safeguard political continuity but also serve as a revising chamber, as it can hardly be said to do in its present form.'[1]

There was one curious result of the conservative qualifications which the Social Democrats permitted Edén to retain in his reform of Parliament. Although for about twenty years the percentage of seats which the Social Democrats won in the First Chamber tended to be considerably lower than their representation in the Second, when the time came for the party to receive its first setbacks in the Second Chamber there was no reflection of this tendency in the First Chamber. In 1941 the Second Chamber Social Democrats reached the peak of their power with 134 seats. These were reduced to 115 in 1945 and 112 in 1949. In the First Chamber, in contrast, the number of Social Democrats continued to increase, rising from 75 in 1941 to 83 in 1945. In 1947 the number was 86, and was still 84 in 1949. In this year the Social Democrats had an absolute majority only in the First Chamber. The conservative qualifications could work both ways!

III. Governments after the third reform of Parliament

Once the reform of Parliament was achieved, the coalition became less harmonious. Personal relations, thanks to Edén's leadership, remained cordial, but there were differences of opinion on social and financial policy. The Ministry resigned in 1920 and Branting took office as Prime Minister of the first Social Democratic Government. Six months later the Second Chamber elections took place. Of the electorate 55 per cent. voted and the Conservatives gained some ground. None of the parties was willing to form a Government on a minority basis, and the Liberals, the centre party, would co-operate with neither Right nor Left; the King therefore fell back on a bureaucratic caretaker Ministry, under Louis De Geer II. Only one member of Parliament was in the Ministry, which lasted

[1] *The Anglo-Swedish Review*, June 1953, p. 102.

until the new First Chamber elections in 1921. In this campaign
the Social Democrats played down their socialization propaganda and scored a victory. Once again the King suggested a
coalition, but when this proved unsuccessful the Social Democrats formed a 'Swedish popular national' government. It was
defeated in 1923 by an adverse vote in the First Chamber, the
last occasion on which this chamber forced the resignation of a
Ministry.

The period 1920–32 was one of minority Governments. On
two occasions the Liberals took office despite their small numbers, relying for success alternately on the Socialists and the
Conservatives, but their 'hopping' (*hoppande*) majority ended
when the other two groups came together and agreed not to
encourage these tactics. It was the inability of the parties to
work together which was the main reason for the absence
of stable parliamentary government during this period. The
Socialist aim of strong government based on a firm majority in
the Second Chamber, was realized after the 1932 elections. The
Right declined in numbers from 73 to 58, the rump of the two
Liberal parties (which had split in 1924 over temperance)
being a mere 24. The Socialists increased the number of their
seats from 90 to 104 and the Farmers' Association, formed in
1917, from 27 to 36. The second Liberal government resigned
after the election and the Prime Minister's implication in the
Kreuger crash,[1] and the Social Democrats, armed with a plan to
deal with the Depression, eagerly took office. They realized that
to have a majority they needed allies, and they surprised the
Liberals and Conservatives by making an agreement called 'cow
bartering' (*kohandel*) in colloquial Swedish and 'log rolling' in the
United States. They made an alliance with the farmers and
obtained an absolute majority in both chambers. Like the old
Farmers' party the Farmers' Association refused to take a share
in government but was not unwilling to support the Socialists in
the harmonious co-ordination of farmer-producers and worker-

---

[1] Kreuger had built up a world business organization based on the Swedish
Match Company. Realizing that he had taken too many legal and financial risks
when he was overtaken by the Depression, he committed suicide in Paris in March
1932. It was then discovered that Ekman had received 50,000 crowns from Kreuger
for the Liberal Party organization. Later, despite his persistent denials, it was
proved that Ekman had also accepted 50,000 crowns as a personal gift from
Kreuger.

consumers especially through the development of co-operatives within and without the Socialist movement. Each party sacrificed some of its ambitions, but the Socialists achieved their main aim of rescuing the country from the slump by a policy of public works and credit-spending which their economists had prepared. In June 1936 the understanding came to an end when the Government was defeated over its defence policy. The Farmers' party took office until the Second Chamber elections in September, after which the Socialists were returned, only four short of an absolute majority. They formed a new ministry in which the Farmers' party had four seats.

During the Second World War there was a coalition of all parties except the Communists. When it broke up after the war the Socialists formed their own government. In 1946 there occurred the death of Per Albin Hansson, who had led the party since Branting's death in 1925, and a third-generation Social Democrat, Tage Erlander, became Prime Minister. The party lost three seats in 1948 and came to depend on the support of other parties, sometimes the Communists, for its majority in the Second Chamber; in the First it retained control. The Communists proved a difficult ally and were abandoned in 1951 when the efforts of 1932 were repeated and a Coalition Government of Social Democrats and Farmers was formed. The decline in the number of Social Democrat and Communist seats in the 1952 election, to 109 and 5 respectively, meant that a majority coalition of these parties in the Second Chamber was impossible. This increased the dependence of the Social Democrats on the Farmers' party, since it could be assumed that no offers of partnership with the Socialists would be made by the Liberals or Conservatives.

Thus two distinct periods emerge from a survey of the thirty years after 1921. Until 1932 there was a succession of minority Governments (*minoritetsparlamentarism*) with a change of Ministry at each election and often in between. This was followed by *majoritetsparlamentarism*, i.e. Government supported by one or more parties and for the most part possessing a majority in both chambers.

CHAPTER XIII

Conclusion

I T was suggested in the Preface that the three reform bills were important not only in themselves but in 'the wider context of the country's social, political and constitutional development'. In conclusion, therefore, it may be appropriate to discuss the background against which the reform of Parliament took place.

1. *The social background; The rise of new classes and ideologies*

In their social context the three reform measures extend over the period of transition from the old semi-feudal world of the *ancien régime* to the modern welfare state. Each bill, in a sense, signified the rise of a new class which claimed political power. First there developed the middle class of bankers, merchants, ironmasters and others like them who benefited from the bill of 1866. They were followed by the lower middle class, many of whom were Nonconformists, who were to a large extent responsible for the agitation leading to the unsuccessful reform bill of 1906 and the Reform Act of 1907. Lastly, there arose the organised working class who, through their unions, demonstrated their new power in the events of November 1918.

The period between 1866 and 1921 may with some justification be called the 'Liberal Era' in Sweden. However, the generic term 'liberal' not only included many different shades of opinion but, as the period wore on, changed its dominant meaning considerably.

The earlier part of the era may more precisely be called the economic-liberal period. The 'victory of Liberalism' in 1866 meant the rise of an economically powerful middle class. As was suggested in Chapter v, the size of this middle class may easily be overestimated. The majority of the electorate remained farmers, as the size of the Farmers' party in the Second Chamber indicated. Amongst the *herrar* in the First Chamber were many who could more accurately be called landowners, or servants of the Crown. However, the period from 1866 to about 1900 was dominated, at least ideologically, by the prosperous middle class of the industrial revolution. It was they who were responsible for the economic changes which took place with increasing speed. Many of the nobility and even farmers, for example Hans Andersson of Nöbbelöv, became entrepreneurs or came to share the capitalist outlook. It is true that among the liberals who supported the 1866 reform there were radicals and moderates as well as economic-liberals. In retrospect, nevertheless, it is apparent that the victory, as Hedin remarked, belonged mainly to the commercial and industrial middle class whose economic policies had suffered from the cumbersome political operations of the Estates. Politically, this class became increasingly conservative.

Consequently, by the time that the lower middle class asserted itself, inaugurating what may perhaps be best termed the political-liberal period about 1900, the older economic-liberalism had become a conservative force. The political-liberal era of 1900–20 may be distinguished from its predecessors by the greater political and social consciousness of those who called themselves liberal. In come ways these later liberals might be compared with the earlier radicals, with whom they were connected through the aged Adolf Hedin. There was, however, no return to the Utopian radicalism of the 1830's, because the political-liberals, like the economic-liberals, owed their influence to their class interests. The 'small folk' as they were than called, rather different from the 'white collar workers' of today, could be compared in some respects to the people who supported Gladstone and later Liberal leaders in Britain between 1880 and the First World War. Staaff himself was no 'Whig' like De Geer, but of middle-class origins, while his choice of colleagues, several of whom came from the lower middle class, indicated the direction of his politics. The rise of this new class was accompanied by a bitterness which had no counterpart in the 1860's. On the part of the political-liberals there was a suspicion of the Crown and the *herrar*, and on the other side a resentment towards the appointment of men like Bergström and Berg to the first Liberal Ministry. It is true that although the influence of. the petite-bourgeoisie and Nonconformists, with their leanings towards pacifism and temperance, distinguished this period, there were still sufficient liberals of an older and more socially acceptable type for Gustav V to imagine in 1914 that he could form an alternative Ministry from them. Their refusal to serve, however, showed how inadequate was their popular support.

The passage of each of the reform bills may perhaps be described as the dramatic signal of a transfer of political power from one social class to another. In 1865 the Nobles and Clergy were well aware that by passing De Geer's bill they were ending a long epoch of Swedish history. Forty years later, when they accepted responsibility for a reform of both chambers, Lindman and his colleagues from the economic-liberal middle class knew that they were being compelled to modify that careful balance of the two houses which had preserved Parliament from the on-slaughts of a Second Chamber in which first the Farmers' party and later the Liberal party had claimed to represent the popular will. Henceforth there was no gainsaying the authority of the Second Chamber. In 1918 the First Chamber and the Liberal party agreed to the introduction of complete universal suffrage, a measure which they knew would benefit the workers and the Social Democratic party.

Yet each class only gave way when it was satisfied that the power it was transferring would not be fully exercised. The formal transfer of power, as implied by the reforms, was not immediately followed by important changes in policy. Thus it followed that despite the victory of the economic-liberals in 1866 there was little apparent change in social policy for many years. Moreover, the political-liberals, although well established in Government by 1914, were not strong enough to withstand the combined opposition of Court and Conservatives in the ministerial crisis over rearmament of that year. Finally, the Social Democrats, despite having been the largest party in the Second Chamber since 1915 and part of the 1917 coalition, were unable to form a strong Socialist Government until 1932.

The slowness of the social and political changes may have been due in part to the innate conservatism of the Swedish people. Certainly, except in the case of a few Left Socialists in 1918, and later of the Communists, the revolutionary solution of political problems seems to have been rejected. Political parties have waited upon the support of the electorate for parliamentary measures. The inability, or reluctance, of any of the dominant groups to exploit their success to the full, has, however, been due also to another factor, namely, the existence of a Fourth Estate in the form of the farmers. Though they have never gained the political power due to them by virtue of their numbers, they have never been without influence upon the conduct of affairs. They proved the main opposition to the economic-liberals after 1866, and during the political-liberal era they formed powerful groups within both the Liberal and Conservative parties. One of the greatest figures of this period, Petersson of Påboda, served as Minister of Agriculture in both Conservative and Liberal Ministries. Even the Social Democrats found them an obstacle to political power, and their most significant decision in 1933 was to try to bring about an alliance of farmers and workers in the creation of the first of their series of strong Governments.

The political emancipation of the lower social classes has now been accomplished, and the period since 1921 has seen the gradual replacement of the older social divisions by a dominant middle class outlook in some respects perhaps comparable to that of the United States. The victory of the workers in 1918 meant the end of a period of class struggle, and was the prelude to a new development—the merging of the former middle, lower-middle and working classes into the comparatively homogeneous society which characterizes Sweden today.

11. *Political developments: The rise of political parties*

The rise of the lower social classes was accompanied by the formation of new political parties. However, although the lower middle class and the workers each had a political party concerned with their interests, there was no equivalent parliamentary organisation as the economic-liberals grew in importance in the 1860's. The traditional explanation of this phenomenon has been that a general antipathy for parties as factions was engendered by the Era of Liberty in the eighteenth century. To this suggestion may be added the observation that in the 1860's the modern urban society from which the Liberal and later on the Social Democratic parties (and indeed twentieth-century Conservatives) drew their support did not yet exist.

Nevertheless, the almost complete absence of any political party organization to further the economic-liberals' cause in the 1860's is striking, especially in comparison with the disciplined order prevailing in the Farmer Estate and later the Farmers' party.

It is perhaps the policy of the farmers which provides a partial explanation of the absence of an economic-liberal political party. The farmers' main object was the abolition of the system of land taxation which bore upon them and not on the other classes. So long as it was necessary for the middle and upper classes to be united on the desirability of this burden resting upon the farmers' shoulders there was little urge for a party organisation which, presumably, would tend to divide them. Hence, much as the economic-liberals might want the farmers' support for parliamentary reform, they were somewhat chary in making an alliance with them. For a time, admittedly, the Burgher Estate pursued a common policy with the Farmer Estate, but as soon as the Farmers showed themselves to be 'radical', that is, to be ambitious for considerable influence over the proposed bicameral legislature, the Burghers withdrew. After 1866 the distinction between the farmers and the other classes was perpetuated, the farmers in the Second Chamber opposing the *herrar* in the First. There was even a school of thought which maintained that the tension between the two chambers in Sweden was the equivalent of the party division within the British House of Commons, and used this analogy to argue in favour of the De Geer bicameral equality. No mention was made of the fact that the Swedish Second Chamber, unlike the British Opposition, was always at a disadvantage, since it did not contain an alternative Government.

Curiously enough, the farmers shared in the general respect for the Swedish parliamentary tradition which, as much as the Estate system, militated against the formation of an economic-liberal party. They did not wish to replace the traditional separation of powers by parliamentary government but supported the rule of the King as executive power. Moreover, the economic-liberals found it expedient to vote with the conservatives. Certainly in the circumstances a liberal party was superfluous, as the short-lived New Liberal party of 1868 suggested.

The first modern mass party to attain political power was the Liberal party under Karl Staaff, when the obstacles preventing the formation of such a party forty years earlier no longer existed. The antipathy to political parties was not shared by the lower middle class, anxious to use the opportunity for political organization afforded by the transformation of the country into an increasingly urbanized society. United opposition to the farmers was no longer necessary once Boström's concessions were accepted in 1892. Above all, there was hardly the same general support of the traditional separation of powers. The willingness of the Liberal party to challenge the 1809 Constitution by claiming that Government should depend upon the goodwill of the Second Chamber meant the division of members of Parliament, and indeed of the whole country, into parties which supported or opposed the rule of the King as Executive.

Yet despite all these favourable omens, the first Liberal Government was defeated in 1906 within a few months of its appointment. This would appear to have been due mainly to over-enthusiasm and overconfidence. While no party had achieved such astonishing success both in Parliament and throughout the country, Staaff and his colleagues were somewhat premature in challenging the First Chamber when still without a majority in the Second. Five years later they returned to power, this time with firmer support and more modest ambitions. Nevertheless, within four years, the second Liberal Government was overturned, and the Liberal parliamentary party defeated at both elections in 1914.

The extraordinary débâcle of the Liberal party would seem to require some explanation. Voters do not abandon a party because it has met with a temporary setback, especially of the sort which lost Staaff his authority in 1914—the opposition of the Crown. The natural response should have been an upsurge of enthusiasm throughout the country for the defeated Ministry. Instead the party lost a third of its seats at the election following Staaff's resignation.

The decline of the party was at least partly the responsibility of its leader, whose understanding of the need for political compromise with his opponents was much less than his ability to win the affection of his devoted supporters. He held to certain principles too long, for example lower-house *parlamentarism*, thus losing the support of all except the hard core of his party, but to retain his parliamentary majority during the 1911–14 Ministry he adopted the very expedients he had condemned in others. It needed more political astuteness than Staaff possessed, and greater flexibility, to preserve an even balance between the two necessities of the Liberal party, moral principles and political power.

The 1914 defeat was the result not only of flaws in Staaff's leadership, but of the heterogeneous nature of the Liberal party. The moderate-Liberals were tempted to join the ranks of the Conservatives, while the more radical, such as Lindhagen, began to feel more at home with the Social Democrats. By 1914 the growth of the Social Democrats had altered the whole basis of the Liberal party's strength. Originally urban in character, it had lost many town seats to the Social Democrats owing to proportional representation, and had instead become increasingly dependent upon the rural vote, the farmers' own party being in temporary eclipse. In the 1912 Parliament nearly half the Liberals were newly elected, and the proportion of town radicals had dropped from over a half to just over a quarter.

The failure of the Liberals is the more interesting when contrasted with the success of Branting in building up the Social Democratic party into the largest in the Second Chamber in 1914, and in keeping it the largest. No doubt the power of the 'small folk' upon whom Staaff relied was bound to end with the rise of the working class, but the swift decline of the Liberals and the remarkable ascendancy of the Socialists was not solely due to the changing electorate. For one thing, the Swedish urban working class was not so large as in more highly industrialized countries such as Britain, and even there the Labour party grew comparatively slowly.

Moreover, it would appear that the personalities of Staaff and Branting affected the fortunes of the parties they formed and dominated. The Social Democrats had in their leader a man who was always able to change his mind when he saw that a policy was out of date, and who could deal most effectively with the various factions which appeared in his party. Whereas Staaff was plagued by Tällberg and his friends, Branting gave the Young Socialists freedom so long as he was in opposition, but never allowed them to dictate his policy or to affect the party's decision to act responsibly in office. The Young Socialists were defeated at the 1914 Congress which accepted *ministersocialism*. In 1917, when it appeared that the party might soon have to accept office, Branting let them break away completely rather than make their inclusion a liability.

Helped by proportional representation, Branting was able to broaden the basis of his electoral support without weakening his party's strength. Faced with the need to acquire votes he so extended the outlook of the party that in 1920 he could say on taking office that his was to be a 'popular national' Government. Farmers and middle class professional people were encouraged to join the party. A baron like Palmstierna, and professors like Steffen and Petrén, were welcomed into the higher counsels of the party, though not without criticism from some younger party members. Many Socialist principles were dropped from the programme, and in practice little attempt was made to nationalise the means of production, distribution, and exchange. If to change one's policy in this fashion is to be unprincipled, then the Branting of 1921 had lost all honour since entering Parliament twenty-four years previously. But the change was perhaps inevitable once the party accepted parliamentary institutions and placed coalition government according to the wishes of the majority of the electorate before government in accordance with the principles of members of the Social Democratic party.

The Social Democrats, therefore, were wiser in their treatment of the groups within the party than the Liberals, and more competent in attracting the expanding electorate. They were also helped by their reluctance to take responsibility for office in their early years, leaving government in the hands of the Liberals. The attempts of the Liberal party to execute Liberal policy twice led to defeats, in which the Social Democrats were not implicated. The party was perhaps fortunate in not forming a government of consequence before 1932, when it was able to take the credit for the revival from the slump and a series of imposing projects. Continued prosperity has kept the party's position strong.

The rise of the Liberal and Social Democratic parties seriously affected the Conservatives' strength. Until the 1908 elections they could still muster about 100 seats in the Second Chamber, but in the 1911 elections these were reduced to 64, the same number as the Social Democrats. When the blow against the Liberals was struck in 1914, the Conservatives gained a number of seats, but in the 1917 elections they held only fifty-seven. But

although the decline of the Liberals after the break-up of the
1917–20 Coalition Ministry was rapid (so much so that for many
years they ceased to be a major party), the collapse of Conservatism was delayed for some time. In the revivals of 1920
and 1928 the Conservatives won over 70 seats. It was after 1928
that their numbers began to fall away, until in the 1948 elections they won only 23 seats. A similar decline in the First
Chamber left them with only 23 seats even there. The Conservative party has ceased to be a government party, but continues
to attract landowners, civil servants, and businessmen, groups
which have diminished in political influence since the Social
Democrats obtained power. Partly because of tradition, and
partly because they still tend to represent different points of
view, the Conservatives have not joined forces with the Liberals
to form a strong united opposition. Yet the 30 seats of the Conservatives in 1952, added to the 59 of the Liberal party under
Professor Ohlin, would have given such an Opposition 89 seats
compared to the Social Democrats' 109.

The other important political party is the Farmers' party. By
no means as unimportant as its numbers might suggest, the
Farmers' party in its different forms has always been a powerful
influence in the Second Chamber. The co-operation of many
farmers with the Conservative party from 1904 onwards tended
to make the farmers seem insignificant as an independent
political force. As a party this may have been so, but as already
explained, as a social force the farmers have remained important.
It was the farmers who enabled Lindman to succeed where
Staaff had failed, who acted as what might now be called a
'front' for the King in his manœuvres against the Liberals in
1914, and whose agreement to support the Social Democrats in
1932 was decisive. Moreover the Swedish farmers, in contrast to
those of many countries, have usually been represented in
Parliament by their own kind. Thus whereas Barthélemy could
say of his countrymen in 1918: 'It is one of the best proofs of the
French peasant's common sense that he does not let himself be
represented by a peasant!' Brusewitz has commented: 'For those
who know something of the importance of the active part
played by the farmers in the Swedish and Scandinavian Parliaments generally, this reads rather oddly.'[1]

[1] *Studier, &c.*, p. 237.

The farmers weakened their position by their long reluctance to take office. Even in 1932 they refused to take part in the Social Democratic government. After their brief experience of office in 1936 they were willing to accept several portfolios, and in 1951 the pre-war coalition of Social Democrats and Farmers' party, which had been abandoned during the war, was re-introduced.

The stability of the Swedish political system in the last twenty years has led some observers to suggest that the liberal period of competing political parties has given way to a settled social order in which Government tends in some ways to ad-judicate the claims of various large social groups, none of which can expect to strengthen its position perceptibly. There even seems to be some indication of a conduct of affairs not unlike the pre-liberal era, when Parliament relied on its committees and Government was a separate power. In the Social Democratic Government of 1950, only nine of the fifteen members of the Cabinet were members of Parliament. Indeed, members of Parliament still look upon committee service as a proper political aim, and those who fulfil sixteen years' service in the chambers are awarded pensions. It would be reading too much into this development to regard it as a return to the old order in which social groups, like the Estates, meet together to be administered by a comparatively disinterested Government. On the other hand, it may be no accident that in a country which has had so short an experience of liberalism and individualism, these ten-dencies towards the traditional representation of interests of the realm should be observed and discussed.[1]

III. Constitutional change: from separation of powers to parliamentary government

The period from 1866 to 1921 not only saw a considerable extension of the franchise as a result of the reform bills, and a change in the composition of Parliament owing to the rise of political parties, but brought about important changes in the interpretation of the doctrine of the separation of powers.

So long as the Estates existed, there was no challenge to the separation of powers. Moreover, even after 1866 the Constitution

---

[1] Heckscher, G., 'Pluralist democracy: the Swedish experience' in *Social Research*, vol. xv, no. 4, December 1948. See also Herlitz, *Grunddragen, &c.*, pp. 291–4.

continued in force much as before, and so it was presumably not the Estate divisions alone which prevented Parliament from challenging the King. The probable explanation of the continued acceptance of royal executive authority is the harmony of interests of the *herrar* and the King in opposition to the farmers. The threat to the Monarchy arose with the development of new classes and parties bent on a share in government as well as representation in Parliament. The farmers, in contrast, would 'go to the Council door and no farther' as one of their leaders, Ifvarsson, expressed it. Staaff on the other hand claimed the authority of a Prime Minister on the British pattern and assumed Gladstone's mantle with his rallying-cry: 'Shall the power of the King and his people rule over Sweden, or the power of the King and the gentry?'

The main transfer of power occurred between 1905 and 1917. It may be described as a change from government by the Monarch to whom his Ministry was responsible, to government by the Ministry, which now became dependent upon Parliament rather than upon the King. The Monarch retained his formal authority, but in practice the Ministers were mainly drawn from Parliament and not from the Civil Service. Until 1905 the King could still choose his own Prime Minister, and even Boström was the personal choice of Oscar II. However, the Ramstedt Government of 1905 was virtually the last civil service Ministry, the limitations of which became apparent during the Norwegian crisis. The only return to a Ministry composed of civil servants occurred when the brief caretaker Government took office between the fall of the Social Democrats in 1920 and the elections which followed. Moreover, the parliamentary Ministries came to depend increasingly, as Boström had foretold, upon the Second Chamber.

The choice of Prime Minister was limited by party alignments in Parliament. The King was not restricted, like the King in Britain, by a two-party system according to which the Leader of the Opposition became Prime Minister after winning an election. The Swedish multi-party system, complicated by the bicameral organisation of the legislature, made the task of the King more difficult. The candidate for office should ideally have been the leading member of the party which had the greatest number of seats. Up to 1941, however, no party had a clear majority, and in these circumstances it was regarded as desirable to give preference to the party which had improved its position most in the election.

The five Governments between 1906 and 1917 illustrate the application of these principles. Staaff was the obvious choice in 1906 because his party had won a great victory in the Second Chamber elections and was the largest in the Chamber. The rise of the Social Democrats to the left of the Liberals, and Staaff's moderation in the Lundeberg coalition, partially removed the stigma of his radicalism. His resignation led to the formation of the second Government under Lindman. Although the Conservatives were less powerful in the Second Chamber than the Liberals, they could, nevertheless, muster nearly as much support, and in addition could rely on the First Chamber. Under the bicameral system, Lindman was therefore qualified for the office, since he was a moderate Conservative though not a member of the lower house. The Liberals remained the largest party in the Second Chamber after the 1911 elections, when the third of the five Governments was formed. It was natural, therefore, for the King to appoint Staaff once more. The latter consulted the Social Democrats because they had improved their position so much during the election that they could justify inclusion in a coalition. However, they declined, much to the relief of both Staaff and the King, who regarded the republican Social Democrats as too extreme to form a Government.

The fourth Government is perhaps the most interesting case. It was formed after the spring election of 1914, in which the Conservatives won a large number of seats. In the regular autumn elections, however, the Social Democrats became the largest party in the Second Chamber, winning one more seat than the Conservatives. Nevertheless, the Conservative Government remained in office. There were several contributory factors to this state of affairs. In the first place, the Social Democrats were still unwilling to embark upon *ministersocialism*, and made no claim to take part in government. Secondly, the obvious centre group, the Liberals, had lost so many seats that they could not be asked to lead a new Government. In the third place, the Conservatives themselves had not lost any seats at the election (the Social Democrats having gained at the Liberals' expense), and still controlled the First Chamber. Above all, the war had begun and party politics temporarily were in abeyance.

By 1917, however, when the fifth Government was formed, the parties of the Left were more aggressive. In the elections of that year, the Social Democrats led the field, followed by the Liberals. The King chose the Liberal leader, since he was from the centre, and he in turn approached the Social Democrats. Edén, who led the Liberals, might have asked the Conservatives to join him, had they been sympathetic to parliamentary reform. In proposing a coalition with the Social Democrats he appeared to Gustav V to be courting the extreme left, but in fact the break-away of the Left Socialists had placed Branting's party in the same left-centre position Staaff occupied in 1906. A successful coalition was therefore formed.

It is the 1917 Government which is regarded as the 'breakthrough of parliamentary Government' in Sweden. Previous Governments could claim the support of one of the chambers, but this Ministry controlled the Joint Vote with the aid of sixty-one seats in the First Chamber. The days of First Chamber Governments relying on an 'annexe' in the Second were over, and with them ended the direct influence of the King.

The decline of the monarchical Executive is also indicated in the absence of interference with the Prime Minister's choice of colleagues. Individual resignations and appointments declined with the advent of parliamentary Ministries. Perhaps the best-known examples of interference in Sweden to set beside those of Queen Victoria in Britain occurred in 1918 when Gustav proposed Hellner as Foreign Minister, and attempted to dissuade Edén from appointing Branting to a ministerial post. In both cases he was anxious to ensure the continuation of the policy of war-time neutrality. Royal interference in the formation of Ministries by the Prime Minister after 1905 seems to have been of slight importance.

Probably the most crucial test of royal authority is the dismissal of a Ministry. By 1906 the King was no longer able to flout the wishes of the electorate by removing Ministers at will. Nevertheless, both in 1906 and 1914 the King was to some extent responsible for the resignation of the Staaff Ministries. Staaff's failure to secure a dissolution of the Second Chamber in 1906 in order to demonstrate the desire of the people to limit the power of the First Chamber may be compared with the British Liberal Government's request for a general election in December 1910 on the House of Lords question. In Sweden, however, the King did not give way, and this led to the Ministry's resignation. Yet the situation was not the same in both countries. Unlike the British Liberal party, the Swedish Liberals did not control even the lower house, and they were attacking not an obvious anachronism but an elected body specially created only forty years previously.

The 1914 resignation is a clearer example of the King's power to dismiss his Ministers, though here again matters were so ordered that Staaff and his colleagues were not dismissed from office but encouraged to resign.[1] Once again, however, the weakness of the King's authority was demonstrated, not only by his failure to obtain an alternative Liberal Government, but by the necessity to dissolve the Second Chamber even though the triennial elections were due in a few months' time. In other words, as Staaff had argued in 1911 and thereafter, Governments required a 'mandate'.

The 1914 crisis marked the end of another of the King's powers as Executive, that of dissolving Parliament. During the free-trade controversy in 1887, Oscar I had dissolved the Second Chamber, but Gustav's first attempt in 1913 failed owing to the obstinacy of Staaff. Yet it is probable that, had the moderate-Liberals supported him in 1914, he would have been no more anxious to dissolve the Second Chamber than he was in 1906 when he called Lindman to be Prime Minister. Perhaps more significant was the controversy over the right of a Prime Minister to demand the dissolution of the Chambers. Gustav gave way to Staaff on this point in 1911, though the need to apply the provisions of the second reform bill to the First Chamber made this a special case. However, in 1917 Edén secured a promise to dissolve the Second Chamber if the First proved obstinate over the third reform bill. Henceforth, the power of dissolution mainly rested with the Prime Minister.

In two other respects, there were signs of the change to parliamentary government. The direct relationship of the

---

[1] The King's role is still debated. S. Clason's letters in *Historisk tidskrift*, 1951, no. 2, pp. 189 ff., and Sven Hedin in *Försvarsstriden 1912–1914* suggest he wished to force a crisis. Hildebrand, op. cit., ii. 110, denies this.

Executive with the people which exists under systems where the separation of powers is in force, ceased in Sweden with the Palace Yard speech in 1914. Secondly, the right of independent Executives to have their own advisers, which caused Staaff so much trouble, particularly during his second Ministry, was challenged in Sweden in 1917 by Edén, after which the King promised not to allow anyone to come between him and his constitutional advisers.

1917 is, therefore, a watershed in modern Swedish constitutional history. Though today the power of the Crown is undiminished, it is no longer exercised personally by the King. So long as the will of the people as expressed by the parties in Parliament is clear, he has little choice in the appointment of Prime Minister, who chooses his colleagues himself. Ministries cannot be dismissed, or forced to resign by a personal appeal to the electorate or by dissolution of one or both chambers. Dissolution, though still a prerogative of the Crown, depends upon the recommendation of the Prime Minister.

IV. *The classification of the Swedish system of parliamentary government*

It is tempting, but it would be misleading, to assume that the Swedish political system was based until 1917 upon the same theory of the separation of powers as the American, and that since then, thanks to Staaff's interest in the British Constitution, it has become a parliamentary government on the British model.

(a) *Sweden and the United States*

In the first place, there are important differences between the American and Swedish conceptions of the separation of powers. Admittedly, there are points of identity. Both have written constitutions 150 years old or more. The Executive, whether King or President, makes important appointments, and, owing to the formal separation of powers, is not responsible for summoning the legislature. The Executive does not control business in the legislature in either country, and even the American houses in practice share the financial power. In Sweden the provisions of the Constitution reinforce practice. The two legislatures are well organised in committees. Until 1913 the United States Senate, like the First Chamber, was indirectly elected by other bodies, and Senators are still, like members of the First Chamber before 1953, required as candidates for election to be of a higher minimum age than members of the lower house. The upper house in both countries acts as a brake on the lower, re-election taking place by stages.

However, these points of identity are accompanied by many more in which the two countries differ. The constitutional documents are dissimilar. Moreover they differ in the form of their amendment: in Sweden the same legislature passes amendments twice, after re-election; usually in the United States the State legislatures are responsible for the second stage. The two heads of State differ fundamentally, the hereditary Swedish monarch being quite unlike the elected American President. Nor are the Cabinets of the two countries similar, even though the President of the United States and the King of Sweden both preside over weekly Cabinet meetings. Cabinet Ministers in Sweden are chosen by the Prime Minister, usually from leading Government supporters in Parliament. Members of the American President's Cabinet are personally appointed by him and instead of being members of the legislature are generally from outside Congress. Unlike the First Chamber, the Senate has the duty of ratifying treaties, of confirming executive appointments, and of trying impeachment cases. Formal legislative power, shared equally between Crown and Parliament in Sweden, tends to pertain to Congress in the United States, where the President has to secure sponsors for the Administration's measures. Swedish standing committees are joint bodies of both·chambers, and have not the same tradition of powerful chairmen appointed by a seniority rule. Moreover, in each chamber there are several parties, elected by a system of proportional representation. Parliament may be dissolved by the Executive in Sweden, but the President has no such power over Congress. The American Senate, with a prestige far greater than that of the House of Representatives, may hardly be compared with the Swedish First Chamber, an upper house which may even become, as in other Scandinavian countries, unnecessary. Finally, there is no Swedish equivalent of the Federal system, or of the Supreme Court.

Yet despite these many important differences of political practice, something of the American attitude to the relations between the Executive and legislature persists in Sweden, if only in general principles. Just as Americans believe that certain matters are properly the responsibility of Congress, and that others are that of the President, so Swedes have a traditional belief that the Executive, even though as the Ministry it is part of Parliament, is in some measure distinct from the legislature. Some such separation of the two powers is inevitable, even in the French political structure. It is found in Britain, where members of the Government are called Ministers of the Crown. It is hardly surprising, therefore, that in a country where the doctrine has been abandoned, and then only informally and for but one generation, the notion of the separation of the executive and legislative functions should survive. In particular, the Swedes take seriously the fact that constitutionally 'the King alone shall govern the realm' and thus Ministers are servants of the Crown but not of Parliament, even though in practice they are dependent upon parliamentary support for their policy. In some respects, restrained as they are by their written Constitution, they have not fully adopted the system of Cabinet Government and parliamentary supremacy known in Britain.

(b) Sweden and France

The similarities between the French and Swedish political structures must not be discounted. In many respects the procedure of Parliament in Sweden is similar to that of Parliament in France. The notion of a Cabinet which does not control the business of both chambers, of Ministers who may appear before both houses, and of a system of ministerial countersignature, may seem decidedly 'French' to the British. When there is added to these an elaborate system of parliamentary committees, interpellations, a multi-party system, proportional representation, and regular elections to both chambers, at first sight the analogy appears to be complete.

In addition there are many historical comparisons. Parliamentary committees had a bad record in the eighteenth century in both countries, although only in France was this sufficiently odorous for permanent committees not to be established until 1902. Like the Swedish First Chamber, the Senate of the Third Republic was indirectly elected by local electoral colleges, re-election of members taking place gradually. Members were to be over forty (in Sweden over thirty-five), and legislation was to be dealt with concurrently with the lower house. Today in neither country do the Socialist parties compare with the British Labour party which, it has been said, 'owes more to Methodism than to Marxism' (though the Social Democratic party long ago abandoned its Marxism), and the so-called 'bourgeois parties' are more narrow in their electoral appeal than the Conservative party in Britain.

In some respects, Sweden and France share characteristics with the United States, and it is the British system which is the exception. For example, all three countries have written constitutions (in Sweden since 1634), and a head of State, whether President or King, who makes appointments personally, and who presides over Cabinet meetings. In Britain alone, the Executive has responsibility for summoning the Legislature to regular sessions. However, only in the U.S.A. has the Executive no power to dissolve the legislature.

Once again, however, the points of similarity are more than matched by the many differences. In the first place, the Swedish constitutional tradition began long before the French, and cannot be said to be derivative. It is, moreover, difficult to make comparisons with France, where constitutions have changed so much in the past 150 years. The two chambers of the Third Republic have been retained, but in different form: the National Assembly is only occasionally restrained by the somewhat ineffective Council of the Republic. A president is very different from a king; for example, the King of Sweden, advised by his Ministers in full session, may declare war, whereas under the Fourth Republic, the National Assembly must give its consent. The authority vested in the French President to dissolve the National Assembly under certain specified conditions is much less than the general power given to the Swedish Crown to dissolve either house.

Sweden is not, therefore, a country in which there is legislative supremacy to the extent that there is in France, where Ministers are responsible to the National Assembly alone and must, under the Fourth Republic, obtain a vote of confidence from the Assembly when taking office. The instability of governments in France, and the necessity of providing for periods when no Ministry can be formed, have no counterpart in Sweden.

Even interpellations, partly owing to the absence of the French Order of the Day procedure which gives Deputies power to change the order of business, have very little importance in Swedish constitutional history. Indeed, owing to the constitutional provision whereby the Ministry is formally responsible to the King, there is no vote of confidence procedure. Perhaps even more revealing is the contrast between the procedures for the verification of credentials in the two legislatures. In France this is very definitely a parliamentary responsibility, whereas in Sweden complaints are lodged with the Crown. Civil servants may sit in the Swedish Parliament, but in France they are no longer active once they are elected.

The Swedish system of two chambers of equal standing has no counterpart in France where, under the Third Republic, the lower house possessed the financial power, and conversely, the Senate could give its consent to the dissolution of the Chamber by the President. French committees are not joint, and the *rapporteur* system has no formal Swedish counterpart. Swedish committees, moreover, cannot bury bills referred to them. Finally, the attempt to control the legislature in France by granting the Executive the power of dissolution may be contrasted with Swedish experience where the power has been granted but on the whole has not been necessary.

In conclusion, therefore, it may be agreed that while there are many formal political institutions in Sweden which have their counterpart in France, the authority of the legislature in Sweden is restricted by the tradition of the separation of powers. It is true that for a time, in the 1920's after the abandonment of the royal Executive, it seemed as if the Swedes had replaced the practice of separating the powers in favour of legislative supremacy, but this was for only a few years. Nor was there ever the instability of Government to be found in France. Though Governments resigned fairly frequently they did so with a certain regularity associated with the elections, and there was little problem of finding alternatives. The success of Sweden in overcoming this period of weakness in Government, if such it may be termed, without abandoning either the multi-party system or proportional representation, suggests that these alone are not responsible for French political instability.

It would seem that it is not enough to compare political

structures when analysing political systems. The French history of competing ideologies, the traditions of the Commune on the Left, and Bonapartism on the Right, have no counterpart in Sweden, where there has never been a mob to man the barricades, and where the conservative forces have accepted democratic changes, even if with some reluctance. The difference in temperament may be a more fundamental explanation of social and political stability than political institutions themselves. There have been few refusals to obey the Chair in the Swedish Parliament, little cause for anxiety over irrelevant and propagandist speeches by members, and no violent scenes. The multiparty system does not operate in the same way. In contrast to the French agglomeration and splintering of parties, there are four main Swedish parties, none of which differs considerably in ideology from the others. Moreover, the co-operation, with two interruptions, of two of these, the Social Democrats and the Farmers, has given a continuity and stability which has lasted more than twenty years. Thus despite the similarity of many of their parliamentary institutions there is a marked contrast in the stability of the two countries' political systems which cannot be accounted for in purely political terms.

(c) *Sweden and Great Britain*

The growth of a fairly strong Executive in Sweden in the period since 1933 suggests the possibility of comparison with Britain. Yet the persistence of traditions usually associated with the Continent or the United States makes close identification of the two systems impossible. In particular, it should be noted that the Swedes themselves show their consciousness of the difference by their use of terminology. They are particularly sensitive to the use of English phrases like 'parliamentary government' to describe their system. This many of them translate as *riksdagsvälde*, the parliamentary absolutism of the eighteenth century which they emphatically deny is the system established by the 1809 Constitution. In Britain the terms 'parliamentary government' or even 'parliamentary sovereignty' are used in a political sense, legal authority residing in the Queen-in-Parliament. However, in Sweden, the legal interpretation alone is in many circles accepted, perhaps because of the greater legalism of the approach to politics. Nevertheless, the actual operation of Swedish politics since 1917 does not conform to the strict legal interpretation of the Constitution, and the differences between Britain and Sweden are in practice less important than those between Sweden and either of the other countries with which comparison has been made.

There are several obvious grounds for comparison between Sweden and Britain, particularly in recent years. Both countries are constitutional monarchies with a long tradition first of royal rule tempered by Parliament and later of a gradual transition to parliamentary government in which the Monarch merely reigns. The Privy Council in Britain may be compared in some respects with the King-in-Council in Sweden; both are formal institutions which have lost power to a Cabinet unknown to the Constitution. In both countries the traditional separation of the Executive from the legislature is preserved in the rule that debate is forbidden when the King is present. In theory the King has the right to introduce legislation and to veto bills from the legislature, but in practice the personal power of the Monarch is now exercised by a Cabinet Government acting in the name of the King. The changes which have taken place are largely matters of convention rather than constitutional law. In many ways the changes in Sweden took place somewhat later than those in Britain.

There are many instances which illustrate the declining power of the Monarch in both countries. For example, although the King retains theoretically the power to dissolve Parliament, he uses it only upon the advice of his Ministers, in Britain since the eighteenth century, and in Sweden since 1914. Today Ministries depend upon the confidence of the electorate and Parliament, not upon the King. The upper house in Sweden was dissolved in 1911 upon the firm request of Staaff, and in 1917 Gustav V was forced to promise dissolution of the Second Chamber in the event of the First Chamber proving recalcitrant over the third reform bill. The House of Lords was twice threatened with the creation of new peers, the equivalent of the First Chamber's dissolution, first in 1832 and again in 1911. Part of the legislative authority of the Sovereign, the royal veto, was last used in Britain in 1707, and in Sweden in 1913.

The Monarch has also lost power in the right to choose his own chief Ministers. The change in Britain began in the eighteenth century, and took place gradually in Sweden after the dissolution of the union with Norway in 1905. But whereas the Swedish Monarch abdicated his right in Sweden finally only in 1917, he was compelled to acquiesce in the wishes of the Norwegian *Storting* as early as 1869. Queen Victoria failed to appoint Hartington instead of Gladstone in 1880, but in 1894 she could still choose Rosebery without consulting Gladstone. Staaff's difficulties with the courtiers of Gustav V may perhaps be compared with Peel's annoyance over Queen Victoria's Ladies of the Bedchamber.

The increasing authority of the Prime Minister led to a diminution in royal interference in the appointment of the Ministry. Queen Victoria's objection to Sir Charles Dilke (that he was divorced and had been a republican), may be compared to Gustav's reluctance to sanction the appointment of Branting (who also had republican sympathies), though Victoria was the more successful in her opposition. Whether Gustav's hint that Edén should choose a sounder man, namely Hellner, as Foreign Secretary in 1917 has any more recent counterpart in Britain is still argued. However, there have been no repetitions in recent times of the older personal diplomacy which caused the over-ambitious Charles XV to attempt in 1864 to aid Frederick of Denmark until dissuaded by anxious Ministers. Queen Victoria's celebrated intervention over General Gordon in 1884 and Gustav V's Palace Yard speech of 1914 symbolize almost the final efforts of Sovereigns to interfere with the policy of democratically elected Governments. Today, the Monarchs in both countries are reduced to the right to be informed, to encourage, to advise, and to warn—and to little more.

Thus collegial Cabinet Government has replaced the royal Executive by a somewhat similar process in each country. The Cabinet has its proper place in Parliament, and enables writers in Britain at least to speak of 'parliamentary sovereignty'. Yet in neither country does the legislature control the activities of the Executive so much as in France, where the Finance Committee challenges the power of the Finance Minister much more than do parliamentary committees in either Sweden or Britain today. However, Ministers depend upon parliamentary support, and in practice upon their disciplined political party (or parties) representing the will of the electorate. The parties themselves are in some respects comparable. In Sweden and Britain there is neither the absence of doctrine which characterizes American parties, nor the extreme Left and Right ideologies which increase the tensions in the French National Assembly. Nor do the parliamentary committees nowadays wield the power that they still do in the United States or in France.

Thermaenius has suggested another point of comparison, namely, that parliamentarism developed in both countries before the introduction of universal suffrage, in contrast to the other Scandinavian countries, where the extension of the franchise led Parliament to establish its predominance.[1] Nevertheless in both countries, reform bills led to changes in the powers of Parliament. The five British bills of 1832, 1867, 1884, 1918, and 1928 correspond in some measure to the Swedish bills of 1866, 1907–9, and 1918–21, periods of considerable social and political changes.

Indeed, the social movements underlying the political transformation show many similarities. In Sweden, as in England, the established church lost much of its influence, particularly over education. At the same time an assault was made on the common aristocratic and paternalist tradition which caused Hedin to lose his temper at the sight of a peasant touching his forelock, and Cobden to sigh that London Society was so dangerously pleasant that 'I am already half-seduced by the fascinating ease of their parties'. In both countries there was comparatively little scandal or corruption, perhaps because the ruling classes kept control of the administration by means of a higher Civil Service drawn from ancient universities. The rise of the middle classes was accompanied by an interest in temperance, free trade, and evangelism as well as by organized Liberalism. The National Liberal Federation in both countries ensured the victory of the radicals over the moderate Liberals, and their formation was followed by appeals to public opinion typified by Gladstone's Midlothian speech in 1880, and Staaff's Gnesta oration. In 1907 the Swedish Conservatives took a leaf out of Disraeli's book by a reform bill which stole the Liberals' clothes. For long, Liberals in both countries were not at ease with the Monarchy: resentment over the assumption of the title

[1] Thermaenius, E., 'Från konstitutionalism till parlamentarisk demokrati', *Det Nordiske Administrative Förbunds 5 Almindelige Möte*, Oslo, June 1933.

'Empress of India' by Queen Victoria had a counterpart in Staaff's annoyance over such issues as Gustav's personal standard. The radical Celtic fringe which troubled orthodox Liberals in the form of Lloyd George was paralleled by the Tällberg *fronde* which upset Staaff's plans. Indeed it was the heterogeneity of the Liberals, amongst other things, which led to their downfall after an uneasy alliance with Socialists who later replaced them.

It is significant from the point of view of recent events that the Socialist movement in both countries has had a solid trade union base which on the whole has been unsympathetic to Marxism. The acceptance of the parliamentary system by the Socialists, and the failure of the Communists to create a strong party has preserved continuity in political development.

Lest these parallels seem to imply close similarity of political structure, it is perhaps worth pointing to some of the differences which prevent such an identification. Attention has already been drawn to the ways in which Sweden approximates more to American or French practice, and so perhaps a few illustrations will be sufficient.

In the first place both the legislature and Executive in Sweden pay considerable attention to the principle of the separation of powers. Secondly, whereas the Queen-in-Parliament in Britain is undoubtedly supreme, it is difficult to draw too close an analogy with a country where there is a written Constitution limiting the freedom of action, at least until an amendment process has been undergone, of both Executive and legislature. It is true that the Swedish political system has been transformed from a royal Executive to a Cabinet Executive without an amendment of the Constitution being necessary, thus making it impossible to speak of the supremacy of the Constitution in quite the same way as that of the United States, which is interpreted by the Supreme Court. Nevertheless, the constant references to the provisions of the Constitution in Sweden suggest that a written Constitution is less flexible than the partly written British Constitution.

There may also be considered the nature of the legislature itself. The two equal chambers, committee system, and the existence of several parties, combine to make the legislative process in Sweden rather different from that in the House of

Commons. Moreover, the prospects of *majoritetsparlamentarism* are not guaranteed in Sweden, where, although the traditional separation of the powers has been abandoned, the supremacy of the British-style Executive is less assured.

It would seem, therefore, that, as a product of its own history and long constitutional development, the Swedish political system, for all its similarities with Britain and other countries, is unique. There remains the task of classifying this particular type of government.

v. *The Swedish system: the diffusion of power*

In the analysis of the British, French, and American systems, three distinctive relationships of the Legislature and Executive emerge: the separation of the two powers; the tendency towards domination by the Legislature; and Executive predominance. In theory the Swedish political structure still approximates to the separation (and balance) of powers, but in practice it has leant first towards legislative supremacy and, in the last twenty years, increasingly towards a more powerful Executive.

Yet such is the nature of the Swedish arrangement that it would appear on the whole to be a compromise between presidential and parliamentary government: a diffusion of power. Power is diffused amongst joint standing committees, each with equal representation of both chambers, amongst two chambers equal even in financial power, and between an Executive and Legislature with equal shares of legislation. Ministers address both houses, civil servants sit in Parliament, and the stipulation that at least two Ministers without Portfolio shall have had experience in the public administration has never been repealed. Perhaps the clearest proof of this diffusion of power is in the handling of Government bills by the Legislature. Whereas French and American committees claim control over Government legislation, and whereas the British Government maintains its position through strict party discipline, in Sweden committees report out the Government's bill together with their alternative proposal. Government and chambers have each to decide which to adopt.

Sweden has perhaps been fortunate in its political heritage. It is strange to recall that when De Geer presented his reform bill to the Council of State in 1862 a messenger entered with a brown paper parcel, addressed to him as Chancellor, in which there were ten Jacobin caps, one for each Minister. The moderate reform which abolished the Estates seemed to many at the time to be revolutionary. Yet only fifty-four years after the bill passed into law, the first Social Democratic Government took office, and the Crown had indeed, to quote Charles XV, been 'landed head over heels in *parlamentarism*'. Curiously enough, the two leaders of the country, King Gustav V and the Prime Minister Hjalmar Branting, had been alive at the time of the first reform and attended school together. The one had been brought up later in the tradition of the monarchies of Europe, distrustful of Liberals and positively afraid of Socialists; the other had gone to prison for his anti-religious opinions. In their youth they represented the extreme Right and almost extreme Left. By 1920, nevertheless, they were friends who trusted each other, and were in their own way moderate in opinions. Karl Staaff had suggested that what distinguished the Swedes from the French in their form of Government was their phlegmatic temperament and unwillingness to be swayed by sudden oratory or passion. It might be added that the spirit of compromise and fairness, exemplified in the careers of Gustav and Branting, helps to explain why in the course of a few decades the Swedish political system should have changed to one of parliamentary government and yet have remained true to its tradition, if not of the separation, at any rate of the diffusion, of powers.

APPENDIX I

(a) Party Strengths, First Chamber

First chamber parties	1908	1911	1912	1915	1918	1921	1922	1925	1929	1933	1937	1941	1945	1947	1949
Right	(about) 130		85	89	88	37	41	44	49	50	45	35	30	26	23
Liberals	15		51	47	45	40	38	{13, 22}	{7, 24}	{4, 19}	16	15	14	14	18
Farmers' Association						19	18	18	17	18	22	24	21	21	21
Social Democrats			12	14	16	50	51	52	52	58	66	75	83	86	84
Left Social Democrats					1	4	1	1	1	1					
Communists							1	1	1	1		1	2	3	3
Others			2								1				1

(b) Party Strengths, Second Chamber

Second chamber parties	1905	1908	1911	1914	1915	1917	1920	1921	1924	1928	1932	1936	1940	1944	1948	1952
Right (including Farmers' party and National Progressives)	90	98	64	86	86	57	72	62	65	73	58	44	42	39	23	30
Liberals	106	98	102	70	57	62	46	41	{5, 28}	{4, 28}	{4, 20}	27	23	26	57	59
Farmers' Association						14	30	21	23	27	36	36	28	35	30	27
Social Democrats	13	34	64	74	87	86	75	93	104	90	104	112	134	115	112	109
Left Social Democrats						11	7	6								
Communists								7	5	8	2	5	3	15	8	5
Independent Socialists											6	6				

Figures are not available for the years before 1905. Elections are held in the autumn in the year preceding the meeting of a new Parliament, and, until the 1918-21 reform, were held triennially.

Chancellors 1858–1876: Prime Ministers 1876–1952

Chancellors

Appointed:

April	1858	L. De Geer	May	1874	E. H. Carleson
June	1870	A. Adlercreutz	May	1875	L. De Geer

Prime Ministers

Appointed:

March	1876	L. De Geer	Oct.	1917	N. Edén
April	1880	A. Posse	March	1920	H. Branting
June	1883	C. J. Thyselius	Oct.	1920	L. De Geer II
May	1884	O. Themptander	Febr.	1921	O. von Sydow
Febr.	1888	G. Bildt	Oct.	1921	H. Branting
Oct.	1889	G. Åkerhielm	April	1923	E. Trygger
July	1891	E. G. Boström	Oct.	1924	H. Branting
Sept.	1900	F. von Otter	Jan.	1925	R. Sandler
July	1902	E. G. Boström	June	1926	C. G. Ekman
April	1905	J. O. Ramstedt	Oct.	1928	A. Lindman
Aug.	1905	C. Lundeberg	June	1930	C. G. Ekman
Nov.	1905	K. Staaff	Aug.	1932	F. Hamrin
May	1906	A. Lindman	Sept.	1932	P. A. Hansson
Oct.	1911	K. Staaff	June	1936	A. Pehrsson
Febr.	1914	H. Hammarskjöld	Sept.	1936	P. A. Hansson
March	1917	C. Swartz	Oct.	1946	T. Erlander

Population Divisions

Percentage of population engaged in	1870	1900	1940	1949
Agriculture and similar occupations . . .	72·4	55·1	34·1	29·7
Industry and handicrafts	14·6	27·8	38·2	39·7
Commerce and trade	5·2	10·4	19·5	20·9
Public service and professions . . .	7·8	6·7	8·2	9·7

APPENDIX 4

Summary of Parliamentary Reforms

	1866	1907-9	1918-21
(a) FIRST CHAMBER			
Eligibility of primary voters			
i. Type of suffrage	Adult and Legal Persons	Adult and Legal Persons	Adult
ii. Minimum age	21	21	23 (21 since 1945)
iii. Property qualifications	Local taxes paid	Local taxes paid	None
iv. Maximum number of votes	Virtually unlimited: later		
(a) Provinces	5,000	40	One
(b) Towns (six)	100 (1869)	40	One
Type of Electoral College			
(a) Provinces	Provincial Councils	Provincial Councils	Provincial Councils
(b) Towns (six)	Town Councils	Town Councils	Electoral Colleges
Minimum age of members of Electoral College	..	..	27 (23 in 1937, 21 since 1945)
Period of election of First Chamber (fraction annually)	9 years	6 years	8 years
Eligibility of members of First Chamber			
i. Minimum age	35	35	35 (23 since 1953)
ii. Property qualifications			
(a) Estate (assessed)	80,000 riksdaler	50,000 crowns	50,000 crowns
(b) Annual income (assessed)	4,000 riksdaler	3,000 crowns	3,000 crowns (abolished in 1933)

Salaries paid since 1907-9.
Proportional Representation introduced 1907-9 in primary and Electoral College elections.
No residential qualifications.

	1866	1907–9	1918–21
(b) Second Chamber			
Eligibility of electorate			
i. Suffrage	Male	Male	Adult
ii. Minimum age	21	24	23 (21 after 1945)
iii. Property qualifications			
(a) Leased property	assessed at 6,000 rdr.	None	None
(b) Owned property	1,000 rdr.		
(c) Annual income.	800 rdr.		
Eligibility of members of Second Chamber—minimum age (other qualifications being similar to those governing the electorate)	25	24	25 (23 after 1949)
Period of election	3 years	3 years	4 years
Members have always received a salary.			
The residence qualification became less restrictive after the introduction of Proportional Representation and large constituencies, 1907–9.			
Approximate size of electorate after reform.	200,000	(Before reform 500,000) 1,000,000	3,200,000

Biographical Notes

The *Svenskt biografiskt lexikon*, work on which was begun in 1917, is the chief Swedish biographical reference book. Unfortunately it has so far only reached ENVALL. A shorter series, *Svenska män och kvinnor*, begun in 1942, which has already reached SHELDON, has been extensively used. For the remaining names it has been necessary to refer to *Svensk uppslagsbok*. Since the post-war edition is not yet complete, the names from SHELDON onwards have had to be obtained from the pre-1939 edition.[1]

(*Svensk män och kvinnor* is available at the Swedish Institute, London.)

ABELIN, Gustaf Rudolf (1819–1903). Volunteer in 1st Life Grenadiers 1837. Lieut.-General 1871. Member of First Chamber 1871–98. Minister of Land Defence 1867–71.

ADLERCREUTZ, Axel Gustaf (1821–80). Son of a Lieut.-General. Law degree at Uppsala 1845. Served in Svea *hovrätt* (Court of Appeal). President of Göta Court of Appeal and Civil Minister 1868. Minister of State for Justice (Chancellor) 1870 to 1874, resigning over defeat of his defence bill. Became a provincial governor. Member of Second Chamber 1877–80, and a leader of Intelligentsia party. Helped found Evangelical movement in 1856.

ADLERSPARRE, Axel (1812–79). Naval cadet at Karlberg 1825–37. 1838–43 served mainly in U.S. ships. In Danish-German War 1849. Captain 1858. Head of *Kommandoexpedition* in Sea Defence Department in 1863. On reserve from 1866. Member of Second Chamber 1867–79. Very independent character and forced to leave *Kommandoexpedition* in 1868 and post as head of *Förvaltningen av Sjöärendena* in 1871. Joined Intelligentsia party. Freetrader. Supported conscription.

AGARDH, Carl Adolph (1785–1859). Son of a merchant. Student at Lund 1799. Professor of botany and practical economics 1812. Member of Clergy Estate 1817–48. Interested in savings banks, water communications, forests, creation of funded debt, domestic capital formation to avoid foreign economic control, political theories of Montesquieu and Geijer. Changeable and not politically influential. Feared democracy and opposed parliamentary reform, but supported Departmental reform, women's betterment, and more Government authority at expense of parliamentary

[1] Since these notes were prepared, further volumes have appeared in these series.

committees. Deeply religious. Ordained priest 1816, Bishop in Karlstad diocese 1835. Opposed to religious reform, Free churches, Catholicism, and Judaism. Preferred Melancthon to Luther, and opposed new Church handbook and catechism.

ALMQUIST, Carl Jonas Lovis (1793–1866). Romantic writer of uneven quality. Unpopular because of free-love views.

ANCKARSWÄRD, Count Carl Henric (1782–1863). 1795–8 Karlsberg cadet school. Lieut.-Col. 1809. Opposed Gustav IV Adolf, but pushed aside when Parliament met. Ultimately won over to Bernadotte, and took part in German expedition 1813. Disliked Russian alliance, broke with him, and was sent home. Opposed bureaucracy in Riddarhus 1817–18. Wanted Oscar to take over government 1840. Favoured a 'manly attitude' to Norway 1859–60.

ANCKARSWÄRD, Count Johan August (1783–1874). Fought in Napoleonic Wars. Liberal in attitude to Land Taxes, *Indelningsverk* and parliamentary reform. Brother of above.

ANDERSSON, Hans of Nöbbelöv, later of Skivarp (1848–1919). Director of Skivarps sugar factory 1901. Farmer in Scania. Member of Second Chamber 1882–1918. Liberal member of Farmers' party and later Old Farmers. Wanted F-boat 1911 onwards. A Leader of National Progressives 1906, supporting Proportional Representation, universal suffrage, and limit to local plural vote. Vice-Chairman of new Farmers' and Burghers' (Conservative) party in Second Chamber 1912. Mainly interested in farming questions. Increasingly conservative.

ANJOU, Lars Anton (1803–84). Son of a vicar. Student at Uppsala 1819. Ordained 1827. Doctorate 1845. Minister for Church and Education 1855. Bishop of Visby 1859. In Clergy Estate 1859–66. Member of Church Assembly 1868–83. Of Walloon descent. Supported teaching of Latin in gymnasia. Moderate conservative and opposed to parliamentary reform 1862–3.

BENEDICKS, Gustaf (1848–1918). Son of an ironmaster. Educated at Falun mining school and abroad. Introduced electricity into father's steelworks. Interested in Sala-Gävle railway, which affected his firm. Bought out by *Stora kopparbergs bergslags A/B* 1903. Member of First Chamber 1892–1909.

BERG, Johan Fridtjuv (1851–1916). Son of an elementary school-teacher. Married the daughter of a smith. Decided not to become a student but to follow father in trying to raise standard of elementary schools. Influenced by Danish Folk High Schools. One of the twenty-two disqualified Stockholm freetraders 1887. Member for Stockholm 1891 in Second Chamber and motioned for shorter working·day. Wanted peace with Norway and called traitor in 1905. Minister for Church and Education 1906.

BERGEGREN, Henrik Bernhard (1861–1936). Elementary education. Son of a bookseller. Joined staff of *Social Demokraten* 1890 and later other newspapers. Interested in workers. Anarchist. Of little importance after First World War. Interests in literature and art. Agitator. Preached force but won friends even among political opponents.

BERGSTRÖM, David Kristian (1858–1946). Son of sluice inspector. Doctor of Philosophy at Lund University 1892. Civil servant then journalist. Chairman of Verdandi society in 1880's and edited its brochures from 1888. His own pamphlet on the franchise a landmark. Formed People's party in Second Chamber 1896. Presented motions on prevention of accidents to workers, arbitration and workers' rights. Minister in Helsingfors 1907–11. Then in Staaff's Second Ministry.

BILDT, Baron Didrik Anders Gillis (1820–94). Son of a Lieut.-Col. Cadet at Karlberg 1835–7. Chief of artillery staff 1854. Governor of Gotland 1858–62. Governor of Stockholm 1862–74. Friend of Charles XV but not so great a favourite as popularly imagined. Independent political views. Sympathy for Poles 1863 and Danes 1864 but seems to have been against active alliance. Minister in Berlin 1872–86. Admired Bismarck. Earl Marshal 1886. In Riddarhus 1847–66. Near Junkers in views. Actively supported reform of Parliament and thought to have influenced Charles XV. Member of First Chamber 1866–74 and 1887–94. Prime Minister 1888–9.

BILLING, Axel Gottfrid Leonard (1841–1925). Son of a country revenue superintendent. Lecturer in Hebrew and theology at Lund University. Refused follow Sundberg as archbishop because no international interests. ('I speak only one language, Scanian'.) Member of First Chamber 1889–1906, 1908–12. Protectionist. First chairman of National party 1912. Known for ability to reach compromise in parliamentary committees except where principle involved, e.g. Latin in schools, relations of Church and State. Supported workers' insurance and arbitration. Responsible for support in First Chamber of proportional representation and universal suffrage to Second Chamber. Left wing in Norwegian question. Supported Dreadnought construction.

BJÖRCK, Albert Wilhelm (1812–85). Son of a professor. Studied law at Uppsala. Assize judge 1843. Went into private practice. Became chairman of Gothenburg reform association. Member of Burgher Estate 1850–66 and Second Chamber 1867–9. Strongest man of opposition in Constitution Committee 1853–4. On Budget Committee 1856–69. Motioned for Burgher vote in his Estate 1853. Less active after 1866.

BJÖRKQUIST, Manfred (1884–). Son of a rural dean. Studied at Uppsala. Superintendent of a folk high school 1910–13. Rector of Sigtuna folk high school 1917. First bishop of new Stockholm diocese 1942. As young layman led the Young Church revival. Made his folk high school popular institution. Collected money for F-boat.

BJÖRNSTJERNA, Count Carl Magnus (1817–88). Educated in England where father Swedish Minister. Joined Lifeguards 1836. Colonel 1858. Member of Second Chamber 1873–84. Junker over parliamentary reform but in favour of reform in economic and legal affairs.

BJÖRNSTJERNA, Oscar Magnus Fredrik (1819–1905). Joined Lifeguards 1836. Major-General 1871. Succeeded Hamilton as Minister to Copenhagen 1864. Member of First Chamber 1874–1901. Opposed parliamentary reform. Upheld *Indelningsverk*. Freetrader.

BLANCHE, August (1811–68). Illegitimate son of army padre. Graduated at Uppsala 1832. Civil servant. Author of twenty-three plays. Influenced by Dickens. Member of Burgher Estate 1859 and later the Second Chamber. Popular figure. Supported abolition of death penalty, women's rights, sharpshooter movement, parliamentary reform, freedom of Norway, Poland, and Italy. Admired Bakunin and Charles XII—yet against Scandinavianism.

BLOMBERG, Knut Hugo (1850–1909). Son of a works manager. Professor of Law at Uppsala 1894. Member of First Chamber 1894–1909. Conservative.

BOSTRÖM, Christopher Jacob (1797–1866). Son of a ship's carpenter. Professor in practical philosophy at Uppsala 1838–63. Taught the princes 1833–7. Dominated nineteenth-century Swedish philosophy. Influenced by Schelling, Plato, and Leibniz. Theory of rational idealism.

BOSTRÖM, Erik Gustaf (1842–1907). Nephew of C. J. Boström. Broke off university studies to take over entailed estate on death of his mother 1863. Elected member of Second Chamber 1875. Began as freetrader and, though one of *herrar* in Centre party, supported farmer opposition to bureaucracy.

BRANTING, Karl Hjalmar (1860–1925). Converted to Socialism at Uppsala when studying natural science. Evolutionary in spirit and supported parliamentary institutions. Editor of *Social Demokraten*

1886. Fined 800 crowns for slander when defending Verdandi behaviour 1887. Sentenced to 3½ months' imprisonment in 1889 when defending Socialist colleague in *Social Demokraten*. First Social Democrat member of Second Chamber 1897. In Parliament as party leader till death 1925.

CARLÉN, Richard Theodor (1821–73). Studied law at Uppsala. Member of Burgher Estate 1862–6. Supported parliamentary and penal reform. As member of Second Chamber interested mainly in legal questions. Opposed Farmer's party's association of taxation and defence. In favour of creation of office of Prime Minister.

CARLSON. Fredrik Ferdinand (1811–87). Taught Oscar I's sons before succeeding Geijer as professor of history at Uppsala 1849. Visit to England influenced his liberalism. Period in Berlin 1834–6 introduced him to von Ranke's historical methods. In Clergy Estate 1850–66 and after 1856 a leading parliamentary figure. Minister for Church and Education 1863. Favoured parliamentary reform, religious freedom and lay influence in Church affairs. Many reforms during his period of office 1863–70, 1875–8. Regarded King as foremost representative of the State and his behaviour as crucial to political development.

CHRISTERSEN, Jarl (1833–1922). Vice-admiral 1892. Minister of Sea Defence 1892–9. Did not succeed in rebuilding fleet, but naval reform 1896 the greatest since reign of Gustav III.

DALMAN, Wilhelm Fredric Achates (1801–81). Son of a courtier. Studied law at Lund and entered Civil Service as chancellery clerk in Riddarhus 1825–66. Also clerk in Department of Justice 1840–66. From 1828 a member of opposition in Riddarhus. In 1850's supported annual Parliaments, Jewish emancipation, inheritance rights of illegitimate children, right of women to reach majority at 25. Partly responsible for decision to publish debates 1828–30. Chief editor of *Dagligt Allehanda* 1833–47. On the board of *Aftonbladet* 1852–9, and later of *Nya Dagligt Allehanda* (founded 1859) and *Stockholms Dagblad* (founded 1824). Against active support for Poland and Denmark 1863–4 and *political* Scandinavianism. Last great effort as publicist was support of De Geer's bill for parliamentary reform. Later became blind.

DANIELSSON, Andreas (Anders) (1784–1839). Son of a wealthy farmer (*rusthållaren*). As youth served as secretary to Quarter Sessions. Because of sound judgement and clarity of expression, elected to Farmer Estate at 25. Chosen as parliamentary representative by twenty-seven districts 1834–5, unique record. At first supported government. Joined opposition 1817–18 and maintained that the Estate had come of age. Supported economy, reduced army and bureaucracy, abolition of Land Taxes, Free Trade, mortgage banks, better education. Friend of Anckarsvärd 1828–30. Dominated Farmer Estate 1834–5, and employed Dalman, Gustav Hierta, Anckarsvärd, &c. to draft motions. Financial difficulties later and died spoilt by success, becoming less a farmer and more a 'politician in galoshes'.

DANIELSSON, Anders Peter (1839–97). Son of a farmer. Simple but not poor home. Little education—six weeks' elementary school and confirmation preparation—but eager to learn. Married at 21 and took over the farm. Literate. Member of Second Chamber 1872–97. Sat on several committees as radical farmer. Vice-speaker 1891–4, 1897. Opposed *herrar*. Interested in reforming Supreme Court, Land Taxes, Second Chamber suffrage. Opposed party leaders in 1879, hence more radical programme 1880. Gradually weakened opposition to defence reform and supported Boström's bill 1892. Protectionist. Unstable in opinions. Increasingly conservative. Like others, did not realize that *herrar*–farmer conflict being replaced by middle- and working-class tension.

DE GEER, Baron Gerard Louis (1854–1935). Son of Louis De Geer. Studied law at Uppsala. Then to Svea Court of Appeal. Left Government service 1892 and became farmer. In First Chamber 1901–14. Moderate party until joined Liberals 1912. Against proportional representation. Favoured Norwegians and social equality. Left Parliament and party on failure to build Ministry 1914. Formed 'professional' Ministry in 1920–1, but not thought strong enough as Prime Minister.

DE GEER, Baron Louis Gerard (1818–96). Son of a landowner. Studied law at Uppsala. Assessor, Scania High Court 1849–55. President, Göta Court of Appeal, 1855–8. Chancellor, 1858–70. President Svea Court of Appeal 1870–5. Chancellor, 1875–6; Prime Minister, 1876–80.

DE LA GARDIE, Count Jacob (1768–1842). Major-general 1812 but lost support of Bernadotte and sent to Madrid embassy for two years. Member of Riddarhus till 1841. *Lantmarshalk* (Speaker) 1835. Supported education, savings banks, archives, care of sick and children. Landowner and physiocrat.

DICKSON, Oscar (1823–97). Commercial education in Lubeck and Gothenburg. Worked in family firm of Dickson Bros. in London and Gothenburg. Head of firm 1855. Bought forests cheaply from Norrland farmers. Supported explorers. Ennobled 1880, baron 1885. Tried to persuade Charles XV to support De Geer's reform bill. Married Countess Julia von Rosen 1857. A multi-millionaire (Swedish crowns).

256 · APPENDIX 5

EDÉN, Nils (1871–1945). Son of a headmaster. Professor of History
at Uppsala 1909–20. Member of Second Chamber 1909–24.
Chairman of Constitution Committee 1913–17. Convinced by
Union crisis of necessity for government to have its roots in the
people. Asked by Staaff to be Minister without portfolio 1911, but
instead became leader of Liberals in Second Chamber. Good
leader and debater. Key position as leader of Second Chamber
Liberals and chairman of Constitution Committee. Agreed to Social
Democrats' proposal to co-operate 1914. For coalition 1917. As
Prime Minister 1917–20, took advice and gave colleagues independence. More government bills in 1918 session than ever
before. Refused accept Prohibition programme, hence Liberal
party split 27 May 1923. Advised not to be chairman of the new
non-prohibition party, and left politics. Had a logical mind,
appealed to reason but did not know his party well.

EKDAHL, Nils Johan (1799–1870). Son of a bailiff. Studied at Lund
1820. Ordained 1822. Vicar in Stockholm parish 1838. Very
intense and orthodox churchman. Turned against George Scott, a
former friend, as Methodism expanded, and after he himself became vicar.

EKMAN, Carl Gustaf (1872–1945). Son of a farmer. Elementary
school education and then a farmhand. Studied at commercial
school 1891. Chief of the Good Templars in his province. Studied
at Kristinehamn practical school 1894–5. Editor of *Malmköpings
Tidning* 1896. Then other newspaper posts. Chief of Good Templar
Order at 26, 1899–1909. Town councillor in Eskilstuna 1902–13.
Member of National Liberal Federation 1902, of First Chamber
1911–28, and Second Chamber 1929–32. Strongly influenced by
Baptist minister who taught him when he was still a farmhand.
Not an especially good journalist. As Prime Minister known for
his 'balancing' policy, which he began in 1918 when he led centre
of Liberal party on Prohibition issue. Opposed to too many concessions to Socialists in 1918 reform bill. Against continuing coalition 1919.

ELOWSON, Gullbrand (1835–1908). Son of member of Farmer Estate
and changed his name from Andersson to Elowson. Doctor of
Philosophy at Uppsala 1863. Schoolteacher in mathematics and
physics. Member of Second Chamber 1887–1908. Liberal, but
supported proportional representation.

ESSEN, Fredrik von (1831–1921). Landowner and ironmaster. In the
army till 1863, then in Court service till 1867. Member of First
Chamber 1866–74, 1876–1906. Belonged to Scania party. Finance
Minister 1888–1894.

FORSSELL, Hans Ludvig (1843–1901). Son of a dean. His doctoral thesis on Gustavus Adolphus's administration considered good enough for a professor, 1866, and laid basis for Swedish economic history. Interested in Macaulay liberalism and also Germany as new Great Power in Europe. Finance Minister at 32 in 1875. Believed Scandinavia must defend itself against Asian invasion of Europe. After argument with Posse, became president of the College of the Exchequer (*kammarkollegium*). Member of First Chamber 1880–97, and correspondent for *Stockholms Dagblad*. Freetrader.

FRIESEN, Sixten Gabriel von (1847–1921). Son of a rural dean. Doctorate in mathematics at Uppsala 1877. Headmaster of Norrmalm Higher Modern School, Stockholm 1880. Member of Second Chamber 1885–87, 1890–1905, and of First Chamber 1905–15. Because of economical bent, neared Farmers' party. Not pugnacious and gave way in leadership of Liberals to Staaff. Later mainly interested in activities of Stockholm City Council.

GEIJER, Erik Gustaf (1783–1847). Son of an ironmaster. Early environment liberal, cultured and religious. As student at Uppsala more interested in music than work. In revenge for father's criticism attempted and won Swedish academy prize for essay on Sten Sture. Became interested in philosophy, in Schelling rather than the French political theorists. M.A. Uppsala 1806. Visited England as tutor to a merchant's son. Professor of history at Uppsala 1817–46. In 1809 preferred English parliamentarism to division of powers. Later wanted organic state, but against influence of nobility. Liberal, freetrader, and admirer of Charles XIV. At first supported Holy Alliance, and opposed Richert. Defended guild system. Scholarship more the general survey than criticism of sources. Abandoned conservatism in 1838, but conflicted with Manchester liberalism. Realized that new middle classes threatened by industrial proletariat. Believed workers should have the vote and lost many liberal friends. Something of a Christian Utopian socialist.

GRIPENSTEDT, Baron Johan August (1813–74). Son of a landowner. Artillery cadet and officer, 1831–41. Member of *Riddarhus* 1840–66. Consultative Minister 1848–56. Finance Minister 1856–66. Member of Second Chamber 1867–73.

GUNTHER, Claes (1799–1861). M.A. Uppsala 1824, then in Civil Service. In Riddarhus supported Richert reform motion. Consultative Minister 1848 until failure of reform bill 1851. Chancellor 1856 to 1858 when Crown Prince Regent appointed De Geer.

GÖTREK, Anders, Peter (Par) (1798–1876). Son of a customs-house attendant (called Godberg). Attended Uppsala university but

took no examination. Bookseller. Bankrupt 1851. Deplored
poverty and drunkenness. Translated Communist Manifesto and
read Saint-Simon. Arrested 1848 but released immediately. Too
volatile in ideas to make his mark.

HAMILTON, Count Henning (1814–86). Member of Council 1858–61.
Minister to Denmark 1861–4. Member of First Chamber 1867–81,
when forced to leave Sweden through scandal.

HAMILTON, Hugo Adolf, Baron (1802–71). M.A. at Uppsala 1824.
Served in College of Exchequer 1824–8. Equerry to Crown Prince
Oscar 1826–39. Refused to be Finance Minister 1840. Director of
Post Office 1845 and its first Director-General 1850. Interested in
farming, elementary schools. Joined opposition in Riddarhus
1828. Worked actively for parliamentary reform. Many artistic
interests and chief of the Dramatic Theatre.

HAMMARSKJÖLD, Knut Hjalmar (1862–1953). Son of a landowner.
Rapid career in law at Uppsala. Temporary professor 1891.
Minister without portfolio 1900–1, and of Justice 1901–2. Then
President of Göta Court of Appeal: Minister of Church and
Education 1905 and member of Karlstad delegation with Norwegians. Minister to Copenhagen 1906–7. Provincial Governor
of Uppsala province 1907–30. Responsible for creation of Supreme
Administrative Court 1909. Chairman of Casablanca Court and
other international courts before First World War. Director of
Stockholms Enskilda Bank 1913–14. Had never been M.P. when
made Prime Minister 1914. Friendly to Central Powers and insisted on neutrality in war. Defeat in Parliament caused resignation 1917.

HANSSON, Per Albin (1885–1946). Elementary school till 12. Shop
assistant. Helped form Young Socialists 1903. Anti-militarist.
Edited *Fram*, Young Socialist newspaper 1905–9 and left because
not radical enough for its supporters. Joined *Social Demokraten*.
Chief editor after Branting 1917. Member of Second Chamber
1918. Defence Minister 1920. Wanted disarmament. Opposed
Ekman's 'balancing' politics. Against class war. As Prime Minister,
gave others a free hand in secondary matters, but strong leadership in general policy.

HARTMANSDORFF, Jakob August von (1792–1856). Son of a regimental
quartermaster. Father died young, and son had economic pri-
vations. After leaving Uppsala, joined Civil Service 1808.
Conservative after life in Norway though he appreciated the Norwegian system of government. Culturally influenced by Germany.
Believed in 'polarity' theory: State to balance private and public
interest. In favour of Departmental reform at early stage and in

committee on reform of administration 1821. Entered Riddarhus 1823. At first an economic-liberal. Conservative in education policy. As Chamberlain (*hovkansler*) 1838, used power of censorship over twenty times. Motion in 1851 for five Estates to prevent farmer-domination. Hamilton abandoned this scheme and Hartmansdorff lost influence.

HEDIN, Sven (1865–1952). Swedish explorer. Last person to be ennobled in Sweden. Friend of Gustav V. Warned Sweden of Russian danger in 1912. Said to be partly responsible for the Palace Yard speech in 1914. Pro-German in sympathies.

HEDIN, Sven Adolf (1834–1905). Son of a vicar. Graduated at Uppsala 1861. Joined *Uppsala Posten* and introduced Ibsen and Björneson to Sweden. Became political. Anti-dynastic, and anti-Russian, especially in 1863. Wanted united Scandinavia on democratic basis. Regarded 1866 reform as too moderate. Disliked Bismarck. After 1871 said that rearmament necessary because of Russian danger, and one reason for support by Centre of his election to Parliament. Supported accident and old-age pensions 1884, Norwegian self-government, Free Trade, abolition of economic legislation, reduction in power of business firms in local elections. Defended small nations' rights and disliked British colonialism, Russification of Finland and German militarism. Pro-French. First professional politician in Sweden, and one of her greatest political figures. Lonely, great in opposition. Strong moral sense and religious, despite opposition to official religion. Defended Strindberg in *Giftas* affair. Opposed Latin in schools, and proposed common primary school for all.

HEDLUND, Sven Adolf (1821–1900). Son of farmer on Crown estate. Studied at Uppsala and entered Civil Service 1846. Began newspaper career 1847. Editor of *Göteborgs Handels- och Sjöfarts Tidning* 1852–1900. Influenced by Geijer and Christian liberals. Independent of Gothenburg's plutocracy. Managed his newspaper on the English model, giving correspondents a free hand. Important topics and cultural questions well presented. In 1870's Hedlund joined Farmers' party and became one of its leaders. Freetrader. Not doctrinaire. Represented best qualities of liberalism—social conscience, good debater. Some interest in occultism. Did not exploit powers of leadership in Parliament, perhaps too impulsive.

HELLNER, Johannes (1866–1947). Son of an elementary schoolteacher. Doctor of Laws, Lund university, 1896, then in Civil Service. Secretary of Karlstad conference with Norwegians and then Minister without Portfolio for Staaff. Became businessman and director of several of largest Swedish firms. Member of First

Chamber 1911–14, and Second Chamber 1914. Foreign Minister 1917–20 and worked to gain admittance of Sweden to League of Nations.

Hierta, Johan Gustav (1791–1859). Son of a Lieut.-Col. Joined army 1809. Adjutant to Anckarswärd 1812, who influenced his politics. In German and Norwegian campaigns 1813–14. Lieut.-Col. 1821. In 1820's joined Riddarhus. Helped Anckarswärd issue newspaper *Medborgaren* 1829–32. Radical and Saint-Simon ideas. Paper stopped publication 1832 after being suppressed several times. Then correspondent for *Aftonbladet* and *Göteborgs Handels och Sjöfarts Tidning*.

Hierta, Lars Johan (1801–72). Second cousin to Johan Gustav Hierta. Son of associate professor in chemistry, Uppsala. Educated in liberalism. Father affected by ideas of Rousseau and the Enlightenment. Studied law at Uppsala and entered Civil Service. Clerk in Riddarhus 1823, having learnt shorthand, then unknown in Sweden. Became interested in politics and decided to start a parliamentary newspaper. Stimulated by July Revolution, began to publish *Aftonbladet* 1830. Not heavy like its predecessors and on French and British lines. By 1832, 3,000 copies sold, a very high figure for Sweden. Liberal and follower of Jeremy Bentham. Practical, sober, no Utopian socialist. Wanted a good government responsible to Parliament, no House of Lords. Paper suppressed fourteen times 1835–40, yet survived, and in 1855 Parliament forbade further censorship. Largely responsible by his efforts for real freedom of the press. Supported Free Trade, human penal code, increased women's rights, economy in administration. A leader of Riddarhus opposition 1840–1. More favourable to Oscar I than to Charles XIV. Attacked by ultra-radicals 1848 for being moderate over parliamentary reform and Schleswig issue. Wounded by this and Almquist tragedy and sold his paper 1851 to a syndicate. Member of Burgher Estate 1859 and Second Chamber 1866. Opposed spending money on railways and defence. Was member of Reform Association. Superficial, doctrinaire, too sensitive to public opinion, not a statesman. Believed in greatest happiness principle of Utilitarians. Left estate of over 3 million crowns.

Höglund, Carl Zeth (1884–1956). Son of a leather merchant. Baptist and liberal. Attended Gothenburg High School and then joined staff of *Ny Tid* 1904–5. Imprisoned for six months for advocating general strike and refusal to mobilize at time of Norwegian crisis. Through his speeches, responsible for the spread of socialism. Supported republic, single chamber, disarmament. Member of

Second Chamber 1915. Imprisoned for one year 1916 for high treason. Formed Left Socialists 1917, but lost seat at election. Attached to Communist International until 1924. Rejoined Socialists 1926. Member of party council 1928 and of Second Chamber. Managing Director of *Social Demokraten* 1932–6. Chief Editor 1936–40. Advocated rearmament against the dictators.

IFVARSSON, Carl (1818–89). Son of a farmer. Member of Farmer Estate 1859–66 and Second Chamber 1866–89. With friends, seized Farmers' seats on committees in 1862–3 sessions, and formed kernel of Farmers' party 1867. Against discussion of defence and Land Taxes together. Supported solution of 1878 but not Posse's in 1883. In opposition minority when partial solution to problem reached 1885. Unable to keep party neutral 1887. Freetrader. Important as member of Budget committee 1865–89. Vice-chairman from 1883.

JONSSON, Olof (of Hov) (1839–1930). Member of Second Chamber 1878–96 and First Chamber 1904–16. Pugnacious, sharp intelligence, ability to work, and much general knowledge. A Norrland farmer, freetrader, and leader of Old Farmers' party 1891. A left liberal. Helped join the two Farmers' parties 1895. Liberals opposed this and secured his defeat in next election. In First Chamber helped build Conservative party organization (*Allmänna valmansförbundet*). On his death left 367,000 crowns and his farm to his parish for district-visiting work and education.

JUHLIN, Anders Julius (1861–1934). Doctor of meteorology at Uppsala. Great administrative ability. Became Civil Minister for Lindman. Proposed reorganization of railways. Director-General of Post Office 1907–25 and responsible for its modern organization.

JÄRTA, Hans (1774–1847). Student at Uppsala and then entered Civil Service, 1791. A 'Jacobin'. Present at masquerade when Gustav III was murdered 1792. Second Secretary in Office for Foreign Correspondence but too radical and so transferred to Lord Chancellor's office 1796. Opposition leader in Riddarhus 1800. As protest against government abandoned his title. Dismissed from government service and went into copper export trade. Against Gustav IV Adolf 1808 but more moderate. Worked only behind the scenes in deposition of 1809. His authorship of 1809 Constitution now questioned. Did not favour balance of power or detailed control of Council by the Estates. Secretary for Commerce and Finance 1809 and wanted trade with England. Retired 1811 because of opposition to Bernadotte as regent. Provincial Governor

1812–22. State pension 1823. Conservative. Read Burke and regarded state as an organism. Lived at Uppsala 1825–36, and developed ideas. Director of National Archives 1837–44. Talented, critical, and polemical. Unable to work well with others and impression slighter than might have been the case.

KARL (CHARLES) XIII (1748–1818). Always envious of brother Gustav IV. Erotic from childhood. Weak personality, and allowed Bernadotte to assume government when still Crown Prince Regent. Was aware of Adlersparre's proposed march on Stockholm in 1809.

KEY, Carl Fredrik Edvin Emil (1822–92). Stepfather A. C. Raab, landowner and liberal politician in Riddarhus. Educated at Lund and entered Finance Department 1848. Literary and artistic interests and later political. Widely travelled. Supported reform and Scandinavianism in 1840's. Not too successful as farmer 1848–83. Supported 1865 reform. Member of Second Chamber 1867–83, and on Budget Committee 1868–83. A leader of Farmers' party but could not persuade them to solve defence question, and so left Parliament. Had also lost money in financing newspaper to help Farmers' party, *Sveriges Medborgaren*. Became Postmaster at Hälsingborg.

KJELLÉN, Johan Rudolf (1864–1922). Son of a parson. Professor of political science at Gothenburg 1901 and Uppsala 1916. Influenced by Ratzel's political geography. Regarded the state as a living organism. Member of Second Chamber 1905–8 and First Chamber 1911–17. Helped to form Young Conservatives. Wanted Sweden to join Germany 1914–18. No pupils of consequence carried on his teaching. Considered an academician by politicians and a politician by academicians.

KLINCKOWSTRÖM, Rudolf Mauritz (1816–1902). Baron. Son of a naval Commander. Served in Navy 1837–77. In Riddarhus 1844–66 and fiercely opposed 1865 reform. Member of First Chamber 1877–99. Supported increased defence, Protection, writing-off Land Taxes.

LAGERBJELKE, Gustav (1817–95). Son of Adjutant-General. Studied law at Uppsala; clerk in Svea Court of Appeal. Clerk in Parliament of 1840–1. Entered Riddarhus 1844. Last *Lantmarshalk* (Speaker) 1862. Provincial Governor of Södermanland 1858–88. Speaker of First Chamber 1867–76, 1881–91. Believed in tradition. Proposed reform of Estates 1847. Clear ideas on railway development. Careful to advise restraint to Charles XV.

LARSSON, Jacob Timotheus (1851–1940). Son of a solicitor. Studied law at Lund and became vice-assize judge 1879. Lawyer in Lund

1879–89. Brought up in strong-principled orthodox Lutheran home. Under Marxist influence became radical and doctrinaire. Radical-liberal member of Second Chamber 1903–8. First Chamber 1910–14, 1917–28. Became Social Democrat 1921. Appointed Navy Minister 1911 because of work on Civil Commission 1908–11, connected with the Services, and became friendly to Social-Democrats. His personal conservatism and pedantic bureaucratic approach to issues contrasted sharply with his advanced radicalism.

LARSSON, Liss Olof (1838–96). Son of Farmer member of Parliament. Left school at 14, but studied in spare time. In 1866 elected to Second Chamber in place of his father who had sat in Farmer Estate. Youngest member and distinguished by his Dalecarlia costume and dialect. A leader of Farmers' party. On Budget Committee 1871–90. Typically economical. Supported 1878 proposal for defence, and opposed Posse's in 1883. Opposed state support for theatres but wanted aid for elementary teaching and temperance. Intolerant in religious questions. Opposed emancipation of Jews. Lay member of Church Assembly 1878. Opposed social reforms like accident- and old-age insurance 1884. Friendly to Norwegian case, and yet on good terms with Oscar II. Protectionist in 1880's and helped form New Farmers' party. Defeated in 1890 election, and entered First Chamber where he was unimportant. One of leading nineteenth-century farmers. A feared opponent.

LEFRÉN, Johan Peter (1784–1862). Son of professor of theology, Åbo university, Finland. Fought in Russian and Norwegian campaigns. Governor of Karlberg Military Academy 1824, and revolutionized the teaching. Great influence on Crown Prince Oscar, and chief of his staff 1828. In charge of Stockholm in March crisis 1848. Ennobled 1818. Good debater in Riddarhus 1823–60. In favour of two chambers based on voting by estates, with extra estate for the unrepresented.

LEIJONHUFVUD, Broder Abraham (1823–1911). Baron. Son of cavalry captain. Major-General 1868. Defence Minister 1870. Member of Riddarhus 1856–66 and Second Chamber 1875–84 representing Stockholm constituency. Blunt, and offended Farmers' party.

LINDHAGEN, Carl Albert (1860–1946). Graduated in law at Uppsala 1883. Served in Svea Appeal Court. Legal adviser to executors of Alfred Nobel 1897–9. Member of Verdandi Association at Uppsala. Entered Second Chamber 1897 along with his friends Branting and Staaff. In Second Chamber 1897–1917, First Chamber 1919–40. Liberal at first. Joined Socialists 1909 but an individualist. Left-Socialist 1917–23. Claimed responsibility for 987 motions, 115 interpellations, 482 reservations in committee, and 3,584 utterances in Parliament. Humanitarian. Important influence 1901 in stopping purchase of land by companies in Norrland. Motioned for republic 1912–14. Fined 1914 for shouting for republic in a street procession. Supported Minorities in Sweden, small states and Asia. Pacifist in First World War. Supported League of Nations.

LINDMAN, Saloman Arvid Achates (1862–1935). Naval officer until 1892. Director of several ironmining companies, and later of some of the largest Swedish firms. Director-General, Telegraph Board, 1904–8. Member of First Chamber 1904–11. Second Chamber 1912–35, where Conservative leader. Naval Minister 1905. Prime Minister 1906–11. Foreign Minister 1917. Prime Minister 1928–30.

LUNDEBERG, Christian (1842–1911). Son of an ironmaster. In army 1858–74. Attended a Farming Institute 1863–5. Managed father's ironworks 1865–72 and then various interests. Member of First Chamber 1885. Vice-Speaker 1899–1908, except when Prime Minister. Speaker 1909–11. Conservative and Protectionist. Chiefly responsible for Union dissolution 1905. Rather against parliamentary reform but finally gave Lindman full support.

LÖWENHIELM, Gustaf Carl (1771–1856). Studied in Strasbourg as schoolboy. Became friend of Metternich. Chief of Staff in Finnish army 1808 and attacked Russians. Wounded. Supported Bernadotte and dispatched 1812–14 to Paris, London, and Moscow. Minister to Austria 1816, and to France 1818 onwards. Interested in Swedish domestic politics and considered as possible Lantmarshalk and Foreign Secretary.

MALM, Olof Bernhard (1851–1939). Son of a farmer. Major-General and chief of Fifth Division 1907. Minister of Land Defence 1907–11. Not a politician. Evangelical.

MALMSTEN, Carl Johan (1814–86). Professor of mathematics at Uppsala 1842. Consultative Minister 1859–66. Provincial Governor 1866–79. Began modern teaching of mathematics in Sweden (differential equations, &c.). Main work as Minister was ending of export duties 1862–3.

MANDERSTRÖM, Christoffer Rutger Ludvig (1806–73). Son of a courtier baron. Studied at Uppsala and then into Civil, and later Diplomatic Service. Permanent Secretary 1840, envoy to Vienna 1855 and Paris 1856. Foreign Minister 1858. In favour of the November Treaty with France and Britain 1855, but against enmity towards Russia. Against support of democratic Danes and believed support of Denmark might mean war with Germany 1857. Yet supported Hamilton over Danish alliance 1864. Member of First Chamber 1866–73. Left foreign ministry 1868 because of attitude of Farmers' party over economy. Brought up in Gustav III French manner.

MÅNSSON, Ivar (of Trää) (1845–1911). Son of a farmer, and Scania farmer himself. Member of Second Chamber 1872–9, 1884–1903. Very economical in politics. Conservative member of New Farmers' party. Supported Boström. In favour of unity of parties 1895. Unofficial leader of Farmers 1896. Last main contribution was his proposal for reform 1902. His summer speeches in Scania were always an event and attracted large crowds.

MÖLLER, Fritz Gustav (1884–). Father died soon after Möller's birth. Errand boy at 13. Attended Malmö higher commercial institute 1905–6. Transferred to journalism and Young Socialist movement. Directed newspaper *Fram* 1911–12. Managing Director of *Tiden* 1913–17. Secretary of Social Democratic party 1916. Important factor in party's organization and policy. Against revolution. Socialization to follow attainment of parliamentary majority. Member of Second Chamber 1918–19. Leader of First Chamber Socialists 1919–24, 1927–32. Member of reform bill committee 1918. As Minister for Social Affairs 1924–6, 1932–51, made his most important contribution to Swedish politics. Party council chose Erlander instead of Möller as leader on Hansson's death 1946.

NILSSON, Per (of Espö) (1816–79). Son of a well-to-do farmer. Member of Farmer Estate 1853–6 and Second Chamber 1867–79. Liberal and humane. Wanted to abolish death penalty, improve popular education, help Poles in 1863. Gradually left independent position to support Farmers' party. Thought Posse and Key not liberal enough. No education. Self-education in history, geography, and folklore. Left library of 3,000 books, a collection of coins and archaeological specimens. His notebook described parliamentary life during his day.

NORDENFALK, Johan (1796–1846). Son of an ironmaster. Graduated in law at Uppsala 1816. Assize judge 1821. Under-Secretary for defence 1828–31. Baron 1838. Refused to become Minister 1840. Accepted office under Oscar I 1844. Liberal, and in favour of reform. Supported mortgage banks for agriculture (First bank 1861).

NORDSTRÖM, Johan Jakob (1801–74). Son of a master turner in Åbo, Finland. Professor of law and economics at Helsingfors Academy 1834. After criticism left Finland and did not return. Became

Director of National Archives in Sweden. Secretary of Constitution Committee 1847–51. Represented Academy of Science in Clergy Estate 1853–63. Intransigent attitude towards Norway 1859–60. Member of First Chamber 1866–74. Legalist politician, in many respects strict conservative. Active in securing foreign railway loans for Parliament.

OSCAR II (1829–1907). Married Sofia, daughter of Duke Wilhelm of Nassau. Crowned in Stockholm and Trondheim. Taught by C. J. Boström 1833–7, F. F. Carlson 1837–46, and two Norwegian tutors. Musical and poetic. Attended Uppsala university, then in navy. Commanded a squadron off west coast for a time during Dano-German war 1864. Admired Napoleon III. Religious, romantic, influenced by C. J. Boström. Wanted to improve on reign of brother, Charles XV. Monarchy to represent the national interest. Drawn towards Germany and Bismarck, believing Germany to be key to defence of Europe. Visited Berlin to show Scandinavia to be pro-German, but not much interest. Wilhelm II wanted Oscar to crush Norway lest North Sea become a British-Slav ocean, but Oscar too passive in Norwegian policy and dissolution inevitable 1905.

PALM, August (1849–1922). Son of elementary schoolteacher who died when Palm 10 years old. Tailor. Visited Denmark and Germany. Became Social Democratic agitator. Addressed first Socialist propaganda meeting in Malmö 1881. Opposed by authorities, temperance and Liberal workers' associations. Issued first Swedish Socialist programme *Folkvilja* 1882 (mainly replica of Gotha programme). Stressed necessity of making trade unions socialist. Opposed by more moderate Branting and Sterky, and lost leadership 1886. Imprisoned for 6½ months 1887 for libel against Parliament, and during this time prepared for constituent congress of 1889. Against anarchism of Bergegren and 'intellectual' leadership of Branting, Danielsson, and Sterky. Favoured General Strike.

PALMSTIERNA, Carl Otto (1790–1878). Son of a colonel. Baron. Joined army 1807, and fought in German and Norwegian campaigns 1813–14. Adjutant-General and Provincial Governor 1836. Political from 1823. Member of Court party 1831 and used by King on delicate missions. Lantmarshalk (Speaker) at important Parliament 1840–1. Chosen by increasingly conservative Oscar I as Finance Minister 1851–6. Active in railway construction. Led extreme conservative junkers 1859–60.

PERSSON, Daniel (of Tällberg) (1859–1918). Father a sessional judge. Auctioneer, forest dealer, lawyer, and local government official as well as farmer, in Dalecarlia. Member of Second Chamber 1890–1918, Old Farmer till 1895 then independent. Liberal 1900. Humorous, radical, economical, advanced in social policy. Temperance advocate. Important force behind 1907 reform. On Defence Committee 1910, 1911–14, but opposed Staaff 1914. Chairman of five-man council when Staaff died 1915. Vice-Speaker 1913–17. Speaker 1918.

PETERSSON, Per Alfred (of Påboda) (1860–1920). Attended folk high school 1876–8, and Swedish Mission Association school 1884–5. Inherited father's property of Påboda 1886. Member of Second Chamber 1897–1908. Economical, anti-bureaucratic. Member of Council for Farmers' party 1904, Budget committee 1903–5, Special Committee for Union question (as Farmers' representative). Minister for Agriculture 1905. Formed National Progressive party 1906. Residential qualification caused resignation from Second Chamber. Member of First Chamber 1910–20. Minister for Agriculture 1907–9, 1911–14, 1917–20. On five-man Liberal council when Staaff died 1915. Poor relations with Lindman, later good terms with Staaff. Important figure in politics 1905–20.

PLATEN, Baltzar Julius Ernst von (1804–75). Trained in merchant navy before joining navy. Served in British fleet 1825–7. Left the Service 1838 and directed Motala workshop, several estates and ironworks and father's Göta Canal. Chairman of its board 1855–7. Minister for sea defence 1849–52. In Liberal opposition. Wanted canal and archipelago fleet. Envoy in London 1857–61. Minister for sea defence 1862–8. Member of First Chamber 1866–73. Finance Minister 1871–2. Honorary doctorate at Oxford 1860. One of richest men in Sweden.

POSSE, Arvid Rutger Fredriksson (1820–1901). Studied law at Lund. Colleague of Louis De Geer in Scania and Blekinge High Court. Landowner 1847. Built castle of Charlottenlund. Director of Scania mortgage association 1854–9. Chairman of Scania Private Bank 1861–1901. Director of South Scania Railway 1865. Member of Riddarhus 1856–66 and, because of seniority of his family, chairman of Budget Committee 1865, 1867–75. Speaker of Second Chamber 1876–80. Prime Minister 1880. Member of First Chamber 1881. Much hated for leadership of Farmers' party in obstructionist opposition.

POSSE, Gösta (1823–88). Brother of Arvid. Obtained doctorate at Lund 1844. Then into Civil Service and 1848 into army, till 1854. Landowner. Chairman of Skaraborg Private Bank 1865–88, Hjo-Stenstorp railway 1873–88. Member of Riddarhus 1853–66 (except 1862–3). Liberal but opposed to parliamentary reform.

Failed to enter Second Chamber and so entered First Chamber 1868–84. Led offshoot of Farmers' party in First Chamber. Long friend of Emil Key.

REUTERDAHL, Henrik (1795–1870). Son of a master barber. Poor home. Educated at Lund. Ordained 1825. Professor of Church History at Lund 1845. Member of Clergy Estate 1844–51. Minister of Church and Education 1852–5. Archbishop 1856–66. Influenced by Schleiermacher. Less liberal after middle-forties, becoming High Church and conservative. Supported Hartmansdorff and opposed sects. Applied Conventicle Edict so severely that it was immediately rescinded (1858). Good scholar and fearless churchman. Intellectual aristocrat, doctrinaire, narrow-minded, and humourless. Softened after becoming archbishop.

RICHERT, John Gabriel (1784–1864). Son of an assize-judge. Studied law at Lund. Assize-judge 1813. Member of 1811 Law Committee 1814–32. Granted pension by Estate in 1834 worth 3,000 riksdaler after 1857. Favoured humane penal code, equal inheritance rights for women (who should reach majority at 25), abolition of privilege. Defended farmers against Skaraborg Provincial Government's punishment for tree-felling. Taught Oscar I law and political science. The main opposition liberal theorist. Not eligible for any Estate. Not a careerist. Refused to be Minister. Professor of legal ratification Lund 1844. Several parliamentary demonstrations against him 1847–8.

RYDIN, Herman Ludvig (1822–1904). Son of a shopkeeper. Was student at Uppsala 1840. Acted as private tutor. Doctorate 1848. Served in Svea and Göta Courts of Appeal. Associate professor in Administrative Law and Economics at Lund 1853. Professor of Law at Uppsala 1855–90. Member of First Chamber 1867–75, of Second Chamber 1875–90 (except 1878–81). Moderate when in First Chamber and in favour of solution to defence question 1873, 1885. Protectionist, and leader of New Farmers' party. Became less liberal, opposing wider suffrage, increased urban representation, and church reform. Wanted intimate co-operation of government and Parliament but not *parlamentarism*.

SANDBERG, Anders (1797–1876). Son of a workman. Studied at Lund university. Ordained 1820. University lecturer in physics 1825. Doctor of Theology 1845. Member of Clergy Estate 1840–66. Economical. Opposed parliamentary reform but on good terms with liberals because of mutual interest in popular education. Made the 1842 education act economically feasible. Wanted prohibition of schnapps.

SANDLER, Rickard Johannes (1884–   ). Graduated at Uppsala and then taught at Brunnsvik folk high school for nine years. Principal 1924. Member of Council of Social Democratic Youth Association 1907–12. In Second Chamber 1911–17, and First Chamber 1919. Foreign Minister 1932–9. Previously Director of Statistical Central Office. Translated *Das Kapital* 1930–3.

SCHWAN, Hans Niclas (1764–1829). Wholesaler. Active Burgher in Stockholm. Director of East India Company 1806–13. Prevented Bank of Sweden from falling into Gustav IV Adolf's hands 1809. Speaker of Burgher Estate 1810–23. Liberal, but good Court connexions. Councillor for Bank of Sweden 1810–28.

SCHWAN, Johan Gustav (1802–69). Joined father's firm; interests included ironworks and shipping. Member of Burgher Estate 1850–66. Active freetrader, especially over French commercial treaty. Brilliant speaker but did not understand parliamentary procedure well. Criticized for speculations in 1857 crisis.

SCHWERIN, Frederik Bogislaus von (1764–1834). Count. Born at Stralsund. Cornet in cavalry at 13. Studied at Prussian military academy Berlin. Went to Sweden 1780. Two years at Uppsala, then Strasburg university. Studied theology at Uppsala 1785, having been assured by Gustav III of the first royal living to become vacant. Court chaplain 1786. Studied at Göttingen 1786–7. Vicar of Sala 1788–1834. Doctor of Theology 1809. A nobleman, junker, learned grand seigneur, but hardly a parish priest. Introduced new farming methods to Sala. Interested in mercantilist economics, the new romanticism in history. The State 'an entailed estate'. 1815 onwards a politician. Hardly of same opinion as the later radicals of the 1830's.

SCOTT, George (1804–74). Son of a Scottish tailor, very religious home. Ended school at 12. Till 1830 shop assistant and office worker. Abandoned Presbyterianism for Wesleyanism 1827. Local preacher 1828. Ordained 1830. Because of his tolerance of people holding different opinions from his own, sent as missionary to Stockholm 1830–42. Originally sent by Samuel Owen to look after small group of English factory workers. Little success there, but much among cultivated Swedes. Supported by English minister, Lord Bloomfield, and made legation chaplain. Preached in Swedish 1831, and a driving force in revival in Lutheran church. Became famous, and with money from United States and Britain, built English Church. Later the Confessionalists and Liberal Opposition turned against him. Fierce press campaign against him and life threatened in middle of service on Palm Sunday 1842. Escaped, and left country. Welcomed on further visit 1859.

SELANDER, Nils Haqvin (1804–70). Son of member of Farmer Estate. Studied astronomy at Uppsala. Entered Academy of Sciences with title of professor 1837. One of its two representatives in Clergy Estate 1844–66.

SPARRE, Erik Josias Filip (1816–86). Doctorate at Uppsala 1836. In Civil Service but known for his non-bureaucratic behaviour. Member of Riddarhus 1844–66. In First Chamber 1867–9, and Second Chamber 1870–86. Opposed reform bill and thought to be Charles XV's alternative to De Geer. Later opposed Farmers' party. Protectionist.

STAAFF, Karl Albert (1860–1915). Leader of Verdandi group at Uppsala 1882–5. Private lawyer in Stockholm 1893–1905. Member of Second Chamber 1896 (People's party). Helped found National Liberal Federation 1902. Consultative Minister 1905. One of four Swedish delegates in negotiations preceding dissolution of union with' Norway 1905. Prime Minister 7/11/1905 to 29/5/06 and 7/10/11 to 17/2/14.

STRÖM, Otto Fredrik (1880–1948). Journalist 1901. At Gothenburg University 1902–3. Party Secretary to Social Democrat party 1911–16. Later a Höglund Left-Socialist. Russian consul 1919–24. Returned from Communists to Social Democrats 1925. Member of First Chamber 1916–21 and 1930–48. Interested in co-operation between farmers and workers, city of Stockholm, townplanning, theatre.

SUNDBERG, Anton Niklas (1818–1900). Professor in dogma and moral philosophy at Lund. Bishop 1864. Archbishop 1870. Conservative. Member of Clergy Estate 1859. Speaker of Second Chamber 1867–72. Contributed much to parliamentary tradition of new chamber. In First Chamber 1877–92. Refused to be Minister. High Church, broad-minded, cosmopolitan.

SWARTZ, Carl Johan Gustaf (1858–1926). Tobacco manufacturer. Studied at Bonn University 1877–8, Uppsala 1879–81. Elected to First Chamber 1900–26, though the Norrköping Town Council was protectionist and he a freetrader. Good Finance Minister. Introduced uniform taxation 1910 and moderate budget 1911. Took initiative in formation of Tobacco Monopoly of 1914 despite his own interests. A cool Prime Minister 1917. Played useful part in reform of 1918–21.

TAMM, Claes Gustaf Adolf (1838–1925). Baron, ironmaster. Left dragoons in 1865 and managed ironworks. Member of Riddarhus 1865–6. Finance Minister 1886–8. Defended Free Trade. Governor of Stockholm 1888–1902.

TAMM, Gösta (1866–1931). Son to Claes. Baron, Farmer. Left

dragoons in 1897 and member of Second Chamber 1903–5. Liberal in favour of proportionalism. Minister of Agriculture for Staaff. Friendly to rearmament and left the Liberals 1914. In Second Chamber 1912–14, 1915–17.

TERSMEDEN, Nils (1795–1867). Civil Servant; in diplomatic service at St. Petersburg 1824–32. Member of Riddarhus 1840–66. Fought reform bill and organized press and pamphlet campaign. M.A. Uppsala 1818.

TERSMEDEN, Wilhelm Fredrik (1802–79). Cousin to above. Left dragoons 1830 to manage ironworks. Member of Riddarhus 1828–66 and held leading position. Opposed Charles XIV. Moderate-liberal. Eager for parliamentary reform. Chairman of Swedish Public Mortgage Bank 1861–75.

THEMPTANDER, Oscar Robert (1844–97). Very competent Civil Servant. Bureau head in Customs Board 1878. Member of Second Chamber 1879–81. Consultative Minister 1880, Finance Minister 1881 at 37. Prime Minister at 40. Later Governor of Stockholm Province. Moderate-liberal. Left State service 1896 to be chief of largest business corporation in Sweden (*Trafik A/B Grängesberg-Oxelösund*) but died 1897.

THYSELIUS, Carl Johan (1811–91). Son of a bishop. Civil servant. Minister for Church and Education 1860–3. President of College of Exchequer 1864. Member of First Chamber 1869–86. Civil Minister 1875–80. Prime Minister 1883–4, and first commoner to hold that office.

TREFFENBERG, Nils Curry Engelbrekt (1825–97). Doctorate at Uppsala 1851. Svea Court of Appeal 1853. Member of Riddarhus 1865–6, Second Chamber 1869, 1873–8. Fierce opponent of Farmers' party. Member of First Chamber 1889–97. Made famous by his threats and pleadings to Sundsvall strikers 1879. One of first politicians to oppose union with Norway. Strong conservative. Reformist lay member of Church Assembly.

TROLLE, Eric Birger (1863–1934). Educated at Lund. Joined Diplomatic Service 1886. Permanent secretary in Foreign Office 1903–5. Foreign Minister in Staaff's Ministry 1905, and Lindman 1907. Resigned with Påboda 1909 and returned to diplomatic service.

TRYGGER, Ernst (1857–1943). Professor of law Uppsala 1889. Prorector 1901–5. In First Chamber 1897. Chairman of National party from 1913. Sharp and logical in debate.

UGGLAS, Curt Gustaf af (1820–95). Lawyer. Moderate member of Riddarhus. Provincial Governor 1858. In First Chamber 1867–93; Finance Minister 1867–70. Governor of Stockholm 1874–88.

Uhr, Anders Wilhelm (1806–1891). Member of Farmer Estate 1850–1, 1859–65. Constitution Committee 1863, 1865–6. In Second Chamber 1867–78. Eager for parliamentary reform and later universal suffrage.

Vennerström, Ivar Teodor (1881–1945). Studied at Uppsala, then journalist. Member of Second Chamber 1915–27. First Chamber 1928–36. Minister of Defence 1932–6. Became Left-Socialist 1916, but returned to Social Democratic party 1923.

Viktoria, Queen (1862–1930). Wife of Gustav V. Formerly Princess of Baden. Granddaughter of Kaiser Wilhelm I. Married 1801. Delicate health and so lived abroad much of the time. Strong-willed and interested in politics.

Waern, C. F. (1819–99). Gothenburg businessman. Uncle of Jonas Waern (ironmaster, Minister 1844). Led Burgher radicals 1830's. Piloted Constitution Committee's bill 1840. Some influence from British Utilitarianism. Admirer of Norway. Friend of Stockholm radicals.

Waldenström, Paul Peter (1838–1917). Doctorate at Uppsala 1863. Ordained 1864. Teacher at Gävle 1874–1905. Doctor of Theology, Yale 1889. Member of Second Chamber 1884–1905, of Church Assembly 1868, 1906–10. Conversion 1858 to Evangelical movement. Formed *Svenska Missionsförbundet* 1878, but remained within Lutheran Church. Ceased to be priest 1882.

Wallenberg, André Oscar (1816–86). Resigned from fleet as captain 1850 having travelled widely. When in U.S.A. 1837 interested in banks. Founded Stockholm Private Bank 1856, the first Swedish commercial bank. Built up credit facilities through *Skandinaviska kredit A/B*. Used the press to mould opinion: part-owner of *Bore* 1848–51, *Stockholms Posten* 1869–70, weekly article in *Aftonbladet* 1865–8. Member of Burgher Estate 1853–63, First Chamber 1866–86. Opposed Farmers' party. Supported metric system, gold standard, bank laws, independence of Bank of Sweden from Parliament, open parliamentary voting, rights of married women over property, the institution of a Prime Minister.

Wallenberg, Knut Agaton (1853–1938). Naval Lieut. 1876. Worked in Credit Lyonnais 1876–8. Managing director of Stockholm Private Bank 1886–1911 and then chairman of the Board. With Hambros, formed British Bank of Northern Commerce. Responsible for State retaining its control of railways and mines in Lapland. Assisted Stockholm Chamber of Commerce and Commercial High School. Moderate, freetrader, conservative. Contributed 500,000 crowns to decoration of Stockholm Town Hall, and 100,000 to Concert Hall.

WALLENBERG, Marcus Laurentius (1864–1943). Naval Under-Lieut. 1882. Then graduated in law Uppsala and assize judge 1890. On board of Stockholm Private Bank 1892. Managing director 1911–27. Interested in financing industry. Opposed to large organizations. Responsible for commercial treaty with Britain 1916–18 in London.

WIDÉN, Johan (1856–1933). Legal examination at Uppsala 1880. Into politics 1900. Represented a town but joined Farmers' party, following father's example. Moderate-Liberal, and joined Liberals 1909 as independent member. Speaker of Second Chamber 1914–17. Failed to form Ministry 1917 and left Parliament. Went into State service in Norrland 1923.

ZWEIGBERGK, Otto Ferdinand von (1863–1935). Graduated at Uppsala 1884. Correspondent for *Dagens Nyheter* 1890. Chief editor 1898–1921. In Verdandi group at university. Greatest period of *Dagens Nyheter* during his editorship.

ÖSTBERG, Gustaf Fredrik (1847–1924). Landowner. Graduated Uppsala 1870. Chief of Stockholm Dairy Co. 1889–1905. Member of Second Chamber 1885–96. First Chamber 1897–1916. Good organizer. Chairman of *Allmänna Valmansförbundet* 1904–5, 1908–12. Helped found Swedish Employers' Federation 1902, and its chairman 1903–7. Important influence in *Nya Dagligt Allehanda*.

Bibliography

PARLIAMENT ACT (RIKSDAGSORDNINGEN) 1866

UNPRINTED SOURCES
Louis De Geer's samling (Riksarkivet).
Bernadotteska Familjearkivet up to 1905.
(Kungliga Slottet. These archives contain very little on parliamentary reform.)
Per Nilsson i Espö's anteckningar (Lund University).

PRINTED SOURCES
Parliamentary papers:
Regeringsformen, 1809.
Riksdagsordningen, 1809; 1866.
Konstitutions-Utskottets Memorial, no. 12, 23 May 1848.
Kongl. Maj:ts Nåd. Proposition, no. 61, 5 Jan. 1863.
Konstitutions-Utskottets Memorial, no. 7, 27 Feb. 1863.
Ridderskapet och Adelns Protokoll, 18 March 1863, 4–7 Dec. 1865.
Preste-Ståndets Protokoll, 18–20 March 1863, 4, 8 Dec. 1865.
Borgare-Ståndets Protokoll, 18 March 1863, 4 Dec. 1865.
Bonde-Ståndets Protokoll, 18 March 1863, 4 Dec. 1865.

Pamphlets, &c:
Aftonbladet, Dec. 1865.
Boström, C. J.: *Äro Rikets Ständer berättigade att för svenska folket besluta och fastställa det nu hvilande så kallade representationsförslaget?* Uppsala, 1865.
De Geer, L. G.: *Några ord till försvar för det hvilande representationsförslaget.* Stockholm, 1865.
Hamilton, H.: *Bidrag till granskningen af Kongl. Maj:ts Nådiga proposition till Rikets Ständer.* Stockholm, 1865.
Hedin, S. A.: *Hvad folket väntar af den nya representationen.* Stockholm, 1868.
Rydin, H. L.: *Betraktelser i representationsfrågan.* Uppsala, 1865.

Letters and Memoirs:
De Geer, L. G.: *Minnen*, i–ii. Stockholm, 1892.
De Geer, L. G.: *Ur Louis De Geers brevsamling*, Stockholm, 1929. (Utg. av L. De Geer).
Hamilton, H.: *Ur Henning Hamiltons brevsamling*, vols. i–ii. Stockholm, 1914. (Utg. av Carlquist, G.)

OTHER WORKS (1809–66):
Andersson, R.: 'Om tillkomsten av de riddarhuskonservativas representationsförslag 1865' (*Statsvetenkaplig tidskrift*, 1949).
Borell, B.: *De svenska liberalerna och representationsfrågan på 1840-talet.* Stockholm, 1948
Brusewitz, A.: *Studier öfver 1809 års författningskris.* Uppsala, 1917.

Fahlbeck, E.: 'Ståndsriksdagens sista skede (1809–66)' (*Sveriges riksdag*, vol. viii). Stockholm, 1934.

Fahraeus, E.: *Administratif och statistik handbok*. Stockholm, 1864.

Gasslander, O.: *J. A. Gripenstedt*. Lund, 1949.

Hallendorff, C.: *Från Karl XV:s dagar*. Stockholm, 1924.

Heckscher, G.: *Konung och statsråd i 1809 års författning*. Uppsala, 1933.

—— *Svensk konservatism före representationsreformen, I Den historiska skolans genombrott i Sverige*. Uppsala, 1929.

II Doktrin och politik. Uppsala, 1943. Skrifter utg. 9 & 17.

Lagerroth, F.: 'Beskattningsmakten i 1809 års RF' (*Statsvetenskaplig tidskrift*, 1938).

Lundh, H. L.: *Skandinavismen i Sverige*, Stockholm, 1951.

Thermaenius, E.: *Representationsreformen*. Svenska Dagbladet 20/12/35.

REPRESENTATIONSREFORMEN 1907–9

UNPRINTED SOURCES

Arvid Lindman's samling, vols. 2, 23, 25 (Riksarkivet). (Fragmentary. Begins 1908).

PRINTED SOURCES

Parliamentary papers:

1906: *Kungl. Prop.* no. 55, 21 Jan.
Motioner: *Första kammaren*, nos. 31–34, 36, 38, 42.
Andra kammaren, nos. 135–7, 139, 140, 143–5, 148–9, 151–3.
Remissdebatt, 27 Feb. (in both chambers).
Konstitutions-Utskottets utlåtande, no. 7, 7 May.
Ibid., no. 10, 16 May.
Första kammarens Protokoll, 14–15 May.
Andra kammarens Protokoll, 14–15 May.

1907: *Kungl. Prop.* no. 28, 30 Jan.
Motioner: *Första kammaren*, nos. 41, 45, 68, 70, 78.
Andra kammaren, nos. 197, 203, 205, 208, 210, 212, 215–16, 252–3, 258, 262.
Remissdebatt, 6 Feb. (in both chambers).
Särskilda Utskottets utlåtande, no. 3, 3 May.
Ibid., no. 5, 12 May.
Första kammarens Protokoll, 10–14 May.
Andra kammarens Protokoll, 10–14 May.

Memoirs:

Billing, B.: *Anteckningar från kyrkomöten och riksdagar, 1893–1906*. Stockholm, 1928.

OTHER WORKS:

Timelin, R. E.: *Ministären Lindman och representationsreformen, 1907*. Karlskrona, 1928. (In the Manchester Central Library.)

Öman, K. I.: *Karl Staaffs första ministär*. Norrköping, 1923.

FÖRFATTNINGSREVISIONEN 1918–21

PRINTED SOURCES

Parliamentary papers:
1918: *Urtima riksdag* (Extraordinary session):
    Kungl. Prop. no. 34, 22 Nov.
    Remissdebatt, 26 Nov. (in both chambers).
    Tredje Särskilda Utskottets utlåtande, no. 1, 14 Dec.
    Första kammarens Protokoll, 17 Dec.
    Andra kammarens Protokoll, 17 Dec.

OTHER WORKS:
Gerdner, G.: 'Ministären Edén och författningsrevisionen 1918'
(*Skrifter utgivna av Statsvetenskapliga föreningen i Uppsala*, 20), Uppsala,
1944.

GENERAL WORKS 1866–1921

WORKS COVERING THE PERIOD 1866–1900:
Fahlbeck, P.: *Sveriges författning och den moderna parlamentarismen*, Lund,
1904.
Hildebrand, K.: *Gustav V som människa och regent*, vol. i. Stockholm,
1945.
Lundberg, F.: *Kunglig utrikespolitik*. Stockholm, 1950.
Petré, T.: *Ministären Themptander*. (Skrifter utg. 21.) Uppsala, 1945.
Rexius, G.: *Den svenska tvåkammarsystemets tillkomst och karaktär*. Uppsala,
1915.
Sundbarg, G.: *Betänkande i utvandringsfrågan*. Stockholm, 1913.
Thermaenius, E.: *Lantmannapartiet*. Uppsala, 1928.
Thomson, A.: *Grundskatterna i den politiska diskussionen*, 1809–66, Lund,
1923.

WORKS COVERING THE PERIOD 1900–21:
Brusewitz, A.: *Konungamakt, herremakt, folkmakt. Författningskampen i
Sverige*, 1906–18. Stockholm, 1951.
Edenman, R.: *Socialdemokratiska riksdagsgruppen*, 1903–20. Uppsala, 1946.
Gerdner, G.: *Det svenska regeringsproblemet 1917–20: Från majoritetskoali-
tion till minoritetsparlamentarism*. Uppsala, 1946.
Hamilton, Hugo.: *Hågkomster*. Stockholm, 1928.
Hedin, S.: *Försvarsstriden 1912–14*. Stockholm, 1951.
Hildebrand, K.: *Gustav V som människa och regent*, vol. ii, 1948.
Håstad, E.: *Det moderna partiväsendets organisation*, Stockholm, 1938.
Höglund, Z.: *Hjalmar Branting och hans livsgärning*, vols. i–ii, 1928–9.
Stockholm.
Höjer, T.: 'Sam Clasons brev under bondetågskrisen' (*Historisk Tid-
skrift*, 1951, no. 2).
Lindgren, J.: *Per Albin Hansson i svensk demokrati*, vol. i, 1885–1920,
Stockholm, 1950.
Maury, L.: *Métamorphose de la Suède*. Paris, 1951.
Nyman, O.: *Parlamentarismen i Sverige. Huvuddragen av utvecklingen efter
1917*. Stockholm, 1950.

Rönblom, H. K.: *Frisinnade Landsföreningen 1902–27. Skildringar ur den liberala organisationsrörelsens historia i vårt land.* Uppsala, 1929.
Spångberg, V.: *Karl Staaff*, vols. i–ii. Stockholm, 1928.
Staaff, K.: *Det demokratiska statsskicket*, vols. i–ii, Stockholm, 1917.
Statens offentliga utredningar (S.O.U.) 1949:20. Betänkande med förslag till religionsfrihetslag.
Thermaenius, E.: 'Från Konstitutionalism till parlamentarisk demokrati' in *Det Nordiske Administrative Förbunds 5. Almindeliga Möte i Oslo 26–8 June 1933*
Thulstrup, A.: *När demokratin bröt igenom.* Stockholm, 1937.
Varenius, O.: 'Riksdagsordningen 46§' (*Statsvetenskaplig Tidskrift*, 1909).
Wåhlstrand, A.: *Allmänna valmansförbundets tillkomst.* Uppsala, 1946.
Wigforss, E.: *Minnen*, vol. i, Före 1914, 1950. Stockholm; vol. ii, 1914–32, 1951.
Zweigbergk, O. von; *Svensk politik 1905–29. Parlamentarismens första kvartsekel.* Stockholm, 1929.

OTHER WORKS:
Andrén, G.: 'Tvåkammarsystemets tillkomst och utveckling', *Sveriges riksdag*, vol. ix. Stockholm, 1937.
Björnberg, A.: (ed.): *Verdandi genom femtio år.* Stockholm, 1932.
Edén, N.: *Den svenska riksdagen under femhundra år.* Stockholm, 1935.
Håstad, E.: *Partierna i regering och riksdag.* Stockholm, 1938.
Heckscher, G.: *Staten och organisationerna.* Stockholm, 1946.
Herlitz, N.: *Grunddragen av det svenska statsskickets historia.* 3rd ed. Stockholm, 1946.
—— 'Riksdagens finansmakt' (*Sveriges riksdag*, vol. xii). Stockholm, 1934.
Kihlberg, L.: *Den svenska ministären under ståndsriksdag och tvåkammarsystem intill 1905 års totala ministerskifte.* Uppsala, 1922.
Lagerroth, F.: 'Staaff eller De Geer?' (*Statsvetenskaplig tidskrift*, 1943).
Lindgren, J.: *Från Per Götrek till Per Albin.* Stockholm, 1936.
Malmgren, R.: *Sveriges grundlagar*, 5th ed. Stockholm, 1947.
—— 'Riksdagen och lagstiftningen' (*Sveriges riksdag*, vol. xiv). Stockholm, 1934.
Olsson, J.: *Kommunal självstyrelse. i Sverige.* Stockholm, 1950.
Reuterskiöld, C. A.: *Sveriges grundlagar*, Vols.
I. Regeringsformen och successionsordningen, Uppsala, 1934.
II. Riksdagsordningen med vallagen samt trychfrihetsförordningen. Uppsala, 1937.
—— Riksdagssessioner och kammarplena (*Sveriges riksdag*, vol. x). Stockholm, 1935.
Spångberg, V.: *Från Arvid Posse till Per Albin Hansson. Svenska statsministrar, riksdagsman och publicister.* Stockholm, 1936.
Statistiska Årsbok 1934–5.
Söderberg, T.: *Bergsmän och brukspatroner i svenskt samhällsliv.* (Det levande förflutna. Svenska historiska föreningens folkskrifter.) Stockholm, 1946–8.

'Studier över den svenska riksdagens sociala sammansättning.' Uppsala, 1936. (*Skrifter utgivna av statsvetenskapliga föreningen i Uppsala, 7.*)

Sveriges styrelse, ed. E. Winge. Stockholm, 1939.

Thermaenius, E.: 'Riksdagspartierna' (*Sveriges riksdag*, vol. xviii). Stockholm, 1935.

Thörnberg, E. H.: *Samhällsklasser och politiska partier i Sverige.* Stockholm, 1917.

Thulin, E.: 'Sammanjämkning och gemensam votering' (*Sveriges riksdag*, vol. x). Stockholm, 1935.

Tingsten, H.: 'Utskottsväsendet' (*Sveriges riksdag*, vol. xi). Stockholm 1934.

—— *Demokratiens seger och kris* (Vår egen tids historia, vol. i). Stockholm, 1939.

—— *Den svenska socialdemokratiens idéutveckling*, vols. i–ii. Stockholm, 1941.

Wohlin, N.: *Den jordbruksidkande befolkningen i Sverige, 1751–1900.* Stockholm, 1909.

(*Sveriges riksdag* i–xvii is in University College Library, London.)

BOOKS AND ARTICLES IN ENGLISH

Bibliographies:

Afzelius, N.: *A Biographical list of books in English on Sweden.* Stockholm, 1938.

Hatton, R.: 'Some notes on Swedish historiography' (*History*, June 1952).

Thorelli, S. S.: 'Political science in Sweden' (*American Political Science Review*, vol. xliv, 4 Dec. 1950).

General:

The Constitution of Sweden, Royal Ministry for Foreign Affairs, Stockholm, 1954.

Andersson, I. and others: *Introduction to Sweden.* Uppsala, 1950.

Arneson, B. A.: *The democratic monarchies of Scandinavia.* 2nd ed. New York, 1949.

Bain, N.: *Scandinavia: A political history of Denmark, Norway and Sweden from 1513 to 1900.* Cambridge, 1905.

Childs, M. W.: *Sweden, the middle way.* London, 1936.

Cole, M. & Smith, C.: *Democratic Sweden.* London, 1938.

Elder, N. C. M.: 'The parliamentary role of joint standing committees in Sweden' (*American Political Science Review*, vol. xlv. 2 June, 1951).

Friis, H. (ed.): *Scandinavia between East and West.* Ithaca, N.Y., 1950.

Grimberg, C.: *A history of Sweden.* Rock Island, Ill., 1935.

Hallendorff, C. and Schuck, A.: *History of Sweden.* London, 1929.

Heckscher, G.: *Pluralist democracy* (Social Research, vol. xv, 4 Dec. 1948).

Herlitz, N.: *Sweden: A new democracy on ancient foundations.* Minneapolis, 1939.

Hovde, B. J.: *The Scandinavian countries*, vols. i–ii. 1720–1865. Ithaca, N.Y., 1948.

Montgomery, A.: *The rise of modern industry in Sweden.* London, 1939.

Reddaway, W. F.: 'Scandinavia: Sweden & Norway 1815–70,' *Cambridge Modern History*, vol. xi, chap. xxiv. Cambridge, 1910.

Royal Institute of International Affairs.

The Scandinavia states and Finland: a political and economic survey. London, 1951.

Stavenow, L.: 'Scandinavia', *Cambridge Modern History*, vol. xii. chap. xi. Cambridge, 1910.

Stomberg, A.: *A history of Sweden*. New York, 1931.

Tingsten, H.: *Political behaviour*. London, 1937.

—— *The debate on the foreign policy of Sweden, 1918–39*. Oxford, 1949.

Stencils available at the Swedish Institute, Stockholm:

Information about Sweden.

Books of reference relating to Sweden. Stockholm, 1947.

Books about Sweden 1946–9. Swedish-American News Bureau, New York, 1949.

Hedin, N.: *Guide to information about Sweden*. Swedish-American News Bureau, New York, 1947.

Hesslén, G.: *Public administration in Sweden*. Stockholm, 1950.

Olsson, J.: *The local government of Sweden*. Stockholm, 1950.

Selected list of Swedish humanistic and legal periodicals compiled by the Swedish Institute for Cultural Relations with Foreign Countries. Stockholm, 1947.

Swedish books and publications on science, medicine, and the humanities 1939–47. Stockholm, 1949.

Index

Abelin, G. R., resigns, 116; threatens to resign, 127; refuses to obey Posse, 128.
Adelskalender, 25.
Adlercreutz, A. G.: Chancellor, 116–17; opposes Ministry, 128.
Adlersparre, A., opposes Ministry, 127–8.
Aftonbladet: founded, 20; helps reformers, 38; attacks Clergy Estate, 72; opposes De Geer's resignation, 113; and formation of Liberal party, 136; supports Lindman, 170.
Agardh, C. A., 32.
Agencies, 11.
Agriculture, Ministry of, created, 159.
— Påboda as Minister of, 148, 159.
alcoholics, law governing, 130; *see also* temperance movement.
Allmänna valmansförbundet (Conservative Party Organization): formed, 162; role of, in 1911 election, 179.
Amendment of Constitution, 7, 57.
— of bills, 57.
Anarchists, 195, 196.
Anckarswärd, C. H.: proposes refusal of appropriations, 13; interested in parliamentary reform, 26, 32, 35; 1830 motion of, 37–40; and Gripenstedt, 80.
Andersson, Hans (of Nöbbelöv), 221; forms National Progressive party, 143; compromise proposal of, 168–9.
Andrén, G., 15 n., 16 n., 29 n., 34 n., 62 n., 76 n., 86 n., 92 n., 131, 135 n.
Anglo-Swedish Review, 217 n.
Anjou, Bishop L. A., opposes parliamentary reform, 62.
Annerstedt, L., 130.
'annexe', in Second Chamber, 134, 232.
anti-militarism: of Social Democrats, 178, 181, 210; propaganda for, 209.
Aphorisms (Boström's), 66.
Arbetarbladet, 162, 170.
Arbetare, 90.
Arbetarkommuner, 200.
army: representation of, in *Riddarhus*,

15, in First Chamber, 78, 89–90; 'vote for uniform', 25, 80; and parliamentary reform, 71; attacked by Hedin, 96–97; involved in parliamentary controversy, 127–8, 181; reliability of, 209. *See also* conscription, land taxes, *Indelningsverk*.
Augsburg Confession, 17.
Australia, 165.

Backstugusittare, 21.
Bagehot, W., 'capitalist conservatism' of, 85.
Bain, N., 45, 129 n.
Bank, Committee, 54.
— of Sweden, 5, 131.
— Stockholm Private, 191.
banks, mortgage, 16.
— private, law governing, 129, 130.
Baptists, 105.
Barthélemy, J., 228.
Belgium, 111.
Benedicks, G., 165.
Bentham, J., 36.
Berg, Fridtjuv, 221; Minister for Church and Education, 143.
Bergegren, H. B., 200.
Bergslag, 197.
Bergström, D. K., 74 n., 221; forms People's party, 136–7; founds National Liberal Federation, 139; Consultative Minister, 143; War Minister, 181.
—, P. A. (*Civilminister*, 1870–5), 117 n.
Bernadotte, Marshal, *see* Karl XIV.
Besvär, 102.
Bevan, A., 200.
Bevillning, 5.
bicameral system, 86–87, 112, 166, 214, 224; *see also* Chambers.
Biesèrt, E., 150.
Bildt, D. A. G., 71; Prime Minister, 118.
Billing, Bishop Gottfrid: supports 'wing-clipping', 109; proposes proportional representation, 139; on Staaff, 150; advises Gustav V, 179.
Bismarck, Otto von, 122.

Waern, C. F., 36.
—J., 12 99; Minister for Oscar I, 38, 42; Finance Minister, 123.
Waldeck-Rousseau, P., 197.
Waldenström, P. P., 105.
Wallenberg, A. O., attitude to reform of, 92, 94, 99, 127.
— Knut A., 122.
— Marcus, 191.
Warning Word, A, 184.
Whig tradition, absence of, 93.
Widén, J., 202.
Wieselgren, P., 105.
Wilson, Woodrow, 210 n.
wingclipping, 109, 145.
Wohlin, N., 14 n., 21 n.
women's suffrage, 205, 212.
workers: in Parliament, 90; and franchise, 91–92.

workmen's compensation, 133.
Wåhlstrand, A., 123 n.
Wäktaren, 67.

Young Socialists, 104; anti-militarist, 178; oppose Branting, 198–200, 226. *See also* Left Socialists.
Yttrande, 130.

Zweigbergk, O. von, 122 n., 123 n., 141, 150 n., 181 n., 183 n., 188 n.

Åkerhielm, G., 118.

Öman, K. I., 131 n., 150 n., 154 n., 155 n.
Örebro, 79.
Östberg, G. F., 162.
Östersund, 162.

PRINTED IN
GREAT BRITAIN
AT THE
UNIVERSITY PRESS
OXFORD
BY
CHARLES BATEY
PRINTER
TO THE
UNIVERSITY

Date Due

CPSIA information can be obtained
at www.ICGtesting.com
Printed in the USA
LVHW022208170323
741893LV00032B/1300

9 781013 711244